LESSING AND THE DRAMA

LESSING AND THE DRAMA

F. J. LAMPORT

Fellow of Worcester College, Oxford

CLARENDON PRESS · OXFORD

1981

Oxford University Press, Walton Street, Oxford OX2 6DP

London Glasgow New York Toronto
Delhi Bombay Calcutta Madras Karachi
Kuala Lumpur Singapore Hong Kong Tokyo
Nairobi Dar es Salaam Cape Town
Melbourne Auckland

and associate companies in
Beirut Berlin Ibadan Mexico City

Published in the United States by
Oxford University Press, New York

British Library Cataloguing in Publication Data

Lamport, F. J.
Lessing and the drama.
I. Title
832'.6   PT2416

ISBN 0-19-815767-3

Set by Hope Services, Abingdon
and printed in Great Britain at
the University Press, Oxford
by Eric Buckley
Printer to the University

Preface

This book is a study of Lessing's lifelong engagement with the practice and theory of dramatic writing. It aims to tell the story of how Lessing's plays came to be written rather than in the first instance to interpret them; though plainly it cannot do the former without in some measure attempting the latter, and the main reason for writing such a book in the first place is that the best of the plays can and do stand on their own feet and speak directly to a twentieth-century audience. Producer, actor, reader, and spectator must interpret the individual plays as best they can; but the literary historian may help them in their task by faithfully performing his, which is to seek to understand them in the context of their author's literary concerns and intentions and of the traditions in which he wrote.

This is only a part of the intellectual biography of Lessing; but it deals with that part of his work and his intellectual life which is both of the most immediate interest to the student of literature and, to my mind, of the greatest value to posterity at large.

My work has profited a great deal from many discussions with critical colleagues and friends, some of whom have read parts of it at various stages of completion, and from teaching Lessing to several generations of often yet more critical undergraduates. To all these people I offer my grateful acknowledgements; and my apologies, if they do not like the uses to which their ideas have been put. My thanks are also owing to my College and to the University of Oxford for granting me invaluable sabbatical leave, and to all the others who have helped the production of this book in any way. And I hope that it will make its contribution to Lessing's memory and to the understanding of his work not least by provoking further discussion, criticism, and dissent. As Lessing himself put it in his essay *Über eine zeitige Aufgabe:*

Befriedigen mich meine Gedanken am Ende: so zerreiße ich das Papier. Befriedigen sie mich nicht: so lasse ich es drucken. Wenn ich besser belehrt werde, nehme ich eine kleine Demütigung schon vorlieb.

F.J.L.

Contents

References

Quotations are taken from Lessing: *Werke*, ed. H. G. Göpfert etc., 8 vols. (Munich, 1970-9), cited as G, supplemented where necessary from the editions of Lachmann and Muncker (LM) and Petersen and Olshausen (PO) (see Bibliography). So that they may be readily traced in any edition, however, references are made to Lessing's plays by act (roman) and scene (arabic) number, to his critical works by chapter, paragraph, etc., and to his letters by addressee and date.

The following further abbreviations are used:

D   R. Daunicht (ed.), *Lessing im Gespräch* (Munich, 1971)
B   G. and S. Bauer (eds.), *Gotthold Ephraim Lessing* (Darmstadt, 1968) (Wege der Forschung, ccxi)

ABNG	*Amsterdamer Beiträge zur neuren Germanistik*
DVJS	*Deutsche Vierteljahrsschrift für Literaturwissenschaft und Geistesgeschichte*
Euph.	*Euphorion*
FMLS	*Forum for Modern Language Studies*
GLL	*German Life and Letters*
GQ	*The German Quarterly*
GR	*The Germanic Review*
JDSG	*Jahrbuch der deutschen Schillergesellschaft*
JEGP	*Journal of English and Germanic Philology*
LYB	*Lessing Yearbook*
MLN	*Modern Language Notes*
MLQ	*Modern Language Quarterly*
NGS	*New German Studies*
OGS	*Oxford German Studies*
PEGS	*Publications of the English Goethe Society*
PMLA	*Publications of the Modern Languages Association of America*
WSA	*Wolfenbütteler Studien zur Aufklärung*
ZfdPh	*Zeitschrift für deutsche Philologie*

I

Introduction

The year 1748 is a year of important beginnings in German literature. In lyric poetry, Ewald von Kleist's *Der Frühling* and the first three cantos of Klopstock's *Messias* are among the first signs of a new poetry of nature and feeling which was to replace the polite conventionalities of the eighteenth-century salon style. C. F. Gellert's *Leben der schwedischen Gräfin von G****, with its introduction of a moral sensibility reminiscent of such models as the novels of Samuel Richardson, marks a similar turning-point in the history of the German novel. And in the theatre, January 1748 saw the first performance, in Leipzig, of a comedy, *Der junge Gelehrte*, by the young theological student, Gotthold Ephraim Lessing.

Leipzig was at this time the centre of the movement under the leadership of Johann Christoph Gottsched to establish in Germany a serious literary theatre on neo-classical lines, after the example set by the French writers of the seventeenth century and their successors.[1] In 1730, at the age of thirty, Gottsched had published his *Versuch einer critischen Dichtkunst für die Deutschen*, in which the various genres — epic, tragedy, comedy, and so forth — are carefully delimited and the 'rules' for each prescribed, after the manner of Aristotle, Horace (a translation of whose *Art of Poetry* accompanies the *Dichtkunst* by way of preface) and their sixteenth- and seventeenth-century commentators and imitators such as Scaliger and Boileau. In tragedy, for example, Gottsched decreed the portrayal of noble characters, the employment of verse, and the observation of the famous 'Unities' of action, time, and place: there were to be no sub-plots, the action depicted should last

[1]   See W. H. Bruford, *Theatre, Drama and Audience in Goethe's Germany* (London, 1950), esp. pp. 51–62; cf. also Kurt Wölfel, 'Moralische Anstalt: zur Dramaturgie von Gottsched bis Lessing', in R. Grimm (ed.), *Deutsche Dramentheorien* (Frankfurt, 1971), i. 45–122.

no longer than twenty-four hours, and the scene should not
be changed. Decorum was to be strictly observed: there was
of course to be no mixture of the genres, such as the inter-
polation of comic scenes into tragedy which made the plays
of Shakespeare seem so barbaric to the neo-classical critics of
continental Europe. In the following year (1731) Gottsched
produced his own tragedy, *Der sterbende Cato*, exemplifying
these precepts: it owes much to Joseph Addison's *Cato* of
1713, but Gottsched tells us in his preface that he has kept
more strictly to the 'rules' than his model, because he does
not want to give the impression 'daß ein Stücke auch ohne
dieselben schön sein könne'.[2] Many of Gottsched's remarks
on drama, and literature in general, make him seem nothing
but a pedant; and it is undoubtedly true that he liked laying
down the law on matters of literary taste and that, like most
of his contemporaries, he preferred the regular and 'correct'
to the imaginative and the experimental. It is furthermore
plain from the *Dichtkunst* and from Gottsched's practical
criticism that he had little or no understanding of the poetic
imagination or of the nature of literary fiction. Gottsched is
greatly concerned with the 'truth' of poetry, but never grasps
that the statements made by poets are neither simply true
nor simply false, but fall into a third category: some of his
pronouncements recall Plato's hostile over-simplifications in
Book X of the *Republic*, where the artist is seen as basically
no better than a liar. But Gottsched was not hostile to art,
even if he did not understand it. He realized that it was an ornament to a civilized nation; indeed, a necessary ornament,
without which no nation could claim to be civilized. France
had dominated continental Europe in the latter part of the
seventeenth century not only through her political strength
as a centralized nation-state but also through the glittering artistic and above all the literary culture which this metropolitan
centralization had produced. The glory of France was the
'classical' drama of Corneille, Racine, and Molière, whose
tradition was still (it seemed) maintained in the eighteenth
century, notably by Voltaire. Gottsched therefore set about
reforming or rather re-creating the German theatre from

[2]   Gottsched, *Sterbender Cato*, ed. H. Steinmetz (Stuttgart (Reclam), 1966),
p. 13.

scratch, according to sound neo-classical theory and the practical example of the French. As Lessing was later to observe, in the course of his famous attack on Gottsched in the seventeenth *Literaturbrief* of 1759:

> er wollte nicht sowohl unser altes Theater verbessern, als der Schöpfer eines ganz neuen sein. Und was für eines neuen? Eines Französierenden; ohne zu untersuchen, ob dieses französierende Theater der deutschen Denkungsart angemessen sei, oder nicht.[3]

But even Lessing concedes that something had to be done; and Gottsched was practical and determined enough to do it. The German literary drama of the seventeenth century had established no lasting tradition. All the German stage had to offer was, as Gottsched tells us in the preface to his *Cato*, 'lauter schwülstige . . . Haupt- und Staatsaktionen, . . . lauter pöbelhafte Fratzen und Zoten':[4] on the one hand, bombastic historical melodramas, crude versions of Baroque tragedy, worlds away from Racinian refinement; on the other, vulgar farcical comedies full of buffoonery and obscenity, often very largely improvised, relying not on a written text but on a stock set of characters and a stereotyped plot — a form of theatrical entertainment with a very long tradition, but again very different from the polite comedy of Molière.

Gottsched was not content with precept or even literary example. He took what was really at that time, for a respectable academic, a remarkable and daring step: he entered into a practical partnership with the living theatre, with a view to establishing serious literary drama in actual performance. He took up a troupe of actors led by Johann Neuber and his wife Caroline. Under Gottsched's patronage and direction the Neuber troupe were to 'purify' the theatre both morally and aesthetically. They were to abolish vulgarity and obscenity, to make theatre-going acceptable in decent society; and they were to abolish improvisation, the mainstay of much theatrical performance, in favour of fidelity to an author's text, and thus to ensure the literary standard of dramatic writing. These intentions were symbolized in the famous (or notorious) ceremonial banishment of Harlequin from the German stage, en-

---

[3] G v. 71.
[4] Gottsched, *Cato*, ed. cit., p. 7.

acted by the Neuber troupe in 1737.[5] By the time the young Lessing arrived in Leipzig, Gottsched's pretensions as universal arbiter of literary taste in Germany had been challenged from a number of quarters; he had become a target for satirical abuse, and Frau Neuber, who had taken over the management of the troupe after her husband's death, had fallen out with their former patron. But his theatrical reforms had been both necessary and effective. Their effectiveness is reflected in *Der junge Gelehrte* and in the success with which it was performed, by the Neuber troupe, in January 1748.

Lessing was not yet nineteen. He was born on 22 January 1729 in Kamenz, a small town in Saxon Lusatia (Lausitz), where his father was a minister of the Lutheran church. Pastor Lessing's first-born son had lived only a few days; his daughter Dorothea Salome was born in 1727, and lived till 1803. After her came Gotthold, and after him ten more children, the best-known to posterity being Karl Gotthelf (1740–1812), Gotthold's first biographer and the first editor of his posthumous papers.[6] Gotthold was intended by his father to follow him into the Lutheran ministry, and after five years at the famous school of St. Afra in Meissen he matriculated at the University of Leipzig on 20 September 1746 as a student of theology. From the beginning, however, he tended to neglect his theological studies, at first in favour of other academic subjects — attending lectures on philosophy and on the art and literature of classical antiquity — then in favour of more worldly pursuits such as dancing, fencing, riding, and the theatre. He made the acquaintance of Frau Neuber and her troupe, and rapidly developed a passionate interest in theatre and drama. This interest was shared and further encouraged by Christian Felix Weisse, a student of classical philology, three years older than Lessing; in friendly rivalry, the two planned dramas and made translations from the French. Twenty years later, Weisse too was a successful dramatist, and Lessing took his *Richard III* as the starting-point for one of the most important theoretical discussions in the *Hamburgische Dramaturgie*. Another

---

    [5]   Bruford, op. cit., p. 61.
    [6]   *Theologischer Nachlaß* (Berlin, 1784); *Theatralischer Nachlaß* (2 vols., Berlin, 1784–6); *G. E. Lessings Leben, nebst seinem noch übrigen literarischen Nachlasse* (3 vols., Berlin, 1793–5).

associate who encouraged Lessing's literary activities was his cousin,[7] Christlob Mylius, seven years older than himself, who had studied medicine and the natural sciences and had something of a reputation, at least in the pious Lessing family circle, as a dangerous freethinker.

The news that their son was associating with actors and atheists deeply shocked Pastor Lessing and his wife, and on hearing that he had actually had a play performed in public, the pastor summoned him home to Kamenz, a grim journey through the icy weather of February 1748, by telling him — falsely — that his mother was dying. The meeting passed off more amicably than might perhaps have been expected, and Lessing returned to Leipzig with his father's permission to change to the study of medicine; but soon the theatre led him into more serious trouble. Suddenly, in April 1748, the Neuber troupe broke up, and Lessing found himself in grave difficulties, for he had stood surety for a number of debts incurred by its members. Mylius left Leipzig for Berlin in May, and Lessing decided to join him; he disappeared from Leipzig, but was forced to break his journey in Wittenberg, where he fell ill. He matriculated at the university there, but stayed only a short time, arriving in Berlin in November resolved to live by his pen. Mylius had obtained an editorial post on the important *Berlinische privilegierte Zeitung*, and Lessing began to contribute reviews to this paper. In 1750, in collaboration with Mylius, he began a periodical publication, *Beiträge zur Historie und Aufnahme des Theaters*.[8] This ran only to four numbers, but it is still of considerable importance, as it marks his appearance as a serious critic and theorist of the drama. For the next ten years, practice and theory go hand in hand in Lessing's dramatic and theatrical concerns.

Der junge Gelehrte is one of a batch of comedies which Lessing completed in the earliest years of his literary career. He also followed with keen interest the development of drama in France, in England, and in other countries, made a number

---

[7] They were not actually blood relations: Mylius's father's first wife had been Anna Dorothea Lessing, sister of Lessing's father, but she died in 1716. Christlob was the fourth son of his second marriage.

[8] 'Aufnahme' here has the common eighteenth-century meaning of 'improvement' or 'encouragement': so too in Schlegel's *Gedanken zur Aufnahme des dänischen Theaters* (cf. below, p. 52).

of attempts at translation from various languages, and studied
many playwrights both ancient and modern. Another theatrical periodical, the *Theatralische Bibliothek*, ran intermittently
from 1754 to 1758; and 1755 saw the appearance of his first
major play, his first completed tragedy and in some ways his
most radically innovatory drama, *Miß Sara Sampson*.

Before he was thirty, Lessing had already made something
of a reputation for himself. He had even published a collected
edition of his works to date, in six volumes, containing apart
from his plays a quantity of verse in various forms and a considerable amount of critical prose writing on a wide range of
topics. Theology, his original intended calling, is not forgotten,
but figures importantly in the *Rettungen* or 'vindications', a
series of essays on writers of the past whom Lessing claims to
have been misunderstood or misrepresented: some of these
essays, particularly the *Rettung des Hieronymus Cardanus*,
contain seeds which were to blossom in the most profound
works of his maturity. In his critical works Lessing had established himself as a polemical writer of vigour, not to say
ferocity, notably in the *Vade mecum für den Herrn Samuel
Gotthold Lange* (1754), a savage demolition of the translations
of Horace by this minor, but successful and well-known poet
of the day.

In March 1754 Mylius died in London, at the age of thirty-
one, on the first stage of a projected scientific voyage to
America; Lessing wrote a preface to Mylius' collected works,
which were published in the following year, but its tone is far
removed from familial piety.[9] Evidently he had become es-
tranged from his former collaborator quite soon after his
arrival in Berlin. In those early years in the Prussian capital he
had however made a number of valued friends: the Jewish
philosopher Moses Mendelssohn; the bookseller and writer
Friedrich Nicolai, one of the leading proponents of the dis-
semination of Enlightenment amongst a wide reading public;
the poets Karl Wilhelm Ramler and Ewald von Kleist. His
friendship with Kleist seems to have been particularly close.
Kleist was to die in the Seven Years' War, but with the others
Lessing continued to correspond until his last years.

---

[9] G iii. 526–44.

In 1756 it appeared that his life was to take a new turn. He was engaged as travelling companion to a well-to-do young Saxon gentleman named Winkler, for a grand tour of Europe which was to include England. However, they had got no further than Amsterdam when the Prussian king Frederick the Great's invasion of Saxony opened the Seven Years' War and sent Winkler hurrying back to Leipzig. Lessing followed him, but in 1758 returned to Berlin and resumed his literary activities: in 1759 there appeared another tragedy, *Philotas*, and the first numbers of another important periodical publication, the *Briefe, die neueste Literatur betreffend* (commonly referred to as the *Literaturbriefe*), in which he collaborated with Mendelssohn and others. These cover a great variety of literary and, in a general sense, philosophical subjects, but only a handful deal with dramatic or theatrical matters; indeed No. 81 expresses a very pessimistic, disillusioned view of the German theatre. It seems that Lessing's active interest in the drama, which throughout the 1750s had manifested itself in experiment, theorizing, and critical discussion, as well as in the production of finished works, was waning. Indeed, he was beginning to feel dissatisfied with Berlin and with his literary career in general. Now however the new turn did come — and it was something very different from a grand tour with Winkler. He took up the post of official secretary to General Bogislaw von Tauentzien, commander of the Prussian forces in Silesia, and remained in Tauentzein's service, based in Breslau (now the Polish city of Wrocław) from 1760 till 1765. Theatre, drama, literature were not forgotten, but no major works of any kind were completed in those five years.

In 1765 Lessing returned to Berlin, this time directing his attention to the fields of antiquarian scholarship and aesthetics with the treatise *Laokoon, oder über die Grenzen der Malerei und Poesie*, the 'first part' of which (though there was never to be a second) appeared in 1766. With *Laokoon* Lessing seems to have hoped to establish himself in an academic career, perhaps to secure the post of librarian to the King of Prussia; but nothing came of this, and later that year the theatre called again. Once more an attempt was being made to run a theatre not purely as commercial entertainment, but under independent direction inspired by a programme of cultural and social improvement. This time the patrons were a group of Hamburg business men, and they invited Lessing to go to Hamburg as resident playwright and critic. He accepted; completed his comedy *Minna von Barnhelm*, which was performed there in 1767; and embarked upon another periodical publication, the twice-weekly *Hamburgische Dramaturgie*, which, from its beginnings as a running commentary on the Hamburg theatre and the plays performed there, grew into Lessing's major work of dramatic criticism and theory. But soon disillusion set in here too, more bitter than before, and he regretted having become involved in the Hamburg project. His interest in classical scholarship continued and bore new fruit in the *Briefe, antiquarischen Inhalts* and *Wie die Alten den Tod gebildet* (1768/9). Indeed, much of the latter part of the *Hamburgische Dramaturgie* also reflects this interest, seeming not so much the exposition of a dramatic theory for the 1760s as a scholarly interpretation of particular passages of Aristotle's *Poetics* — though Lessing's exegesis is indelibly stamped with his own assumptions, very much those of his age and generation, about the nature and functions of the drama. He never again worked in direct collaboration with the theatre, despite offers from Vienna and Mannheim where similar schemes to that in Hamburg were projected, though in both these cities under court patronage. But he continued to observe with interest the renaissance in German drama which was now actually under way, and to which he himself had in no small measure contributed; and in 1772 with *Emilia Galotti* he gave the German theatre its first mature tragedy, which was further to influence profoundly the rising generation of German dramatists.

From 1770 until the end of his life Lessing held the post of librarian to the Duke of Brunswick, and spent most of his time at the ducal library in Wolfenbüttel, though he made a number of journeys further afield, including in 1775 one to Vienna and Italy. The Bibliotheca Augustana in Wolfenbüttel was and is one of the great German libraries, and Lessing found much to do in bringing its treasures to light. In particular he returned to the study of theology, and to the encouragement of theological debate through the publication of obscure or neglected works which he had found in the library. Wolfenbüttel itself soon appeared no more congenial than Hamburg; relations with his aristocratic patrons were not smooth, his old friends were far away and although he made new ones, notably Johann Arnold Ebert and Johann Joachim Eschenburg, he felt lonely and frustrated. He suffered from illness and depression. For one year the gloom was dispersed by a ray of brightness. In October 1776 he married Eva König, the widow of a friend whose family and business affairs he had undertaken to look after. He was forty-five, she forty; they had been engaged for five years, but unable to marry owing to Lessing's endemic financial hardship. It was not a marriage of passion, but of mature, rational affection. On Christmas Day 1777 their son was born; but he died within a few hours, and on 10 January 1778 Eva died too. Lessing recorded his bereavement in letters of savage grief; the only 'laudanum' which could assuage his pain, as he wrote to Eschenburg on 14 January, was the cut and thrust of theological controversy, into which he now threw himself with redoubled vigour. And he now infuriated his opponents so much that they responded by persuading the Duke to withdraw the freedom from censorship which Lessing as ducal librarian had hitherto enjoyed. It appeared that he was to be silenced. But then, inspired by what in a letter to his brother Karl of 11 August 1778 he calls a 'närrischer Einfall', he returned to the drama. He could no longer express his religious views directly, but he gave shape to them in his last play, *Nathan der Weise*, completed in the winter ôf 1778/9. Apart from the treatise *Die Erziehung des Menschengeschlechts*, which appeared anonymously in 1780, it was his last published work. He died on 15 February 1781.

Lessing has been called the founder of modern German literature.[10] The title is deserved, but it needs some qualification. His formidable gifts were, it has often been said, critical and analytic rather than imaginative; and they were in large measure devoted to matters of a more general scholarly or intellectual kind. As a European figure he is principally remembered as a key contributor to those two central activities of the Enlightenment, the revaluation of classical antiquity and the criticism of traditional Christianity: in particular his theo-

[10] H. B. Garland, *Lessing: The Founder of Modern German Literature* (London, 1937, revised edn., 1962).

logical work is of abiding interest, and he is one of the most important figures in the evolution of the philosophy of history. Concerns such as this may well seem far removed from imaginative literature in the usual sense of the term, though he is one of the greatest masters of German prose, and his critical works, with their relentless probing, their irony, their seizing upon particular issues, and the sharpness of their polemic, often seem more revelatory of Lessing the man and his real response to the world about him than his literary works, where he is concealed by the stylized requirements of particular genres; in a famous essay the Romantic critic Friedrich Schlegel declared that his polemical works contained more genius and true poetic spirit than his imaginative compositions.[11] And within the more purely literary realm his claim to founder's status must still be strictly circumscribed. He played little or no part in the renaissance of lyricism, in practice or in theory; his own verse compositions are bounded almost entirely by the conventions of their time, and his critical remarks on a writer like Klopstock, who was trying to break free of those conventions, often betray an almost complete incomprehension of the latter's attempt to use language in a new and creative way. He played no part in the founding of the modern novel: he seems to have taken no cognizance of Gellert's work in this field, and though he does pay Wieland's *Agathon* an unsolicited compliment in his *Hamburgische Dramaturgie* (No. 69) — 'der erste und einzige Roman für den denkenden Kopf, von klassischem Geschmacke' — it is in fact a rather left-handed one, for he immediately continues, 'Roman? Wir wollen ihm diesen Titel nur geben, veilleicht, daß es einige Leser mehr dadurch bekömmt.' Regrettably, he does not seem to have had any real feeling for, or interest in, the imaginative possibilities of narrative prose. It is in the drama that his literary pre-eminence lies; here, however, it is unchallengeable.

After a fairly conventional start and some experimentations whose intrinsic success seems doubtful, he produced three mature masterpieces, *Minna von Barnhelm*, *Emilia Galotti*, and *Nathan der Weise*, which set a standard for modern German drama in three forms: comedy, tragedy, and the

---

[11] Friedrich Schlegel, 'Über Lessing', in B 8–35, esp. 14 f.

modern drama of ideas to which the traditional generic labels
are no longer applicable. Here too his achievement is European
rather than merely German. For a while in the decades following his death the 'classical' evolution of Goethe and Schiller
produced in Germany the last belated flowering of verse
drama in the Renaissance tradition, Lessing had pointed the
way to a drama of contemporary social realism and of critical
debate which was to come to the fore in the nineteenth century and to hold sway in our own.

Moreover, Lessing's claim to be considered the founder of
modern German literature seems to have a great deal to do
with his choice of genre. There may be something of the
chicken and the egg here, in that the success of Lessing's own
plays and the intense application of his critical intelligence to
the nature and purpose of dramatic art themselves contributed
in no small measure to the prestige of the drama in German
literature. Yet there is more to it than that. The examples of
Elizabethan England and the 'grand siècle' in France suggest
that the dramatic form is in some way particularly suited to
the expression of a newly emergent national culture; Gottsched
seems to have perceived as much, though without speculating
upon the reasons. They are indeed complex, and we shall
consider some of them later in appropriate contexts. But one
which we may suggest here has to do with the ability of the
dramatist to adapt traditional *forms* for the expression of new
content, new attitudes or new sensibilities. It is noteworthy
that Klopstock and Wieland, the pioneers of the new lyricism
and of the novel, are both in many ways more consciously innovatory writers than Lessing. In the terms of one of the most
fundamental and wide-ranging in its implications of the literary controversies of post-Renaissance Europe, he was an
'ancient' rather than a 'modern':[12] though his practical
dramatic activity is experimental and exploratory, in theory
he seems to regard himself primarily as a restorer and purifier
of tradition. As we have noted, in 1759 he attacks Gottsched
for destroying the German theatre and trying to re-create it
from scratch, rather than *reforming* it as he should have done.
In the *Hamburgische Dramaturgie* ten years later he effectively

[12] See G. A. Highet, *The Classical Tradition* (2nd edn., Oxford, 1951), pp.
261–88.

condemns European (at all events, continental European) drama since the Renaissance as an aberration, and urges a return to the standards of the Greeks. Klopstock and Wieland were confidently forward-looking; but today it is they who seem old-fashioned, the real birth of modern German poetry and the modern German novel having to wait for Goethe, while Lessing appears as the first of the moderns.

The relation between Lessing's dramatic theory and prac- tice is another topic to which we shall have repeated occasion to return. Too often one hears it said that Lessing's plays were written to illustrate or exemplify various aspects of his dramatic theory. In fact the relationship between them is complex and often contradictory. The early comedies show the young dramatist trying out the basic tools of his craft, largely if not entirely within already established patterns. Lessing's interest in the more advanced developments of the contemporary theatre is reflected in *Miß Sara Sampson*, which one can thus call a piece of practical dramatic criticism. It is an experiment in 'bürgerliches Trauerspiel', which is not to say that it was written in illustration of a theory of that genre: indeed, as we shall see, in this case theory follows practice rather than the other way about. *Minna von Barnhelm*, com- pleted before the inception of the *Hamburgische Dramaturgie* and unaccompanied by a theory of comedy such as the *Drama- turgie* was to elaborate for tragedy, seems a work altogether more independent of theoretical considerations, written, one is tempted to believe, to express Lessing's view of the post-war situation and of contemporary German society; in fact, as I shall argue, it is at least as much a work intended as a model of a particular dramatic genre — practical criticism again, though here practice neither precedes nor follows theory but, largely, replaces it. *Emilia Galotti* is often thought to be a model tragedy written according to the precepts of the *Ham- burgische Dramaturgie*. There is much truth in this view, even if those precepts are never systematically formulated but have to be inferred from a variety of scattered pronouncements; at the same time, what is most interesting, and most valuable, about *Emilia Galotti* arises from the conflict between the requirements of an exemplary form, defined in the *Drama- turgie* in an uncompromisingly conservative or traditional sense, and the vividly contemporary content, the very untraditional sensibilities, and (some would say) the very progressive 'message' of the work. The play offers a remarkable test case for theories on the controversial topic of literary 'intention',[13] for what Lessing was trying to *do* and what his play *means* seem to be different things.

In all these plays we are aware of the direction of Lessing's critical intelligence towards dramatic and theatrical possibilities: the plays and the theoretical pronouncements together make up the picture of Lessing's engagement with the drama, its traditions and its received forms, and its potentialities as an instrument of cultural revival. *Nathan der Weise* stands apart. Alone of Lessing's mature dramas it was written because Lessing had a particular message to convey, rather than because he wanted, whether by way of experiment or of exemplification, to write a particular kind of play. The form is here determined by the content, rather than the other way about, and the critical intelligence is directed not primarily at the cultural potential of the drama in general, but at the real-life issues with which this particular play is concerned and, secondarily, at the potential of the theatre as a 'pulpit' for conveying a specific message — in direct contradiction to some of the most subtle of Lessing's earlier theorizing. Even the choice of the dramatic medium seems to have been made for purely external and fortuitous reasons, Lessing having been forcibly prevented from conveying his message in the medium of critical prose which had seemed in those last years the most congenial to him. And the particular form is one which transcends the traditional genre-boundaries to which, again, Lessing the dramatic theorist had appeared to be so firmly committed. It is no worse a play for this — it is indeed, in my view, Lessing's greatest: the personal urgency of its thematic content brings us closer to Lessing the man than any of his other dramatic works, and in the freedom of its form the practical innovator is no longer compromised by the theoretical conservative. But this in turn means that from the point of view of form, and of the history of Lessing's engagement with dramatic form, it is of unique interest, completing our picture from a new and unexpected perspective.

[13] See D. Newton-de Molina (ed.), *On Literary Intention* (Edinburgh, 1976).

II

Lessing and Comedy

The young Lessing turned, it seems, naturally to comedy rather than tragedy. Writing to his father on 28 April 1749, defending himself for pursuing such frivolities as literature and the theatre when he was supposed to be devoting himself to his theological studies, he declares that he would not be ashamed to earn the title of a German Molière; and by the time he was twenty he had written no less than six comedies of his own, plus two translations or adaptations from the Roman comic playwright Plautus. From the same period of his life only two fragmentary attempts at original tragedy survive. The writing of *Miß Sara Sampson* in 1755 then ushers in a long, complex but intellectually if not chronologically continuous process of grappling with the problems of tragedy, which leads through the experimentation of the late fifties and the theorizing of the *Hamburgische Dramaturgie* to the completion in 1772 of *Emilia Galotti* — conceived in that first period of experimentation, in January 1758 or earlier. Lessing's return to comedy in *Minna von Barnhelm* interrupts this process, which needs to be seen as a unity; conversely, *Minna von Barnhelm* itself should be seen in relation to the possibilities of the comic form which Lessing had so vigorously explored in his youth.

A consideration of the more straightforward genre may also help us in our approach to the more problematic one. It is a commonplace of literary history that eighteenth-century tragedy, in England and France no less than in Germany, often shows a sense of strain, of conscious effort: the tragic characters of Addison and Voltaire strike poses and utter declamatory rhetoric which, we feel — as we do not with Shakespeare or Racine — are remote from the genuine experience of their authors or the audiences for whom they wrote. So much eighteenth-century tragedy seems essentially to be *about* nothing more than 'tragedy': the imitation of an antique, in-deed an antiquated, dramatic form for no better reason than its inherited literary prestige. To a twentieth-century audience, eighteenth-century comedy too may sometimes seem man-nered and remote. But its remoteness is no more than that of the eighteenth century itself; with tragedy, we sense a double remove. The world of the comedies is the world of their authors and their audiences, its perceptions and responses theirs.

These are, as always, varied. Comedy, if a less problematic form than tragedy, is not less complex. It involves a number of different — sometimes apparently contradictory — elements, held in careful balance. The balance can be tipped quite sharply in one direction or another; but there will come a point beyond which it can be tipped no further, or the result will no longer be comedy. What one might call the affective bias of comedy may be negative or positive, satirical or sym-pathetic. That is, the comic dramatist may encourage us to laugh *at* his characters, as examples of human folly or weak-ness, sometimes to the point of suggesting that all humanity and its doings are ridiculous or even contemptible; or he may encourage us to sympathize *with* them, to recognize in them images of what is admirable in humanity and to rejoice with them when their virtue is rewarded. At the one extreme, comedy tips over into farce; at the other, into sentimentality. The writer of literary comedy will generally seek to avoid these extremes. The classical tradition of European comedy, represented at its peak by Molière, tends however strongly to the satirical pole, presenting us with a rogues' or fools' gallery of misers, misanthropists, libertines, humbugs, and their vic-tims; whereas Shakespearian comedy, though not without its clowns and rustics to make us laugh, concentrates far more of our attention on sympathetic characters, the vicissitudes of fortune which beset them, and their ultimate achievement of happiness. Classical comedy often has (or at any rate often claims) a didactic intent: its exposure of folly and vice is held to furnish warning examples, and hence to fulfil a social function.

The mixture and disposition of the dramatic elements in comedy — character portrayal, plot, language, and stage spectacle — also varies a great deal: far more so than in tragedy, where plot (the tragic *event*) is of vital importance and all the other elements essentially subordinate to it. Classical European comedy is based very largely on the portrayal of character types, and here the plot is subordinate and often quite arbitrary: the dramatist merely has to devise a series of situations in which the characters can exhibit themselves. On the other hand, some comedies depend very much on plot, on the creation of elaborate patterns of relationships between the characters which are sorted out satisfactorily only at the very end. This is obviously true of Shakespearian romance; but also of the Italian *commedia dell'arte*, ancestor of the pantomime, with its set of stock characters (lovers, old men, cunning, rascally, or oafish servants, and so on), stereotyped plots, and often largely improvised dialogue, which is a vital element in the continental European comic tradition.[1]

Because of the variety of its basic elements and of their possible combinations and permutations, the relative unimportance of plausibility and consistency, and the fact that incongruity can itself be a source of amusement, comedy is able to absorb a considerable amount of heterogeneous matter. In particular it often incorporates a good deal of what may be called realism, in the portrayal of the manners, fashions, and prejudices of a specific society, and topical allusions to persons and events of the day. This realism is not necessarily of a very profound kind; it is often over-stressed by those critics who are interested above all in the satirical element in comedy, particularly those with ideological axes to grind. Not every concrete or topical reference is necessarily evidence of passionate social or moral concern on the dramatist's part. His business is to amuse his audience, and one of the means at his disposal is familiar reference, often placed in an unfamiliar or unusual context. It is nevertheless true that realism in comedy is very often associated with satirical intent.

In eighteenth-century Germany, Gottsched and his school naturally favoured the classical style of comedy: comedy of a satirical mode based upon the portrayal of particular folly or vice, typically embodied in a central character or group of

[1] Cf. W. Hinck, *Das deutsche Lustspiel des 17. und 18. Jahrhunderts und die italienische Komödie* (Stuttgart, 1965).

characters and often identified (as with Molière's miser or misanthrope) in the title of the play. It might be a folly specific to a particular age and a particular society, like the bogus Pietist religiosity of Frau Gottsched's *Die Pietisterei im Fischbeinrocke*, or a more universal failing like the ineffectual busybodiness of Johann Elias Schlegel's *Der geschäftige Müßiggänger*. The affective emphasis of this kind of comedy is strongly negative, so much so that German critics often refer to it as 'comedy of derision' ('Verlachkomödie'):[2] its foolish and vicious characters are generally presented as incorrigible, and we see them exposed and humiliated, but rarely converted, reconciled, or even forgiven. Like Brecht two hundred years later, Gottsched and his school held that it was their business to make their audiences see, but that whether their characters themselves saw was immaterial.[3]

At the same time, however, the early eighteenth century witnessed an important manifestation of the alternative mode of comedy, in which it is the positive affective elements which are stressed. This originated in France, where it was known originally as *comédie attendrissante*, then (at first amongst its detractors, but later more generally) as *comédie larmoyante*; the designations appear in German as 'rührendes' and 'weinerliches Lustspiel' respectively, but in Germany it was the former which gained and retained general currency, the latter being perhaps more obviously and strongly pejorative than its French equivalent. The 'rührendes Lustspiel' shares with its eighteenth-century satirical counterpart the social utilitarianism characteristic of the age: that is, whereas Gottschedian comedy stresses folly and vice, sentimental comedy stresses virtue, and its scenes of reconciliation and ultimate harmony take place not (as in Shakespearian romance) in a remote, fantastic, or unreal setting which is to be understood as a symbol of a higher, cosmic configuration, but in the familiar settings of contemporary society.

Both these characteristic modes of eighteenth-century

---

[2] Cf. H. Steinmetz, *Die Komödie der Aufklärung* (Sammlung Metzler, xlvii, Stuttgart, 1966), p. 20; H. Arntzen, *Die ernste Komödie. Das deutsche Lustspiel von Lessing bis Kleist* (Munich, 1968), p. 21.

[3] Cf. Brecht, *Gesammelte Werke* (Werkausgabe, Frankfurt, 1967), xvii. 1150 (note to *Mutter Courage und ihre Kinder*).

comedy employ a largely realistic style: thus the use of verse (obligatory for tragedy) was abandoned. In both modes, though, we find that realism is checked by a number of devices of deliberate stylization. Most noteworthy of these is the naming of the characters. A few (most commonly, servants) have ordinary German Christian names like 'Anton' or 'Peter', but none have ordinary German surnames; some, chiefly of course in satirical comedy, have characterizing or 'humour' names denoting their particular aberration, like Frau Glaubeleichtin and Magister Scheinfromm in *Die Pietisterei im Fischbeinrocke* (Frau Glaubeleichtin's husband has naturally to be called Herr Glaubeleicht, though this doesn't fit his character or his — fortunately very minor — function in the play). But most commonly the characters of early eighteenth-century German comedy bear those curious featureless, interchangeable neo-classical names familiar to us from Molière: Adrast and Oront, Damis and Lelio, and so on.

The 'rührendes Lustspiel' was attacked by Gottsched and his followers as tending to blur the traditional distinctions between the dramatic genres (a matter of great concern in academic literary criticism) by seeking to evoke responses (pity and admiration) proper not to comedy but to tragedy. It was vigorously defended by Gellert, who, in addition to writing a number of such comedies himself, made this genre the subject of a Latin inaugural lecture, *Pro comoedia commovente*, delivered on his accession to a chair at the University of Leipzig in 1751. This was later translated into German and brought to the attention of a wider public by Lessing in his *Theatralische Bibliothek*.

Lessing, as a student in Leipzig, liberated from the puritanical confines of home and family, and setting out to become a German Molière, was keenly aware of all the modes of comic writing which were being practised in his day, both traditional and innovatory. The early comedies explore most of the contemporary possibilities of the genre: within the territory which they define, Lessing served his dramatic apprenticeship. For the most part they are conventional, but here and there new ground is broken. *Der junge Gelehrte* stands firmly within the satirical tradition, with its pedantic prig of a central character, who remains at the end just as incorrigibly pedantic and priggish as at the beginning, and its arbitrary, conventional love-interest. Its satire is specific, topical (much allusion is made to the Prussian Academy's essay competition of 1747), and, Lessing claimed, derived directly from his own experience: for, in the introductory remarks to the play written for its publication in his collected works in 1754, he wrote, 'Unter diesem Ungeziefer aufgewachsen, war es ein Wunder, daß ich meine ersten satyrischen Waffen wider dasselbe wandte?'[4] The young scholar Damis is, at twenty, master of seven languages — though he doesn't know Wendish, the Slavonic language spoken in Lessing's native Lusatia (I.1). He always has a book in his hand and a philological speculation in his head: a new note on Homer (I.2) or a query about rabbinical Hebrew (1,5). But all his learning is useless, unrelated, meaningless, and he has no knowledge of life or the real world: as he is told by his servant — 'Er hat alles gelesen, nur kein Komplimentierbuch' (I,1), his father — 'Ich glaube, ihr Gelehrten, je mehr ihr lernt, je mehr vergeßt ihr' (II, 15), and the maid Lisette — 'Sie sind noch nicht klug, und sind schon zwanzig Jahr alt!' (III, 3). In the final reckoning even the world of learning rejects him: the essay with which he confidently expects to win the Academy's prize is full of 'kritischen Kleinigkeiten', but completely ignores the 'Hauptsache' (III, 15). Such plot as the play has concerns the scheme of Damis's father to marry him to his ward Juliane, and the foiling of this scheme by Juliane's lover Valer, with the enthusiastic help of the servants, always in this kind of play willing and able to get the better of their masters. The convention offers possibilities of social criticism, but these remain latent, and the audience's emotional sympathies, in so far as they are aroused at all, lie with the characters of higher rank, in this case Juliane and Valer. But the plot is clearly of subordinate importance to the satirical portrait of the central character, further supported by a good deal of incidental wit and repartee.

The satire of *Der Misogyn* and *Die alte Jungfer* is more general, and the plot-element is more important; but the former, with its vigorous and attractive heroine who dresses

---

[4] G iii. 524.

as a man to help her lover escape from the tyranny of his mis-
ogynistic father, tends to a balance of satire and sentiment,
while *Die alte Jungfer*, in which all the main characters — the
'old maid' of the title, and the two men who are after her
money — are ridiculous, and none sympathetic, moves in the
direction of farce. *Damon, oder die wahre Freundschaft*, on
the other hand, is almost pure sentimental comedy: Damon
the hero is the true friend, Leander, the false friend and rival
in love, is not a comic figure at whom we may laugh, but rather
a villain to be reviled and feared (though finally forgiven), and
the business of making the audience laugh is entrusted almost
exclusively, and at all events excessively, to a minor character,
Oronte, with a catch-phrase, 'Versteh Er mich', repeated *ad
nauseam*.

Of these four comedies, *Der junge Gelehrte* is undoubtedly
the most accomplished, though the published text of 1754
may well have been revised and refined from that performed
in 1748. *Der Misogyn* is also a pleasing, if conventional, piece;
Lessing himself evidently thought well of it, for in 1767 he
revised it, extending the original one act into three, and developing the role of Laura, the hero's sister, who (of course)
herself falls in love with the disguised heroine. *Damon* and *Die
alte Jungfer* are unquestionably inferior; indeed Lessing excluded them from his collected works, and was much put out
when in 1769 they were reprinted without his consent.[5] But
it is noteworthy, and probably not coincidental, that they are
also the two which stray furthest from the centre of the comic
range, the one in the direction of farce, and, more important,
of exclusively negative affective content (there being no characters who are sympathetic) and the other in the direction of
sentiment (there being no major character who is comic).
Lessing soon decided that it was in the middle of the range
that true comedy lay, and continued to maintain this view
both in practice and in theory.

Die Juden and *Der Freigeist* break new ground in their
modification of the satirical element, and in this are both the
most original of the early comedies and the most characteristic
of their author. Satirical comedy generally rests upon an

---

⁵   Cf. Lessing's letter to his publisher Voss, 5 January 1770.

agreement between the author and his presumed or intended audience. This is true even of the anti- 'establishment' satire of our own times, which even at its most radical — indeed, then more so than ever — is principally aimed at an already disaffected audience and preaches thus largely to the converted; those who do not share the author's assumptions may well be shocked, but they are unlikely to reconsider their views, and the author may be quite content with shocking them. Author and audience are likely to agree that a miser or a misogynist, or the religious humbugs of *Die Pietisterei im Fischbeinrocke*, are fit objects for satire. But in *Die Juden* and *Der Freigeist* Lessing is neither simply working on a basis of shared assumptions with his audience (from which it is not a very long step to flattering their prejudices) nor trying to shock them. He is attempting a critical examination of controversial issues of the day — issues, that is, upon which the members of his audience might well be expected to have differing views, and issues which were very dear to his own heart and mind: in *Die Juden* anti-Semitic prejudice, and in *Der Freigeist* the relationship between religious belief, or lack of it, and moral conduct. He is seeking to persuade his audience similarly to examine these issues, forgetting such prejudices as they may have, and to come to a rational point of view. And as a means or aid to such persuasion he is seeking to amuse and entertain his audience, to present them not merely with negative objects of satirical laughter but with positive objects of appreciation, with sympathetic characters and admirable modes of behaviour — yet without going too far in the direction of sentiment or the portrayal of unalloyed virtue.

In the latter respect *Die Juden* perhaps fails — or was felt to have failed by some of Lessing's contemporaries; but maybe he had rather succeeded, to some extent in any rate, in forcing them to reconsider their prejudices. The rascally, bearded 'Jews' who attack and attempt to rob the Baron and his daughter are revealed as two of his own 'Christian' servants in disguise; and the anonymous 'Reisender' who rescues them turns out to be a Jew. Reviewing the play in the *Göttingische gelehrte Anzeigen*, the noted Orientalist and theologian Johann David Michaelis claimed that it was improbable that a Jew should be so unexceptionably virtuous, so brave, noble,

and generous, as the traveller in Lessing's play. Lessing replied
to the criticism in a short essay in his *Theatralische Bibliothek*.[6] The Jewish traveller is certainly shown as sympathetic
and admirable in every respect. (It has been alleged that he is
intended as a portrait of Moses Mendelssohn, but the play
was almost certainly written before Lessing and Mendelssohn
met.) This means of course that he, who must be regarded as
the central figure of the play, is in no way a comic character;
nor on the other hand is the prejudice of anti-Semitism itself
shown as comic, though some of its manifestations may have
comic overtones, as in the traveller's servant Christoph (who
embodies that prejudice in a caricatured form) or, more sinis-
terly, in the two robbers. The satirical effect of the play is
thus more indirect and generalized than in the traditional
type of satirical comedy: the arousal of laughter is largely a
matter of incident, stage business (the changing hands of the
traveller's purloined snuffbox), and verbal repartee, and is
almost entirely confined to the peripheral characters of the
servant class. Even the union of lovers, on which, as so often
in comedies, the curtain falls, is similarly confined to Christoph and the Baron's maid Lisette. For the Baron's daughter
cannot marry the Jewish traveller, even though this might
seem the obvious conclusion of the plot.

Der Freigeist is both in content and dramatic treatment
more complex, and must be accounted the most important
and original of the early comedies. In his letter of self-defence
to his father of 28 April 1749 Lessing undertook to write 'eine
Komödie . . . die nicht nur die Herren Theologen lesen sondern
auch loben sollen', a satire on freethinkers and deriders of
religion. Accordingly, Adrast, the titular protagonist of the
play, is shown to be obstinately and unreasonably prejudiced:
he believes that all clergymen are knaves and scoundrels, out
to cheat him. The living refutation of this prejudice is provided
by Theophan, a young clergyman described in Lessing's notes
for the play as 'so tugendhaft und edel, als fromm'. But those
notes also describe Adrast as 'ohne Religion, aber voller tugendhafter Gesinnungen'.[7] His prejudice prevents him from
judging Theophan correctly, but it does not otherwise prevent

⁶ G i. 415–22.   ⁷ G ii. 651.

him from being a good and admirable character. One wonders whether the theologians really had cause to be so pleased: the clergyman is certainly shown in a favourable light, but the freethinker is essentially as good a man as he; and though he is cured of his prejudice against clerics, there is no indication that he needs to embrace the Christian faith. What counts is a man's moral conduct, and to this, it seems, tenets and beliefs are irrelevant. Lessing does not suggest that it is Theophan's piety that makes him 'tugendhaft und edel'. And just as in *Die Juden* the servant Christoph is a caricature of an anti-Semite, so here both freethinker *and* cleric are caricatured in their servants Johann and Martin. These are, as the maid Lisette observes, 'die wahren Bilder ihrer Herren, von der häßlichen Seite! Aus Freigeisterei ist jener ein Spitzbube; und aus Frömmigkeit dieser ein Dummkopf' (II, 4). Indeed Theophan himself is not perfect — though that makes him not a worse but a better human being; Adrast, who throughout the play has refused to accept Theophan's protestations of friendship, is finally persuaded of his sincerity when he loses his temper, thus showing that he is not a stuffed dummy in a clerical collar but a real person.[8] The play is thus not simply a vindication of the churchman. It is in a way a vindication of the honest freethinker too; perhaps even, if one is to look for a biographical source, of Mylius and of Lessing's association with him. The message is not in the least doctrinaire, but for all that unequivocal and unmistakably Lessingian: a plea for a humane society based upon tolerance and good sense, and embracing all men of good will whatever their faiths or opinions.

This has important dramatic consequences. Adrast's prejudice blinkers him, but it does not prevent him from being basically an admirable character; that is, it makes him an object of satire while still essentially sympathetic. Usually these functions are divided: Damis in *Der junge Gelehrte*, Wumshäter in *Der Misogyn* are totally ridiculous figures, and our sympathy is reserved for the lovers whose union they unsuccessfully try to obstruct. And at the final curtain Damis and Wumshäter

---

[8]   Cf. F. A. Brown, 'The Conversion of Lessing's "Freygeist"', *JEGP* lvi (1957), 186-202, and V. Nölle, *Subjektivität und Wirklichkeit in Lessings dramatischem und theologischem Werk* (Berlin, 1977), pp. 22 ff. The scene is also, of course, quite simply an example of the old comic device of role-reversal.

remain unrepentant and incorrigible, and are simply pushed aside in the general rejoicing: *Der junge Gelehrte* ends with the servant Anton crying 'Je nun! wem nicht zu raten steht, dem steht auch nicht zu helfen. Bleiben Sie zeitlebens der gelehrte Herr Damis!' – to be answered by Damis throwing a book at him. But in *Der Freigeist* Lessing has firstly to make Adrast see the error of his ways, and secondly to include him in the general happy resolution. This means that more weight is thrown upon the plot. The plot of *Der Freigeist* is based on a symmetrical pattern, involving a change of partners. Adrast and Theophan are betrothed to two sisters, Adrast to the gay and frivolous Henriette and Theophan to the quiet and serious Juliane, but the real inclinations of both the men and the girls are not towards their like (as it might seem) but towards their complementary opposite. The action of the play brings this into the open, and at the end the girls' father cheerfully gives his consent to the exchange:

Seid ihr aber nicht wunderliches Volk! Ich wollte jedem zu seinem Rocke egales Futter geben, aber ich sehe wohl, euer Geschmack ist bunt. Der Fromme sollte die Fromme, und der Lustige die Lustige haben: Nichts! der Fromme will die Lustige, und der Lustige die Fromme.

(V, 7)

The plot is thus made to reinforce the play's message of tolerant humanity, its advocacy of a world in which men (and women) of good will can live happily together despite differences of character and creed; and its patent artificiality in no way detracts from this function.

The two Plautine comedies *Die Gefangenen* and *Der Schatz* are both similarly plays with a positive, rather than a negative or satiric, affective intention and strongly dependent upon plot: both are celebrations of friendship and loyalty, and both rely dramatically upon misapprehensions and mistaken identities and the eventual revelation of the truth. The first, a translation of Plautus' *Captivi*, was published in the *Beiträge zur Historie und Aufnahme des Theaters* in 1750 accompanied by an essay on Plautus' life and works and a critical discussion of the play; *Der Schatz* is a lively, free adaptation (in one act) of Plautus' *Trinummus*. (Both, incidentally, have all-male casts.) Lessing's interest in Plautus is very much of a piece with the concerns demonstrated in his own comedies. Plautus introduced into Latin literature a form of drama derived from the Greek 'New Comedy': less fiercely satirical than the Old Comedy of Aristophanes, more 'domestic' and even at times sentimental in tone, with a new stress on virtue to be admired and emulated as much as on folly or vice to be derided and shunned. At the same time Plautus does not neglect to make his audience laugh: indeed he was very much a popular dramatist, aiming to please a wide public. Because of this, he was regarded by more refined critics as vulgar: thus Gottsched, echoing Horace, declares that 'Plautus . . . bequemte sich zu sehr nach dem Geschmacke des Pöbel [*sic*], und mengte viel garstige Zoten und niederträchtige Fratzen hinein.'[9] Plautus was also criticized for technical 'irregularities', such as failure to observe strictly the dramatic unities. Lessing defends him against such charges as these, asserting in the *Beiträge* that the *Captivi*, despite its incidental faults, is 'das schönste Stück, das jemals auf die Bühne gekommen, und zwar aus keiner andern Ursache . . . als weil es der Absicht der Lustspiele am nächsten kömmt'. This purpose he defines as 'die Sitten der Zuschauer zu bilden und zu bessern. Die Mittel die sie dazu anwendet, sind, daß sie das Laster verhaßt, und die Tugend liebenswürdig vorstellet.'[10] Lessing thus sees Plautus as occupying just that middle ground of comedy to which he himself characteristically aspires.[11]

The works we have been discussing were all written between about 1747 and 1750, though *Der Schatz* was not published until 1755. In 1754, in his second theatrical periodical, the *Theatralische Bibliothek*, Lessing summed up the tendency of those years to move away from purely negative satiric comedy of the type favoured by Gottsched. The *Abhandlungen von dem weinerlichen oder rührenden Lustspiel* comprise translations of the French critic Chassiron's hostile *Essai sur le comique larmoyant* of 1749 and of Gellert's apologia *Pro comoedia commovente*, with an introduction and a conclusion by Lessing himself. Having presented the two opposing points

[9] Gottsched, *Versuch einer critischen Dichtkunst* (4th edn., Leipzig 1751, reprinted Darmstadt, 1962), p. 634. Cf. G iii, 377.

[10] G iii. 503 ff.

[11] Cf. V. Riedel, *Lessing und die römische Literatur* (Weimar, 1976), pp. 39 ff.

of view, he argues that although 'rührendes Lustspiel' seeks to arouse more sentiment than is, strictly speaking, admissible in comedy, the new form is still 'nützlich und für gewisse Denkungsarten angenehm'. But more generally and more importantly, he argues that true comedy, as exemplified by Plautus and even by Molière, has never lacked touching scenes: 'Ja, ich getraue mir zu behaupten, daß nur dieses allein wahre Komödien sind, welche so wohl Tugenden als Laster, so wohl Anständigkeit als Ungereimtheit schildern, weil sie eben durch diese Vermischung ihrem Originale, dem menschlichen Leben, am nächsten kommen.'[12]

True comedy, then, in Lessing's view, aims to amuse, to instruct, or to improve — the unquestioning assumption of moral purpose runs through all Lessing's dramatic theorizing — but also to move, and to be true to life. It also aims to appeal to the widest possible public. In the conclusion to the *Abhandlungen* Lessing identifies two extreme forms of comedy: farce ('Possenspiel'), which aims to arouse only laughter, and 'rührendes Lustspiel' which aims only to arouse emotional sympathy — 'weinen und an stillen Tugenden ein edles Vergnügen finden zu lassen', as he had defined it in the prefatory section of his remarks. True comedy will however arouse both. Lessing then goes on to suggest that farce is for the mob, *comédie larmoyante* for spectators of a higher social class and a more refined — indeed over-refined — taste, but true comedy of universal appeal:

Der Pöbel wird ewig der Beschützer der Possenspiele bleiben, und unter Leuten von Stande wird es immer gezwungne Zärtlinge geben, die den Ruhm empfindlicher Seelen auch da zu behaupten suchen, wo andre ehrliche Leute gähnen. Die wahre Komödie allein ist für das Volk, und allein fähig einen allgemeinen Beifall zu erlangen, und folglich auch einen allgemeinen Nutzen zu stiften.[13]

(ii)

At this point, however, Lessing's attention turned away from comedy and towards tragedy. Indeed the most immediately fruitful remarks in the *Abhandlungen von dem weinerlichen*

---

[12] G iv. 55.   [13] Ibid. 56.

oder rührenden Lustspiel, as far as his own dramatic career is concerned, occur in the introductory section, where he observes that the innovation of the sentimental mode in comedy has its parallel in contemporary tragedy, in the introduction of the domestic tragedy or 'bürgerliches Trauerspiel'. This form had originated in England and spread to France; as yet there were no German examples, but in the following year Lessing took up his own hint with *Miß Sara Sampson* and, no doubt stimulated by his initial success in the genre, devoted his dramatic energies, practical and theoretical, for the remainder of the 1750s almost exclusively to tragedy. The first signs of a turning back towards comedy may perhaps be detected in Lessing's translation, which appeared in 1760, of the plays and accompanying theoretical essays of Diderot. True, Diderot the dramatist is usually thought of not so much as a writer of comedies but as a reformer of tragedy; indeed his efforts in this field run closely parallel to Lessing's own. As early as 1748 Diderot had voiced his discontent with the traditions of French classical drama and advocated the adoption of a simpler, more natural style, in a passage in his novel *Les Bijoux indiscrets* (translated by Lessing at a later date in Nos. 84 f. of the *Hamburgische Dramaturgie*). Then, in 1757, in the *Entretiens sur le Fils naturel,* and 1758, in the essay *De la poésie dramatique,* he had gone further and proposed the introduction of a new dramatic form which he calls the *genre sérieux.* This, lying midway between traditional tragedy and comedy, has as its aim the faithful dramatic representation of real life — like Lessing's 'wahre Komödie'. And though Diderot seems indeed to have more to say about tragedy than about comedy, his two plays, *Le Fils naturel* and *Le Père de famille,* serious and sentimentally touching rather than amusing as they both are, nevertheless have happy endings, and both bear the designation *comédie.* Lessing's aim in *Miß Sara Sampson* and in his subsequent experimental and theoretical investigation of tragedy was, as we shall see, the establishment of a form of serious drama which should be true to life and not, like conventional high tragedy, totally remote from the everyday experiences and concerns of an eighteenth-century audience. His study of Diderot confirmed that aim, but may have suggested to him that it was more likely to be achieved on a basis of comedy than of tragedy. It was, after all, the aim which he had established for 'true comedy' in 1754, and for which he had established a practical formula four or five years before that in *Der Freigeist*. Accordingly, in his last and greatest prose comedy, *Minna von Barnhelm*, we find him returning to that basic formula. It is a comedy which seeks to arouse both sentiment and laughter; it is essentially a comedy of plot, of misunderstandings and multiple reversals of situation culminating in a final happy reconciliation, but with nevertheless a strong element of satire both general and specific; its characters, at any rate the principals, are sympathetic, even admirable, but not without their human failings and weaknesses. In respect both of its affective and its dramatic elements, as we have called them, *Minna von Barnhelm* occupies a position very near the centre of the comic range.

It did not however appear for another seven years, and these years included the most eventful period of Lessing's life and the most radical departure from its normal pattern. The experiences of those years left a deep impression on the play, which seems of all Lessing's completed dramatic works the closest to life and the most directly imitative of it: the others are all (irrespective of whether they are worse or better than *Minna*) more evidently literary or intellectual in inspiration, and none of them is set so concretely, if at all, in the Germany of his own day.

In an often-quoted passage in his autobiography *Dichtung und Wahrheit*, Goethe refers to *Minna von Barnhelm* as 'die wahrste Ausgeburt des siebenjährigen Krieges'.[14] The war between Prussia and the alliance of Austria, Russia, and Saxony broke out at the end of August 1756 and was concluded by the Peace of Hubertusburg signed on 15 February 1763. Lessing was a native Saxon who had been living in the Prussian capital, Berlin, since 1749; but such conflicting loyalties as he may have felt seem to have caused him, at any rate initially, little distress. The King of Prussia had upset his plans for a grand tour of Europe with Winkler; in return, he expressed, in a letter to Ramler of 18 June 1757, the hope 'daß nichts als

[14] *Dichtung und Wahrheit*, Book vii: Goethe, *Werke* (Hamburger Ausgabe), ix. 281.

schlechte Verse auf seine Siege mögen gemacht werden'. He continued his literary activities more or less undisturbed. The theme of patriotic heroism finds expression in the tragedy *Philotas*, completed in 1759, but this is of all his plays the most abstract and remote from real life. The first of the *Literaturbriefe*, of the same year, maintains that the war can be regarded as 'nichts als ein blutiger Prozeß unter unabhängigen Häuptern, der alle übrige Stände ungestöret läßt'.[15] But even there Lessing concedes that this is perhaps only a polite fiction — and very soon the truth was to prove otherwise. For it was also in 1759 that one of the most valued friends he had made in Berlin, the Prussian officer-poet Ewald von Kleist, was fatally wounded at the battle of Kunersdorf; and at home in Saxony, his eighteen-year-old brother Erdmann Lessing ran away to join the army, and died in the following year. In October 1760 Berlin was briefly occupied by enemy troops, who destroyed the palace of Charlottenburg and did a considerable amount of damage in the city. Lessing could no longer pretend to ignore the war, or go on living his detached, literary existence, but felt, as he wrote to Ramler on 6 December 1760, 'daß es bald wieder einmal Zeit sei, mehr unter Menschen als unter Büchern zu leben'. And so he took up the post of secretary to Tauentzien, which he held until the beginning of 1765, nearly two years after the war had ended. Legend has it that it was Lessing who read the public proclamation of peace in Breslau.[16]

Minna von Barnhelm is set in Berlin in August 1763, that is, in the immediate aftermath of the war; and the play's plot — the Saxon heiress Minna von Barnhelm's love for the Prussian Major von Tellheim, Tellheim's flight from her, and their eventual reconciliation — springs directly and centrally from the events of the war and after: the Prussian officer's generous treatment of the conquered Saxons, his apparent disgrace when as a direct result of this generosity he is charged by the Prussian authorities with corruption, and his final restitution. We are plainly and unmistakably in the real, contemporary German world with real, contemporary German characters: no longer in the vague, unspecified setting of the early comedies

---

[15] G v. 31 f.   [16] D 171.

with their shadowy Orontes and Lelios. The play contains other, more specific topical allusions. The name of Tellheim's sergeant-major, Paul Werner — 'Ich bin ein guter Wachtmeister; und dürfte leicht ein schlechter Rittmeister, und sicherlich noch ein schlechtrer General werden' (III, 7) — is that of a Prussian general of the day, and was indeed, when the play was performed in Hamburg, changed to 'Weller' out of deference to the Prussian authorities.[17] The date of the action, 22 August 1763 (II, 2), has been identified as that on which one of the major financial scandals of the war, an affair of corruption similar to that of which Tellheim is falsely accused, was publicly exposed.[18] There may be other such references, whose significance is totally lost for us today but would have been obvious for Lessing's contemporaries. Lessing deliberately emphasized his play's intended closeness to real life when he wrote on the title-page 'Verfertiget im Jahre 1763' — when in fact it was not completed until the winter of 1766/7. Goethe describes it as 'die erste aus dem bedeutendsten Leben gegriffene Theaterproduktion von spezifisch temporärem Gehalt, die auch deswegen eine nie zu berechnende Wirkung tat'.[19] But the closeness to life which gave it such innovatory significance is not merely a matter of surface allusions as these.

The insistent anchoring in contemporary reality may however lead us to suspect that the play's primary meaning is satirical. There is undoubtedly a strong streak of anti-Prussian satire running through it; a mark of Lessing's courage, at the very moment when Frederick the Great had successfully defied the united might of Austria and Russia and their allies, earned recognition for Prussia — an upstart state scarcely a century old — as one of the European great powers, and laid the foundation for the later Prussian domination of Germany and the militaristic character of that domination. The play's Saxon heroine holds her head high: proudly and indignantly she answers the landlord's leering 'Aus Sachsen! Ei, ei, aus

[17] Cf. G ii. 671.
[18] For this and other real-life source-material for the play, see D. Hildebrandt (ed.), *Lessing: Minna von Barnhelm* (Dichtung und Wirklichkeit, xxx, Frankfurt and Berlin, 1969); also the same writer's *Lessing. Biographie einer Emanzipation* (Munich, 1979), pp. 289 ff.
[19] Loc. cit.

Sachen, gnädiges Fraulein? aus Sachsen?': 'Nun? warum nicht? Es ist doch wohl hier zu Lande keine Sünde, aus Sachsen zu sein?' (II, 2); and to Tellheim's 'lebhafteste Rührung' at the King of Prussia's ultimately revealed justice and magnanimity she responds with studied indifference, observing that 'Ihr König, der ein großer Mann ist, auch wohl ein guter Mann sein mag. — Aber was geht das mich an? Er ist nicht mein König' (V,9). Tellheim's military sense of honour could well lead him into a course of destructive and tragic action, like the hero of Fontane's novel *Schach von Wuthenow*, where a similar individual trait is again associated with the character and political destiny of a whole nation. That it does not, is largely the work of the Saxon ladies who persuade him to take his boots off (literally, III, 10) and to recognize that in matters of personal affection 'so gar militärisch wollen wir es miteinander nicht nehmen' (IV, 6). Prussian military discipline turns men into caricatures, 'Drechslerpuppen' (IV, 5); Minna's uncle observes that 'Ich bin sonst den Offizieren von dieser Farbe (*auf Tellheim's Uniform weisend*), eben nicht gut. Doch Sie sind ein ehrlicher Mann, Tellheim; und ein ehrlicher Mann mag stecken, in welchem Kleide er will, man muß ihn lieben' (V. 13). The uniform conceals the real man. And the same Prussian uniform is worn, we must recall, by the rascally French adventurer Riccaut: satire is plainly intended here upon the kind of uncritical acceptance of French manners and culture, and contempt for more homely but more solid German virtues, of which the Francophile Frederick the Great set such a conspicuous example.

The note of anti-Prussian satire in the play was perceived from the start, for the Prussian authorities tried to prevent the play's first performance in Hamburg (which, as a free city, was outside Prussian jurisdiction, but in some degree susceptible to Prussian influence). Yet in its over-all effect this satirical, negative element is outweighed by the positive. And not merely does the play's topical significance lie principally, as Goethe suggests, in a plea for reconciliation between Saxon and Prussian, the different political nationalities within the German-speaking world; the Prussian character itself, as exemplified in Tellheim, Werner, and even Just, is presented, for all its shortcomings, in an overwhelmingly positive light.

This is clear above all in Major von Tellheim. He is a noble, compassionate, and generous character, who inspires love and admiration in Minna and profound loyalty and affection in his subordinates Just and Werner. But his very compassion and generosity have been misconstrued, and have thus led to his present apparent disgrace. His honour publicly impugned, he withdraws into proud, private isolation: he flees the woman he loves and who loves him, and will not accept help from his friends, not wanting to be in debt to Just (I, 8) or to Werner (III, 7). He even refuses to accept the repayment of a debt legitimately owing to him, as we see in the scene with Madame Marloff (I, 6); and in this excess of generosity there is a touch of pride and self-regard, hinted at perhaps in the rhetorical stylization of the scene. Indeed, Tellheim's self-reliance is not merely obstinate, as Just and Werner, in the scenes to which we have referred, try with different degrees of success to make him see. It is also something of a pose, a self-dramatization, as Minna tells him: 'Das klingt sehr tragisch!' (II, 9). He is in fact not being true to himself, but playing a role, even if it is for the most part with only himself as audience. Paradoxically, the watchword which is constantly on Tellheim's lips in his haughty withdrawal from social and human relationships, 'Ehre', is itself an essentially public, social concept, indeed exaggeratedly so: for it is, or at all events can easily degenerate into, a mere external, a name, a word without any definable substance or meaning:

VON TELLHEIM (*hitzig*). Nein, mein Fräulein, Sie werden von allen Dingen recht gut urteilen können, nur hierüber nicht. Die Ehre ist nicht die Stimme unsers Gewissens, nicht das Zeugnis weniger Rechtschaffenen —

DAS FRÄULEIN. Nein, nein, ich weiß wohl. — Die Ehre ist — die Ehre.
(IV, 6)

The contrast of conscience and reputation is drawn most sharply in Lessing's 'bürgerliches Trauerspiel' *Miß Sara Sampson*. There the heroine Sara begs Mellefont to marry her, even if secretly, so that their relationship will be legitimized before her own conscience, whatever the world may think (I, 7); while for her wicked rival Marwood, virtue, the voice of conscience, unsupported by public reputation, is 'ein albernes Hirngespinst, das weder ruhig noch glücklich macht' (II, 7).

In *Minna von Barnhelm*, true to the vision of comedy, in which the happy ending usually marks some kind of social re-integration, Lessing suggests that *both* are necessary. The private and the public man must be united: Tellheim's flight from society, from his love and his friends, would lead to self-destruction. He must not flee from Minna, but nor must he flee *with* her from the rest of a supposedly hostile mankind — at least, Lessing will not put his willingness to do so to the test (V, 6). He must learn to receive as well as to give: to accept the help of his friends and to abandon the petulant folly of 'Alle Güte ist Verstellung; alle Diestfertigkeit Betrug' (V, 11). And of course he must not, as he threatens to do (V, 9), spurn the public restitution of his honour which is finally made to him. At the end Tellheim's good name, and his money, are restored, and Lessing does not in any way suggest that they are not worth having; we have seen the dubious side of honour, or the dangers to which a false or exaggerated sense of honour may lead, but the compliment of Minna's uncle, 'Sie sind ein ehrlicher Mann' (V, 13) is finally to be understood quite unironically.

Tellheim is thus essentially, though not without his faults, a character to inspire affection and admiration. We may well recognize in him features of Ewald von Kleist, a poet and a man of deep sensibilities, prone indeed to melancholy and de-pression, but generous and loyal, a soldier and a man of honour; perhaps too of General von Tauentzein, the just and honest soldier whose faithful services were not always appre-ciated by his superiors in Berlin and Potsdam. Tellheim is essentially not intended as a satirical character, certainly not one to be derided. Lessing himself, in No. 28 of the *Hamburgische Dramaturgie*, draws a crucial distinction between 'lachen' and 'verlachen': we can, he says, 'über einen Menschen lachen, bei Gelegenheit seiner lachen, ohne ihn im geringsten zu ver-lachen'. The distinction arises out of a discussion of Rousseau's remarks on Molière's *Misanthrope*. Rousseau cites the play in the course of a general polemic against the theatre, his *Lettre à M. d'Alembert sur les spectacles*, written in 1758: Alceste, the misanthrope of Molière's play, who cannot bear the false-ness and hypocrisy upon which society is founded and is not capable of even the whitest of lies, is in Rousseau's view quite simply an honest and virtuous man — 'un véritable homme de bien' — and it is wrong and wicked of Molière to make us laugh at him. For Molière as for his audience, Alceste's good qualities were vitiated by his unsociability; Lessing's perception of the character is closer to that of his own contemporary, but he does not make Rousseau's over-simplified moral judgment. Even a good man will have his faults, and to perceive these, even to laugh at them, is not to condemn *him*. There is a rather similar distinction drawn in *Minna von Barnhelm* itself, between the 'Lachen' which, Minna tells Tellheim, 'erhält uns vernünftiger, als der Verdruß', and the 'schreckliches Lachen des Menschenhasses' (IV, 6); between kinds of laughter which reflect an essentially positive and an essentially negative view of humanity. Tellheim is indeed a character not unlike Molière's Alceste; but whereas Molière is content to leave Alceste in the absurdity of his self-imposed isolation from his fellow-men (though the play does, of course, end with Philinte proposing yet one more attempt to save Alceste from himself), Lessing must show Tellheim restored to the society which he had threatened to abandon. Another very similar character had been depicted by Diderot in *Le Fils naturel*; there too the hero Dorval turns his back on society but is persuaded by Constance 'que l'homme de bien est dans la société, et qu'il n'y a que le méchant qui soit seul' (words at which Rousseau characteristically took offence, taking them to be some kind of satire on himself).[20] Indeed the exchanges between Dorval and Constance (IV, 3) are strongly echoed in the scenes between Minna and Tellheim. But Lessing, perhaps seeking a mean between the serious sentiment of Diderot and the purer, but crueller, comedy of Molière, has transposed the relationship of his hero and heroine into a much brighter, lighter key.

These distinctions have been ignored by a good many critics, who have argued that if Tellheim is to be seen as a comic character then he must be the object of satire, or contrariwise that if he is not the object of satire then he cannot be a comic but must be an exclusively serious or even a tragic character.[21]

[20] See Rousseau, *Confessions*, Part ii, Book 9.
[21] Cf. the summary of earlier criticism in Arntzen, op. cit., pp. 25 ff.; J. Schröder, 'Lessing: *Minna von Barnhelm*', in W. Hinck (ed.), *Die deutsche Komödie* (Düsseldorf, 1977), 49–65. In an extremely (I think, excessively) sophisticated argument, P. Michelsen has maintained that Lessing deliberately makes us see Tellheim's

Against this view we must insist upon the simple point that Tellheim and Minna and all the others are comic characters because they are characters in a comedy: the serious themes, the characters whom we admire and for whom our sympathy is engaged are all contained within a larger, comic whole. And in terms of its structure and dramatic economy, *Minna von Barnhelm* is not really a comedy of character in the main line of the continental European tradition, even to the extent that *Der Freigeist* with its flawed but essentially sympathetic protagonist still was. Whether Lessing himself was fully aware of this is not clear, for in the *Hamburgische Dramaturgie* he continues to maintain the traditional neo-classical view that 'in der Komödie die Charaktere das Hauptwerk, die Situationen aber nur die Mittel sind, jene sich äußern zu lassen, und ins Spiel zu setzen' (No. 51). And if the distinction in No. 28 is drawn with his own play in mind,[22] then Lessing seems to be implying that the character of Tellheim is the principal focus of attention in *Minna von Barnhelm*. Here as elsewhere, however, Lessing's practice may well differ from his theory; for *Minna von Barnhelm* is surely in essence a comedy of plot. (It is worth observing that its title does not designate an object of satire as do the titles of Molière's plays or those of the Gottschedian type which we have mentioned, including the majority of Lessing's own early comedies.) The plot is not designed simply to exhibit a central character, as is, say, that of *Der junge Gelehrte*, but to bring about an eventual happy ending after a series of complications and misunderstandings, leading at their climax to the very brink of disaster, but still capable at the last of resolution and illumination; and the spectator's interest is principally concentrated on how the dramatist leads his characters into these complications and out of them again.

During the war, in Saxony, Minna and Tellheim have fallen in love and become engaged. The war called him away; now that peace has come, she has set out to find him, accompanied

---

situation, through Minna's eyes, as less serious than it really is (what can 'really' mean here?): 'Die Verbergung der Kunst. Über die Exposition in Lessings *Minna von Barnhelm*', *JDSG* xvii (1973), 192–252. Cf. also A. Hoelzel, 'Truth and Honesty in *Minna von Barnhelm*', *LYB* ix (1977), 28–44.

[22] Cf. P. Hernadi, 'Lessings Misanthropen', *Euph.* lxviii (1974), p. 113.

by her uncle, who (unlike the hostile guardians in *Der junge Gelehrte* and *Der Misogyn*) welcomes the prospect of their marriage. Since he left Saxony, Tellheim's fortunes have fallen; but on the very day when the action of the play takes place, the charges against him have been quashed and his honour and money restored. Now however – as the curtain rises – the complications begin. Tellheim is turned out of his room to make way, as we duly learn, for Minna herself; his change of address delays his receipt of the King's letter of restitution (V, 6); he therefore believes himself still disgraced, and while he is disgraced he will not marry Minna. Meanwhile Minna's uncle is delayed by an accident to his carriage, which means that she has to face Tellheim on her own – but also that we are not too surprised to see him arrive in the nick of time when it looks as though her gamble on Tellheim's love is on the point of disastrously misfiring. The ring brings the lovers together, only, it seems, to part them again: it is Just's pawning of the ring with the landlord which reveals Tellheim's whereabouts to Minna, but also makes possible her deception of him which, well-meant though it is, almost has such unhappy consequences. Minna tries to convince Tellheim of the falseness of his attitude by playing on him a trick which she thinks he will see through as soon as it has served its purpose; but as it is not his nature to take anything less than totally seriously, he does not. He realizes that he adopted that false attitude 'als ich nicht wußte, was ich dachte und sprach' (V, 5), but he has only surrendered one illusion to embrace another, potentially just as damaging to their relationship. The delivery of the King's letter, which ought to resolve the confusion, (as indeed some critics think it does),[23] in fact introduces a further complication, for Tellheim proposes to refuse restitution so that he can share Minna's imagined misery – proposes, that is, in fact to make her share *his* misery, which will be real enough if he tears up the letter. Still Minna hopes that he will realize the truth of his own accord; but she is finally forced to reveal it herself: ' – hören Sie denn nicht, daß alles erdichtet ist?' (V, 12). And with Tellheim reinstated in the

---

[23] Cf. Michelsen, op. cit., p. 242 f.; H. Steinmetz, 'Minna von Barnhelm oder die Schwierigkeit, ein Lustspiel zu verstehen', in A. von Bormann, etc. (eds.), *Wissen aus Erfahrungen. Festschrift für Hermann Meyer* (Tübingen, 1975), 135–53.

King's favour and Minna's uncle at last arrived on the scene, the protagonists' normal social and family relations, which for the duration of the play (the conventional, we may almost say magical, twenty-four hours of the neo-classical unity of time) have been suspended, are restored. The 'mistakes of a night' (as in *She Stoops to Conquer*), the confusions of the 'folle journée' (as in *Le Mariage de Figaro*) are sorted out and normality reconstituted. The dramatist has created all these complications, all these reversals and retardations, only to show that they are capable of being overcome; behind and above them all, now allowing his characters freedom to indulge their individual whims and obstinacies, now checking their freedom when they go too far, we sense his benevolent guiding hand.

This pattern is illustrative or symbolic of what, above and beyond the 'correction' of a particular flaw in human character or human behaviour, or the political reconciliation of Prussia and Saxony, is the play's real theme: the workings of a benevolent Providence in human affairs and the part played in relation to it by individual will and initiative. We shall find this theme in all Lessing's major plays: in the tragedies the providential design is broken, by helpless passivity or by rash action or by a combination of both; in *Nathan der Weise* it is once again harmoniously completed. The idea of Providence is very close to the centre of Lessing's philosophy of life. So too is that of the inadequacy of actions based upon false notions of human self-sufficiency — honour or heroism, virtue or religion.[24] Man must trust in the benevolence of Providence, in the existence of a grand design which will finally ensure that all turns out for the best. As we have seen, Tellheim tries to rely upon himself — but in a sense which implies a lack of faith in Providence: we hear him telling Madame Marloff, 'Sie finden mich in einer Stunde, wo ich leicht zu verleiten wäre, wider die Vorsicht zu murren' (I, 6);[25] and sure enough, he sinks deeper into isolation and gloom, to that 'schreckliches Lachen des Menschenhasses' which provokes Minna to cry — they are not mere words — 'Wenn Sie an Tugend und Vorsicht

---

[24] Cf. H. C. Seeba, *Die Liebe zur Sache. Öffentliches und privates Interesse in Lessings Dramen* (Tübingen, 1973).

[25] Dorval strikes a similar note in *Le Fils naturel*, II.5 and III.7.

glauben, Tellheim, so lachen Sie so nicht!' (IV, 6). Minna
however never loses her faith in an ultimate benevolent design
in human affairs, and is willing to act on the basis of this
faith, even if this looks like *tempting* Providence — or, as we
have already said, taking a gamble on it. Lessing — a passionate
gambler, who in those years in Breslau had spent many an
evening, often far into the night, at the gaming-table — saw
nothing wrong in this. Minna's initiative does not *in itself*
succeed — indeed, it almost leads to catastrophe; but it is *rewarded* with success because it is undertaken in the right spirit.

The theme of taking a gamble is introduced in the important scene in Act IV when Minna is confronted with the
French adventurer Riccaut de la Marlinière, who in circumstances not wholly unlike Tellheim's — 'reformé et mis sur le
pavé' — is making his living at the card-table. The scene is not
merely anti-French satire; if it were, it would be dramatically
gratuitous (as some contemporaries, who were presumably
fully aware of its satirical significance, thought it was). It
usually comes across in performance as the funniest scene in
the play; but in that it raises, albeit in strongly comic form,
such a serious theme, it demands to be taken seriously, and
the laughter it arouses is seen in retrospect to be not merely
satirical.[26] Riccaut, of course, goes too far: he is not merely
a gambler but a cheat. But Minna refuses to join Franziska —
mockingly rebuked by her in the previous scene as a 'Sitten-
richterin' — in outright condemnation of this undoubted
rogue: 'Mädchen, du verstehst dich so trefflich auf die guten
Menschen: aber, wenn willst du die schlechten ertragen
lernen? — Und sie sind doch auch Menschen. — Und öfters
bei weitem so schlechte Menschen nicht, als sie scheinen. —
Man muß ihre gute Seite nur aufsuchen' (IV, 3). (Tellheim is
similarly censorious about Riccaut (IV, 6) and doubts his re-
liability as a bringer of good news, which is however subsequently vindicated — as Minna and Franziska pointedly
observe (V, 6).) Franziska's reply — 'Nein, gnädiges Fräulein;

---

[26] Cf. F. Martini, 'Riccaut, die Sprache und das Spiel in Lessings Lustspiel
Minna von Barnhelm', in B 376–426, originally in *Formenwandel. Festschrift für
Paul Böckmann* (Hamburg, 1964); and K. S. Guthke, 'Der Glücksspieler als Autor.
Überlegungen zur "Gestalt" Lessings im Sinne der inneren Biographie', *Euph.*lxxi
(1977), 353–82.

ich kann beides nicht; weder an einem schlechten Menschen die gute, noch an einem guten Menschen die böse Seite aufsuchen' — shows that she is not satisfied: she reiterates her disapproval both of Minna's lenient treatment of Riccaut's failing and of her unrelenting pursuit of Tellheim's, and as the intrigue develops we are repeatedly reminded that it is a dangerous game Minna is playing, one of which Franziska declares she would not have been capable. But despite its perils, Minna has ultimately no regrets: 'Nein, ich kann es nicht bereuen, mir den Anblick Ihres ganzen Herzens verschafft zu haben!' (V, 12).[27] Her treatment of Tellheim is of a piece with her treatment of Riccaut: she makes no absolute moral categorizations but treats both as human beings in all their complexity. Minna's love for Tellheim is the stronger when she has seen 'den Anblick Ihres ganzen Herzens', even if she does not actually need to 'an einem guten Menschen die böse Seite aufsuchen', as did Adrast in *Der Freigeist*, before she can convince herself that he *is* a human being. This is a more complex moral awareness than Franziska's; and it is this greater moral sophistication, this sense of the complexity of human character and human relationships and of their place in the moral order of the universe, that Lessing is seeking to convey in *Minna von Barnhelm* as he had done in that earlier play. No doubt Minna too has her faults; but Tellheim would not wish to marry 'ein Engel, den ich mit Schaudern verehren müßte, den ich nicht lieben könnte' (V, 9). And perhaps at the end of IV, 2 the laugh is not entirely on Riccaut with his scorn of the crude moral rigour of the German language: 'Corriger la fortune, l'enchainer sous ses doits, etre sûr de son fait, das nenn die Deutsch betrügen? betrügen! O, was ist die deutsche Sprak für ein arm Sprak! für ein plump Sprak!'

Minna von Barnhelm is thus a comedy in which the eventual union, after misunderstandings and complications, of the two principal protagonists is to be taken as an image of a moral universe, in which human relations are governed by a benevolent providential design and in which individual human action and initiative, undertaken in faith in that design, will ultimately be rewarded. It has some satirical elements, but its

[27] Not, surely, an 'etwas fadenscheinige Erklärung' (Steinmetz, 'Minna von Barnhelm', p. 147).

message and its affective impact are overwhelmingly positive; and in the structure of the play the satirical elements are accordingly subordinate to the pattern of the plot and the working-out of the happy ending. That pattern is reinforced in a number of other ways. The betrothal of Minna and Tellheim is paralleled by the betrothal of Franziska and Werner. These characters are of course, in accordance both with dramatic tradition and with social reality, of lower status than the principals, and despite the friendliness, even intimacy, of their relations with the latter, we are never allowed to forget this fact.[28] They are also of a lower degree of moral sophistication; though while Franziska is, as we have noted, more literally scrupulous than her mistress, Werner is rather less so than Tellheim. He too has a distinctively military code of honour (his admiration and affection for Tellheim are strongly tinged with it), which allows him to despise Just as a mere 'Packknecht' (I, 12) and to find 'an Justen . . . nicht viel Besonders' (III, 4), at the very moment when Franziska has been taught to recognize Just's honesty as superior to the soldierly accomplishments of Tellheim's other servants. He also appears to find it not at all improbable, or even dishonourable, that his superior officer should have made promises of marriage which he had no intention of keeping – 'besonders in Sachsen' (III, 5) – though he says later that he didn't mean it (III, 11). On the other hand, he is Tellheim's equal in generosity, and in the important scene III, 7 is able to expose the doubtfulness of Tellheim's moral position: 'Erst ziemte es sich nicht; nun wollen Sie nicht? Ja, das ist was anders.' In fact, although the distinction of 'high' and 'low' characters is still maintained by Lessing in *Minna von Barnhelm*, Franziska and Werner, unlike the servants of the early comedies, are individualized, and not merely conventional figures; they are also *serious* characters, for whom Lessing seeks to engage our emotional sympathies; there is no hint of the antagonism which traditionally characterizes master-servant relationships in comedy, where often we take pleasure in a wily servant's outwitting a foolish master; and in the double betrothal which

---

[28] Hildebrandt's assertion (*Minna von Barnhelm*, p. 26) that Lessing 'demokratisiert das ganze Komödienpersonal' is a typical overstatement. Cf. Arntzen, op. cit., p. 27.

ends the play there is an echo of the pairing-off of complementary opposites which concluded *Der Freigeist*. There, we recall, 'der Fromme will die Lustige, und der Lustige die Fromme'; here the sharp, rather literal-minded Franziska gets the bouncily cheerful sergeant-major, while the over-serious Tellheim is to marry the teasing, capricious Minna. Other subordinate characters are similarly rounded out and portrayed as figures of positive human worth: Just most obviously, but Riccaut too, as we have seen — perhaps even the landlord, despite Just's savage comment, 'Lieber Bestie, als so ein Mensch!' (I, 4). For in the world of this play, governed by a benevolent Providence, 'es gibt keine völlige Unmenschen' (I, 8).

The language of the play also reinforces its themes with insistent patterning, in which words and ideas are passed back and forth and held up, as it were, to illumination now from one side, now from another. Though there is, particularly in the scenes between Just and the landlord, a certain amount of pure verbal repartee of a kind common in the early comedies, the function of which is quite simply to amuse, the dialogue is densely packed with allusions to its central themes. Words like 'Ehre' and 'ehrlich' turn up repeatedly, so too 'Schuld' and 'Schuldner' with their implications both financial and moral. Repeated or echoed exchanges bring out the moral pattern of the character relationships upon which the play is founded: Tellheim's 'Ihre Güte foltert mich' (II, 9) — itself an echo, more emotionally direct and less rhetorically stylized, of Madame Marloff's 'Verzeihen Sie nur, wenn ich noch nicht recht weiß, wie man Wohltaten annehmen muß' — is further intensified in III, 7 with his painful outburst, 'Daß mich doch die besten Menschen heut am meisten quälen müssen', to be turned back on him again by Franziska in III, 10 with 'Aber das ist gar nicht artig, daß Sie Leute, die Ihnen gut sind, so ängstigen'. Phrases uttered by one character recur, sometimes rather surprisingly, in the mouth of another: Minna's 'Der König kann nicht alle verdiente Männer kennen' (II, 2) is contradicted by the landlord, but later repeated by him to Werner, who observes 'Das heißt Ihn Gott sprechen!' (III, 4); while in Riccaut's echo, 'Mann kenn sik hier nit auf den Verdienst', the false gender puns upon the connection of merit and money. Riccaut's comment on Tellheim, however, 'Nit wahr, das iß

ein brav Mann?', quite unironically echoes Werner's 'Ist es
nicht ein braver Mann?' (III, 5). The landlord's conventional
formula of servility, 'Darf ich mich unterstehen zu fragen,
wie Ihro Gnaden die erste Nacht unter meinem schlechten
Dache geruhet? — ', is punctured by Franziska's literal 'Das
Dach ist so schlecht nicht . . .' (II, 2), but her own insistence
on the title 'Jungfer' (II, 2) is similarly turned back on her by
Just in III, 2; this whole scene between Just and Franziska
plays upon the literal and metaphorical meanings of words,
and this continues throughout Act III. At the end of the very
important scene III, 7 it is Werner who unmasks a pose by an-
swering with a literal 'no' to a question rhetorically expecting
a 'yes':

— Wenn ich manchmal dachte: wie wird es mit dir aufs Alter werden?
wenn du zu Schanden gehauen bist? wenn du nichts haben wirst? wenn
du wirst betteln gehen müssen? So dachte ich wieder: Nein, du wirst
nicht betteln gehen; du wirst zum Major Tellheim gehen; der wird seinen
letzen Pfennig mit dir teilen; der wird dich zu Tode füttern; bei dem
wirst du als ein ehrlicher Kerl sterben können.

VON TELLHEIM (*indem er Werners Hand ergreift*). Und, Kamerad, das
denkst du nicht noch?

WERNER. Nein, das denk ich nicht mehr. —

Exchanges such as these are particularly appropriate in a play
where the resolution of conflict and the happy union of the
characters are obstructed not by fate or chance, not by malice
or wickedness, but by misunderstandings often enshrined in
words, of false or doubtful meaning ('Die Ehre ist — die Ehre').

In gesture too we find pattern and repetition. Hands
speak an eloquent language of giving and receiving, of the
offering, refusing, or accepting of assistance and friendship:
Tellheim, who has the use of only one hand, must learn to accept that he needs the hands of others. Madame Marloff leaves
Tellheim with tears of gratitude; but when Just arrives a
moment later, he tries to pretend that he has *not* been weeping
(I, 8). This incident also illustrates how Lessing turns sentiment in the direction of laughter, and thus, in accordance
with his theory, preserves a careful balance of effects. Touching
scenes are followed by amusing ones, and the emotional tem-
perature is never allowed to rise too high. The pain of Minna's

reaction to Tellheim's flight (III, 3) is muted by its indirect presentation through the mouth of one of the play's most purely comic characters (while the use of this character for the purpose makes him for his part a less wholly negative figure) and flanked by some of its most straightforwardly witty (though again, thematically very serious) scenes. The stage direction at the end of V, 12, when Tellheim '*vor Wut an den Fingern nagt, das Gesicht wegwendet, und nichts höret*', suggests indeed a situation verging on tragedy; but the form of Minna's speech, broken with nine dashes, surely implies a lively physical pursuit which makes us *see* the situation, literally, in the correct — that is, comic — perspective.

Lessing's striving for a balance of elements and effects in *Minna von Barnhelm* has its equivalent in his tragedies. There too we shall find him combining traditional and modern elements, above all by infusing the traditional forms with modern content in the shape of modern characters with modern sensibilities in modern situations, characters whom his spectators can readily see as 'like themselves' and to whom they can readily respond emotionally. That is, Lessing imbues both comedy and tragedy with a considerable measure of realism. In tragedy this was a much more radical innovation and correspondingly led to greater problems. But the realism of *Minna von Barnhelm* is not without its problematic consequences.

As we have observed, comedy traditionally incorporates quite often a considerable amount of realistic detail, largely of satiric intent but frequently of a rather superficial kind. *Minna von Barnhelm* is however unusual in that it is basically a comedy of very positive affective intent, less satiric in essence than the majority of Lessing's earlier comedies, yet one which is anchored firmly in a very specific contemporary reality — far more so, in fact, than the early works. This unusual mixture is clearly what gives the play its distinctive character and accounts in considerable measure for its success; yet it also gives rise to certain doubts, at least for many a twentieth-century reader or spectator. The history of literary and theatrical realism over the last two hundred years is, overwhelmingly, a history of ever more *critical* scrutiny and representation of reality, of an ever greater concentration on the imperfections of the world and of human nature. So today we naturally tend to interpret realism as a sign of critical or satiric intent, and are disappointed when things turn out otherwise. Finding in *Minna von Barnhelm* such a detailed portrayal of the situation of a discharged Prussian officer after the Seven Years' War, we feel that Lessing must or at least *ought* to have intended, as Franz Mehring said he did, 'die schneidendste Satire auf das friderizianische Regiment'; and so we feel slightly cheated when Frederick the Great does restore Tellheim to public favour, and puzzled (except in so far as we are pleased to regard it as wilful misinterpretation) when we discover that many critics — and imitators — of the play found it attractive on account of what they thought its *positive* presentation of the Prussian military character.[29] Finding in it a depiction not only of the problems of a post-war situation but also of a reconciliation between representatives of once warring nations, perhaps we expect the play to carry a more explicitly pacifist message, and are accordingly disappointed when the principal male characters cheerfully go off at the end to find another war to fight in,[30] good enough though this may be as a comic ending in the traditional mode. Having had, as Minna tells Tellheim, 'den Anblick Ihres ganzen Herzens', we perhaps feel that we have seen too much to be satisfied by the convenient arrival of uncles and royal messengers with bland messages of comfort: the denouement seems artificial, and if again this artificiality is typical of comic procedures, we feel that the realistic elements of the play have led us to expect something different and 'truer to life'. For we have come to associate realism with an increasingly negative view of reality, and to find it hard to accept happy endings as a true dramatic representation of the world we know: either they must be presented as frankly romantic or utopian, or they must be heavily salted with irony.

Lessing however thought otherwise. For him the happy ending of the play is neither ironic nor utopian: it is representative of a providential order, but he believed profoundly that

---

[29] Cf. Seeba, op. cit., pp. 21 ff., quoting Mehring and others.

[30] I assume that Tellheim intends after all to accept the King's offer of further service in the Prussian army. Cf. Seeba, op. cit. pp. 84 f. Serving officers were not encouraged to marry, but a number did, and some were even accompanied by their wives on campaign: cf. Hildebrandt, *Minna von Barnhelm*, p. 167, and C. Duffy, *The Army of Frederick the Great* (London, 1974), p. 46.

that order ruled the world in which we actually live — which
is why it was supremely appropriate for him to create the unusual kind of comedy which he did. The ending of the play is
not for him a turning away from the reality in which it has
hitherto been so firmly rooted; not a comic dramatist's manipulation of that reality, but a showing forth of its higher
truth. If we have difficulty in accepting that, it is because we
have difficulty in sharing his providential optimism. It has
however been generally agreed that the optimistic design of
comedy with a happy ending offered a more appropriate
medium for the representation of Lessing's vision of reality
than the harsher form of tragedy, whose optimism lies, if
anywhere, in a more paradoxical assertion of the value and
dignity of human striving even in the absence of any providential plan; and accordingly *Minna von Barnhelm* has generally been accounted a more perfect and successful play than
any of his completed tragedies. To this view we can readily
assent. It lacks the sharper, crueller cutting edge of Molière,
the higher poetry of Shakespearian romance, but it can stand
comparison with the best comedies of its own century and of
more recent times. It is certainly immeasurably superior to
the plays of Diderot which probably of all other dramas
approach it most closely both in theme and in dramatic intent.

(iii)

What however was that dramatic intent? It is undoubtedly
true that one of the reasons for the success of *Minna von
Barnhelm* and for its superiority to the early comedies, to
Miß Sara Sampson and even, arguably, to *Emilia Galotti* is its
greater closeness to, and its more direct reflection of, real life
and Lessing's own experience. The inspiration of the tragedies
is more obviously literary, and their settings, though contemporary, are geographically remote; *Minna* is set in Berlin in
August 1763 and the play draws attention to its real-life immediacy by proclaiming itself to have been written in the
same year. It might seem that Lessing's intention was indeed
to portray contemporary reality and his own view and interpretation of it, and that he chose the drama as the most natural
and apposite form in which to do so. But to conclude thus

would be to over-simplify. Lessing, like Diderot, was undoubtedly concerned that serious drama should have a serious
message — that it should reflect contemporary reality, that it
should place before the spectators characters whose lives
and concerns they could recognize as similar and relevant to
their own; and that it should communicate the essence of
eighteenth-century rational optimism and justify the ways of
Providence to man. Lessing, like Diderot, was concerned to
disseminate Enlightened thought and Enlightened attitudes
amongst his fellow-countrymen. Both men saw the theatre as,
potentially, a particularly effective vehicle for such dissemi-
nation. But they also saw that the theatre of their day was
not fulfilling that potential. It was merely providing entertainment — whether overtly, in the works produced frankly for
the mob, or covertly, in those designed for a more sophisticated
taste, which in their artificial conventionality were just as remote from the seriousness of real life. Both men wished to
see the theatre producing works, as Lessing had put it, 'fähig
einen allgemeinen Beifall zu erlangen, und folglich auch einen
allgemeinen Nutzen zu stiften'. Both therefore wrote plays
designed as models to show how this could and should be done.

Minna von Barnhelm is thus a 'model play' just as much as
the two plays of Diderot which Lessing had translated, even
though it is not accompanied by any very highly developed
theory or constructed according to any particular theoretical
programme.[31] The initial idea for it he may well have sketched
in Breslau in immediate response to the ending of the war,
not however as an idea which demanded immediate expression
so much as one which would *make a good play* if the occasion
for play-writing should arise. Even though we find him telling
Ramler on 20 August 1764 that 'Ich brenne vor Begierde, die
letzte Hand an meine Minna von Barnhelm zu legen' — the
first recorded reference to the play — it still had to make way
for other projects. Chief among these was *Laokoon*, which
appeared in the spring of 1766, at an apt moment to support
Lessing's claim to the vacant post of librarian to the King of
Prussia. Characteristically, however, Frederick the Great
passed over both Lessing and his obvious German rival, Winc-

---

[31]   The best treatment of the play from the point of view of its literary ancestry
is in Hinck, *Das deutsche Lustspiel . . . und die italienische Komödie*, pp. 287–301.

kelmann, in favour of a Frenchman; further cause, perhaps, for Lessing to be disillusioned with Prussia, but still he continued with his classical studies. It was however towards the end of that year that he received the invitation to go to Hamburg as resident critic and playwright to the new 'National Theatre'. The decisive impulse to complete his new play was his return to professional involvement with the theatre: now, as he wrote to Gleim on 1 February 1767, it was the projected continuation of *Laokoon* which would have to take second place to the completion of 'meine theatralischen Werke, welche längst auf die letzte Hand gewartet haben'. There were indeed amongst his papers a number of sketches, both comic and tragic, which he could have taken up. But for the inception of a National Theatre, with the hopes which that implied, none would be more suitable than *Minna von Barnhelm* with its 'national' subject-matter and its optimistic message.

It was accordingly completed early in 1767 and performed, after the delay caused by the Prussian authorities' intervention, on 23 September of that year. It was extremely well received, repeated a number of times in Hamburg, and soon performed with success in other German cities — including Berlin.[32] But it was already becoming apparent to Lessing that the Hamburg venture was not going to meet his expectations. The 'National Theatre' was a failure; Lessing parted from it with some bitterness, and began to feel a deep distaste for any further involvement with the theatre. Within the field of drama his interest began to turn, as it had done before, to tragedy — the more elevated and 'literary' form. There are, it is true, a number of reflections on comedy in the *Hamburgische Dramaturgie*, notably the crucial distinction between 'lachen' und 'verlachen' to which we have already referred; the early comedies were revised for a new edition; and work was well advanced on two more, one at least of considerable experimental interest — but both were then, it seems quite abruptly, abandoned.[33]

We must however enquire a little further into the nature of those hopes which Lessing and Diderot — and indeed the

[32] Cf. Hildebrandt, *Minna von Barnhelm*, ed. cit. pp. 175 ff.
[33] Cf. below, pp. 153 ff.

founders of the Hamburg 'Nationaltheater' — invested in the
theatre as a medium of Enlightenment. We have already seen
that Gottsched aimed to begin the literary renaissance of
Germany by a reform of the theatre: in theory he may have
regarded epic poetry as the highest literary genre, but in practice he seems to have perceived that the days of the epic were
gone. Beyond this, however, he takes his hierarchy of literary
values more or less uncritically from classical authority, and
does not seek to establish any reasons for them. Lessing
seems to be going little further in principle when, for example,
in the preface to *Das Theater des Herrn Diderot*, he urges
that Germany must pay attention to Diderot's theories 'wenn
auch wir einst zu den gesitteten Völkern gehören wollen,
deren jedes *seine* Bühne hatte'.[34] Yet, in fact, men such as
Lessing and Diderot — and d'Alembert, whose advocacy of the
establishment of a theatre in Geneva had provoked Rousseau's
attack — were developing a new awareness of the peculiarly
social nature of theatre. The spectator at a play is not, like
the silent reader of a printed page, simply receiving a private
communication: he is participating in a social act. The theatre
is a place where the individual members of a society gather
together and in doing so realize that they are, each and every
one of them, parts of that greater whole: where a society is
aware of itself *as* a society. Pre-eminently this was true in
ancient Greece, whose theatres could accommodate thousands
of spectators; as Diderot observes, in modern Europe, 'il n'y a
plus, à proprement parler, de spectacles publics'.[35] But it is
still possible for the modern theatre to reflect and respond to
the character of the society which constitutes its audience.
This is where Gottsched had failed. Despite his practical condescension to work with the Neubers, he had tried to impose
on the drama an essentially literary taste, one, that is, derived
from books and from critical and theoretical precept, paying
scant attention to what the public actually liked. Here Lessing
had at an early stage in his career perceived Gottsched's mistake
— and was delighted to find in Diderot, as he tells us in the
preface to his translation, a French critic who, far from regar-

[34] G iv. 149.
[35] 'Deuxième entretien sur *Le Fils naturel*', in *Œuvres esthétiques*, ed. P. Ver-
nière (Paris, 1959), p. 121. Quoted by Lessing in the 81st *Literaturbrief*, G v. 259.

ding the 'classical' drama of his nation as the *non plus ultra* of theatrical art, similarly found it excessively remote from the audiences of his own day. Both men sought, therefore, to discover forms with a specific appeal to those audiences.

In Germany the problem was particularly acute – but the challenge correspondingly great.[36] The German-speaking world was fragmented into dozens, perhaps even hundreds, of nominally sovereign political units. These ranged from substantial territorial monarchies, like Prussia or Saxony, to free Imperial city-states, like Hamburg (urban republics owing nominal allegiance only to the Holy Roman Empire), small principalities like Brunswick, where Lessing was to spend the last ten years of his life, and even smaller, quite insignificant entities. One's estimate of the total number depends on how seriously one takes the claims to independence of the smallest territories. There was considerable variety in their political constitution; there were also jealously-guarded differences between the established religions of the different lands – some Catholic, some Lutheran, some Calvinist – which made Vienna, the political capital of the Empire, seem (quite apart from its geographical remoteness) to belong to another world than the Protestant cities of northern Germany. In these circumstances it is hardly possible to speak of 'German society' in the eighteenth century. The theatre could hardly fulfil its social role if there were no society for it to reflect: as Lessing bitterly observes at the end of the *Hamburgische Dramaturgie,* 'Über den gutherzigen Einfall, den Deutschen ein Nationaltheater zu verschaffen, da wir Deutsche noch keine Nation sind!' The theatre was being asked to create its own public: the theatre to create a society and even a nation, rather than the other way about.[37]

Yet the dream – which was to persist, and to reach in Goethe and Schiller some measure of fulfilment – was not completely without foundation. Obviously the German language itself transcended all the political frontiers. But more than this, there was in fact coming into being a theatre-going (and reading) public of increasing homogeneity throughout

[36] Cf. W. H. Bruford, *Germany in the Eighteenth Century* (Cambridge, 1952).
[37] Cf. T. J. Reed, 'Theatre, Enlightenment and Nation. A German Problem', *FMLS* xiv (1978), 143-64.

the urban centres of the German-speaking world — one which, moreover, increasingly resembled the similar public which was growing at the same time in France and in England. It was a public which embodied many of those attitudes, beliefs, and ideals which we have come to regard as most characteristic of eighteenth-century Europe. It was a public in which taste and manners were no longer dominated by the aristocracy — though the hereditary ruling classes retained an unshaken grip on affairs of state till the end of the century. The tone was coming to be set more and more by members of the middle classes, professional and (particularly in England) commercial, whom urbanization and other changes in the structure of society were making increasingly important and who were correspondingly demanding greater cultural, and in due course political, influence. This is the true significance of those remarks at the end of the *Abhandlungen von dem weinerlichen oder rührenden Lustspiel*. The 'Volk', to whom the new drama must appeal, excludes the 'Pöbel' on one hand, and on the other those 'Leute von Stande' who refuse to adopt its attitudes: it is in fact the new largely and characteristically middle-class public. It is to the tastes and sensibilities of this public that Lessing seeks to adapt the traditional dramatic genres.

In the case of comedy this was relatively simple. In traditional neo-classic dramatic theory and practice, comedy was already regarded as the appropriate dramatic genre for the depiction of middle-class, particularly urban, characters and their concerns. The affective bias of such comedy was generally negative; but the common stock of comedy also included positive affective elements, and a greater stress on these could easily lead to the presentation of middle-class characters and attitudes as sympathetic, even admirable, rather than ridiculous. (We note, though, that the principals of *Minna von Barnhelm* are both titled persons — like Gellert's Swedish countess, heroine of what is often claimed as the first 'bourgeois' novel in German.) Stylistically, the new comedy must of course avoid vulgarity — not for any schoolmasterish reason, but simply because it would not appeal to a public priding itself on some degree of refinement in matters of taste. That this refinement could easily go too far is evidenced in the refusal of the actor playing Just in the Berlin performance of

Minna in March 1768 to pronounce the word 'Hure' (I, 12), on which Lessing comments in the brief, unpublished essay *Delicatesse*.[38] Here Lessing was going further than this contemporaries may have wished in the direction of realism. But in general the move towards greater realism — the rounding out of hitherto conventional theatrical roles such as the pert maid or the surly manservant, the use of familiar German names throughout, the anchoring in a recognizable contemporary world — is itself well calculated to appeal to a middle-class taste which, sometimes to the point of philistine literal-mindedness, rejects the fantastic, the implausible, the unreal, anything which seems too obviously stylized or conventional.

In tragedy the problem was very much greater. There was a much more fundamental stylistic conflict between tragedy, as it had always been understood, and the kind of truth to life which seemed to be the necessary hallmark of modern drama. To the resolution of this conflict Lessing devoted the major part of his efforts in the field of the drama, both in practice and in theory.

[38] G iv. 719.

III

Tragedy (I): *Miß Sara Sampson*

(i)

The comic playwright of the eighteenth century could achieve a measure of originality without radical departure from the comic tradition of the past, by changes in the disposition and emphasis of elements in themselves traditional. The task of the tragic playwright was much more difficult; in Germany particularly so.

The German tragic stage had little or no tradition on which it could build. The seventeenth century had seen the emergence of a distinctive German form of tragic drama in the so-called Baroque style. But the works of even the best dramatists of this period, Gryphius or Lohenstein, are greatly inferior to the drama of contemporary France or of Elizabethan England, and are certainly no longer viable on the stage today as are those of Racine and Shakespeare. They seem essentially undramatic, lacking in genuine conflict, clumsy in contrivance and in execution. Gottsched had introduced into Germany 'classical' tragedy in the French manner; but this was not the only endeavour made at this time to discover tragic forms more appropriate to eighteenth-century Germany than those of the Baroque tradition. In 1740 Caspar Wilhelm von Borck translated Shakespeare's *Julius Caesar* into German (in alexandrines, the verse of classical French drama); Gottsched's young protégé Johann Elias Schlegel had undertaken his critical *Vergleichung Shakespeares und Andreas Gryphs*, the first piece of serious German Shakespeare criticism, by no means as uncompromisingly hostile to Shakespeare as Gottsched would have wished. Schlegel had lived and worked in Denmark, and in his *Gedanken zur Aufnahme des dänischen Theaters* he had raised the important question of the differences in national character and literary taste: what is well

received in one country will not necessarily be suitable or acceptable in another.[1] In 1750, in the preface to the first
number of the *Beiträge zur Historie und Aufnahme des
Theaters*, we find Lessing too attacking the exclusive domination of the German stage by French taste, urging that the
German public should be acquainted with the dramatic work
of the ancient Greeks and Romans, of the Italians, the Spaniards, the English, and the Dutch, and asserting that, allowed
to follow its natural bent, the German temperament would
prefer the English style. It must be observed that Lessing in
his early critical ventures is not hostile to the French drama
as such; this is a later development. What he does attack from
the start is rather the continued and exclusive domination of
the French drama and the unwarranted prestige of its inferior
practitioners and imitators.

A growing dissatisfaction with the traditional form of
tragedy is however not merely a German, but a general
Western European phenomenon of the period. As we have
observed, eighteenth-century high tragedy often seems forced
and strained. Dramatists continued to write tragedies for
reasons of literary prestige, but the results seem more and
more unnatural.

Tragedy is paradoxical. It recognizes that the universe is
untidy and inscrutable, a place where good may conflict with
good and evil with evil and where ultimate explanations, or
even the certainty that such are possible, are not forthcoming.
It does not explain why — to pose the question from the
point of view of the ancient world — the moral law, or the
gods' commands, should be so inconsistent that Orestes can
only honour the memory of his father by committing the
hideous crime of murdering his mother. It does not explain
why — to pose the question from a more characteristically
modern point of view — a task such as this should be imposed
on one like Hamlet who is singularly unfitted to perform it.
It faithfully records such dilemmas as these. At the same time

[1] Schlegel's *Gedanken* were published posthumously in 1764 (cf. below,
p. 124), having been written and privately circulated in 1747. It has however been
suggested that Lessing may have seen a copy (C. E. Borden, *J. E. Schlegel als Vor-
läufer Lessings* (Diss. Berkeley, 1937): cited in D. R. George, *Deutsche Tragödientheorien vom Mittelalter bis zu Lessing* (Munich, 1972), p. 362).

it does not preach mere resignation, but celebrates the striving of the human spirit to free itself from the labyrinth. The tidy mind of the Enlightenment found it hard to grasp this paradoxicality. Tragedy looks evil in the face and does not attempt to explain it away: even a necessary evil — Orestes' killing of his mother, or, to take an example which was to exercise Lessing, Virginius' killing of his daughter — does not by virtue of its necessity cease to be an evil. But this eighteenth-century Europe was reluctant to concede. The philosophy of 'optimism' expounded by Leibniz (later caricatured by Voltaire in *Candide*) proclaims that all is for the best and that we live in the best of all possible worlds. Evil and suffering are merely illusory, or at all events have their places in an all-embracing harmonious design. Tragedy must therefore be a 'theodicy', to use the word Leibniz coined to describe his own attempt to vindicate the justice and benevolence of divine Providence. It must show, as Pope had declared in his summary of the optimistic philosophy in the *Essay on Man*, that

> All Nature is but Art, unknown to thee;
> All Chance, Direction, which thou canst not see;
> All Discord, Harmony not understood;
> All partial Evil, universal Good:
> And, spite of Pride, in erring Reason's spite,
> One truth is clear, Whatever IS, is RIGHT.[2]

Often the paradoxes of tragedy seem to be reduced to simple moral equations: if the world is ruled by a benevolent Providence, then virtue must always be rewarded, and suffering can only be the punishment of wickedness. Tragedy must be made to teach some kind of moral lesson.

The philosophy here outlined was accepted by Lessing.[3] He once, according to Mendelssohn, proposed writing a continuation of *Candide* in which Voltaire's satire would be refuted.[4] He seems to have found it hard to accept the real existence of evil in human nature. In *Miß Sara Sampson* the seducer Mellefont is described as 'mehr unglücklich, als lasterhaft' (V, 10),

---

[2]   Pope, *Essay on Man*, i. 289–94: *The Poems of Alexander Pope*, ed. John Butt (London, 1965), p. 515.

[3]   Cf. J. Clivio, *Lessing und das Problem der Tragödie* (Zurich, 1928), and H. Steinmetz, 'Aufklärung und Tragödie. Lessings Tragödien vor dem Hintergrund des Trauerspielmodells der Aufklärung', *ABNG* i (1972), 3–41.

[4]   D 581.

the victim rather than the instigator of misfortune; the actual agent of Sara's death, her jealous rival Marwood, is presented as a melodramatic caricature and finally declared by Sara to be nothing but the instrument of Providence, the 'Hand, durch die Gott mich heimsucht' (ibid.). Similarly in *Emilia Galotti* the would-be seducer, the Prince, is presented as weak and misguided rather than wicked; in *Nathan der Weise* Lessing disarms the malevolent and dangerous Patriarch by turning him into a figure of fun. In the *Hamburgische Dramaturgie* Lessing describes Richard III, as portrayed by Weisse, as the greatest monster ever to have appeared on the stage:

> unstreitig das größte, abscheulichste Ungeheuer, das jemals die Bühne getragen. Ich sage, die Bühne: daß es die Erde wirklich getragen habe, daran zweifle ich. (No. 74)

His tragic protagonists must be esentially virtuous figures; at the same time he must persuade us that they in some sense morally deserve their fate, or we could not bear to witness it — just as eighteenth-century English audiences could not bear the suffering of the virtuous Cordelia in *King Lear*, but preferred Tate's revision.[5]

The paradoxicality of tragedy and its resolute confrontation of evil made it, then, hard for the Enlightened mind to comprehend. But the size and scale of tragic events, and the form of expression appropriate to them, were difficulties just as serious. Tragedy had traditionally concerned itself with events of great magnitude, and as a not unnatural corollary of this had generally chosen for its protagonists characters of elevated rank: kings, princes, and mythological heroes. Standing higher, they had further to fall and their fall was the more spectacular; standing out from the anonymous multitude, they attracted the attention and hostility of the gods, directors of events, as a solitary tree attracts lightning; living not merely the private lives of ordinary men, their fates had consequences which affected others beyond themselves; hieratic figures surrounded by ritual, they could appropriately — though superficial verisimilitude was not an essential consideration — be given a stylized, elevated form of speech in which great events could

---

[5]   Cf. Johnson's note to *King Lear*, in J. Wain (ed.), *Johnson as Critic* (London, 1973), p. 217.

find adequate expression and response. *Éloignement,* the distancing of the tragic event and its enactors from the audience in status, in time, or in place, was an important principle of the tragic style: formally enunciated and strictly observed by the French classical dramatists of the seventeenth century, it is in fact invariably followed by Shakespeare too, for even plays like *Romeo and Juliet, Othello,* and *Timon of Athens,* whose protagonists are not of princely rank (*Timon* is described by Johnson as a 'domestic tragedy'[6]) have geographically remote settings. Lessing's two full-length tragedies, *Miß Sara Sampson* and *Emilia Galotti,* both make a similar compromise with the principle of *éloignement* which suggests an acknowledgment, if unwilling, of its importance. Before his day, there had been one attempt by a serious German playwright to write a tragedy whose protagonists were not kings or princes or mythological personages, but an ordinary pair of unhappy lovers: Gryphius' *Cardenio and Celinde* (1654). Gryphius' play is *éloigné* by its Italian setting, by its introduction of supernatural events, and by its use of verse; even so, Gryphius apologizes in his preface for the fact that 'die Personen so eingeführet sind fast zu nidrig vor ein Traur-Spiel', and Gottsched in his reform of the German theatre continued to insist rigorously on the use of elevated characters. But in the eighteenth century people began to feel the remoteness of tragic events and characters an impediment to, rather than a necessary part of, the true tragic effect. They wanted to see on the stage characters whom they would not have to look up to, admire, and wonder at from afar, but whom they could pity and identify themselves with on a more familiar level. As Lessing wrote in the *Hamburgische Dramaturgie,* 'Die Namen von Fürsten und Helden können einem Stücke Pomp und Majestät geben; aber zur Rührung tragen sie nichts bei' (No. 14).

Not surprisingly, this development is first seen in England, where even the Elizabethan theatre had had its 'domestic tragedies' of ordinary life. Sometimes these were based, as in the case of the well-known *Arden of Faversham,* on fact: a kind of sensational journalism in dramatic form, recounting grisly

---

[6] Ibid., p. 218.

murders with (like its modern journalistic equivalents) at least the claim that it was only drawing the public's attention to such shocking crimes and their punishment as a warning example, in the interests of morality. Eighteenth-century England saw a revival of interest in Elizabethan domestic tragedy and the production of new works of this kind, the most famous being George Lillo's *George Barnwell or the London Merchant* of 1731. Such plays were calculated to appeal to a middle-class audience, sometimes even to the point of overt bourgeois propaganda. Thus in Lillo's play the virtuous merchant Thorowgood eulogizes the activity of his profession: 'See how it is founded in reason, and the nature of things; how it has promoted humanity, as it has opened and yet keeps up an intercourse between nations, far remote from one another in situation, customs and religion; promoting arts, industry, peace and plenty; by mutual benefits diffusing mutual love from pole to pole' (III, 1). But the preference for 'domestic' over heroic tragedy also indicates a lack of interest in affairs of state, a turning away from public to private concerns, a deliberate cutting-off of the greater resonances evoked by the fall of princes and heroes.

The choice of this kind of subject-matter has a necessary stylistic corollary, and the one cannot simply be labelled cause and the other effect. Not only in literature, but in painting, for example, and in architecture the eighteenth century turned away from the grand manner to a simpler and more everyday style. The elevated diction of tragedy was found bombastic and stilted (Greek tragic actors had indeed walked, not literally on stilts, but on high-heeled and thick-soled 'buskins' (*kothornoi*) which made them physically taller than ordinary mortals), and what had been soaring flight in the poetry of a Racine or a Shakespeare could well appear mere artifice and exaggeration in the hands of their inferior successors. Just as much as the paradoxical content of tragedy, its larger-than-life language was found offensive by the tidy and rather literal eighteenth-century mind. As the lady in James Thurber's story *The Macbeth Murder Mystery* — that superb little parable on 'realism' and literary convention — observes of Macduff's words on discovering Duncan's body, 'You wouldn't say a lot of stuff like that, offhand, would you — if you had found a body? Unless you had practised it in advance. "My God, there's a body in there!" is what an innocent man would say.' The trouble is that the ordinary 'offhand' remarks of ordinary 'innocent men' may not constitute an adequate linguistic response to the events of tragedy, which, as many writers of supposedly realistic drama have willy-nilly discovered, call for some more elaborate and stylized form of expression. Even the domestic tragedies of the Elizabethans were in verse. In the eighteenth century we find a determined will to realism, and so Lillo's *London Merchant* is written in prose; though here too verse is used to conclude acts and scenes — to provide a purely formal verbal emphasis to a curtain — and above all when the characters turn to address the audience general moral reflections on their fate and on the course of the action.

The prose domestic tragedy of middle-class life began after a while to find imitators on the Continent: the first French example is Landois's one-act *Sylvie* of 1740, *The London Merchant* was translated into German in 1752, and 1755 saw the independent appearance of two German originals, Christian Lebrecht Martini's *Rhynsolt und Sapphira* and Lessing's *Miß Sara Sampson*. Despite its success, however, the 'bürgerliches Trauerspiel' remained, at least in the hands of its eighteenth-century practitioners, an inherently unsatisfactory form, bearing in many features the marks of compromise between stylistic elements which are hard if not impossible to reconcile. The natural desire of the eighteenth-century European bourgeoisie for serious dramatic representation of their own lives and concerns in a recognizably realistic manner could not easily be satisfied in terms of a highly stylized and artificial form of drama taken over (even if at several removes) from the ancient Greeks. The attempt to do so is explained by the assumption, scarcely questioned before the work of Diderot, that serious drama necessarily meant tragedy: as we have seen, eighteenth-century comedy was becoming increasingly serious in content and in manner, but from the point of view of the theoretical critic, tragedy remained the superior genre.

In Germany the situation was aggravated by the virtually complete lack or disappearance of a national tradition in the drama: the resulting cultural inferiority complex made it even more imperative for German writers to produce tragedies, so that Germany could at last hold up her head in the literary world. Gottsched, concerned above all with the cultural prestige of his nation, and unaware of or unsympathetic towards the increasing demand for contemporary bourgeois realism, had gone on imitating the old forms, and encouraging his followers to imitate them, without asking whether these old forms were really appropriate or meaningful. Many of his pronouncements on tragedy suggest, perhaps more than in the case of any other literary genre he discusses, a lack of any real understanding of its nature. Unable to comprehend the tragic poet's confrontation of evil and suffering, Gottsched endeavours earnestly to demonstrate his moral purpose:

Der Poet will also durch die Fabeln Wahrheiten lehren, und die Zuschauer, durch den Anblick solcher schweren Fälle der Großen dieser Welt, zu ihren eigenen Trübsalen vorbereiten ... Der Poet wählet sich einen moralischen Lehrsatz, den er seinen Zuschauern auf eine sinnliche Art einprägen will. Dazu ersinnt er sich eine allgemeine Fabel, daraus die Wahrheit eines Satzes erhellet. Hierzu suchet er in der Historie solche berühmte Leute, denen etwas ähnliches begegnet ist ...[7]

And a purely formal convention like the unity of place Gottsched attempts, with grotesque literal-mindedness, to justify on the grounds of verisimilitude:

Die Zuschauer bleiben auf einer Stelle sitzen; folglich müssen auch die spielenden Personen alle auf einem Platze bleiben, den jene übersehen können, ohne ihren Ort zu ändern.[8]

Lessing shared many of Gottsched's basic assumptions, including his moralism, though his theories show from the beginning a progressive attempt to refine from simple didacticism a more subtle and complex account of the drama's moral effect. And more and more he came to realize the necessity of innovation if the traditional form, whose timeless validity he no more questioned than Gottsched, was to be successfully adapted to modern needs.

Of Lessing's first ventures in the field of tragedy, two frag-

[7]   Gottsched, *Dichtkunst*, ed. cit., pp. 606, 611.
[8]   Ibid., p. 615.

ments survive. Both date in all probability from before 1750, and, as we might expect at this early date, are in the currently approved French classical style: tragedies of state, with elevated characters speaking lofty sentiments in measured alexandrines. The first is *Giangir, oder der verschmähte Thron*, on one of those Oriental subjects sometimes chosen by seventeenth-century dramatists (as in Racine's *Bajazet*) as an alternative to those from classical antiquity. Here there is no hint of any descent from the grand manner, any attempt to bring tragedy closer to a mid-eighteenth-century audience. However, in the second fragment, *Samuel Henzi*, Lessing seems immediately to break new ground in his choice of characters and setting, for these are taken from contemporary real life. Samuel Henzi was a Swiss, a citizen of Berne, executed in 1749 for conspiracy against the ruling oligarchy. There is plenty of the stuff of tragedy here, for the story contains conflict and paradox, confusion of good and evil as well as their simple opposition. Henzi is a just man and his cause — the defeat of tyranny — is a righteous one; but he falls, or so the tragic playwright chooses to motivate his fall, through the irreconcilability of his noble ends with the evil means necessary to achieve them. It is a central theme of political tragedy: the conflict between the public and the private conscience.

Lessing completed an act and a half (570 lines) of *Samuel Henzi*, and in 1753 published the fragment in his collected works. It is the only one of his unfinished dramatic works which he ever did publish, apart from the single scene of *D. Faust* which appeared in the *Literaturbriefe* in 1759, and in the latter instance he did not acknowledge his own authorship. The contexts are similar: the *Henzi* fragment also appears in a series of fictitious 'letters' — essays, in fact, on a variety of literary and other subjects — and the purpose of its publication is, as with the *Faust* scene, to provoke debate on new or hitherto unconsidered possibilities for serious drama. Here the issue is, precisely, that of real, contemporary subject-matter:

Ich erinnere mich ganz wohl, daß man . . . damals das Gespräch auf die neuste Geschichte wandte, und daß ich in dem ganzen Umfange derselben keine Begebenheit anzutreffen erklärte, welche mich mehr gerührt habe, als die Enthauptung des Herrn Henzi in Bern. . . . Ich behauptete

sogar, daß er einen würdigen Helden zu einem recht erhabnen Trauerspiele abgeben könne.[9]

Some will say, Lessing continues, that it is against the rules of
tragedy to choose such a modern subject; but this objection
is unfounded. Such a choice will indeed raise problems with
regard to accuracy and the responsibility of the dramatist to
respect historical fact (problems to which Lessing returns in
his later dramatic theorizings). But there is no absolute reason
why a modern figure should not be a fit subject for tragedy.
We may perhaps detect here the first signs of Lessing's search
for ways of bringing tragedy closer to the audiences for
whom he was writing. But the fragment itself is not so much
tragedy in modern dress as modern life dressed up as tragedy.
Samuel Henzi is quite unambiguously laid out as a tragedy of
state in the grand manner — we note that Lessing himself uses
the word 'erhaben'. It is written in alexandrines, and the neo-
classic unities of time and place were to be strictly observed,
though this would have been hard to manage with any degree
of verisimilitude. The characters wear modern costume; but
there is nevertheless an overwhelming sense of assimilation to
the prototypes of high tragedy. They are not kings or princes;
but republican Switzerland is made strongly reminiscent of
republican Rome, for which as a setting for tragedy there was
ample precedent. There is indeed in Lessing's hero, whatever
the character and motives of the historical Henzi may have
been, more than a hint of the Roman Brutus; though this in
itself is interesting as possible evidence of a literary ancestry
other than French classicism, for it suggests that Lessing may
have known Shakespeare's *Julius Caesar*, at least in Borck's
German translation.

Lessing was thus already, possibly before 1750 and certainly
by 1753 when the fragment was published, beginning to think
of ways in which tragedy might be given specifically contemporary appeal. But *Samuel Henzi*, and the brief discussion
with which it is introduced in the *Briefe* of 1753, are only a
very tentative exploration in that direction. Critics have with
the benefit of hindsight claimed *Henzi* as a forerunner of Lessing's later 'bürgerliches Trauerspiel', but, as an anonymous

[9]   G iii. 326.

German critic pointed out as early as 1756, it belongs emphatically to the heroic rather than the 'bürgerlich' or domestic mode;[10] and it in no way manifests that radical rejection of the ‿rench classical manner which characterizes Lessing's later tragic theory and practice.

Some dissatisfaction with the prevailing fashion in tragedy is however voiced in the early critical essays. As we have noted, even as early as the *Beiträge* Lessing was urging his countrymen to look further afield than France in search of forms and styles of serious drama which would more readily suit the German natural taste. He must soon have come across examples of the new middle-class domestic tragedy. Certainly in the introduction to the *Abhandlungen von dem weinerlichen oder rührenden Lustspiel*, in the *Theatralische Bibliothek* of 1754, Lessing notes that the innovatory spirit had been at work not only in comedy, but also in tragedy. Just as the French had introduced the 'rührendes Lustspiel', so the English had introduced the 'bürgerliches Trauerspiel':

Hier hielt man es für unbillig, daß nur Regenten und hohe Standespersonen in uns Schrecken und Mitleiden erwecken sollten; man suchte sich also aus dem Mittelstande Helden, und schnallte ihnen den tragischen Stiefel an, in dem man sie sonst, nur ihn lächerlich zu machen, gesehen hatte.[11]

Lessing suggests that the two forms differ as do the national characters of the French and the English.

He promises for another occasion a full discussion of the 'bürgerliches Trauerspiel', but this never, as such, materialized; and the passage in the *Bibliothek* can hardly be cited as *advocating* the new form. Its existence is merely recorded, as one of the developments in contemporary drama which had come to Lessing's notice. Once again, with the benefit of hindsight we can see these remarks as a step towards the adoption of the domestic tragedy in *Miß Sara Sampson*, but it must be doubted whether at the time they represented any positive commitment or intention in that direction.

[10] *Neue Erweiterungen der Erkenntnis und des Vergnügens*, xxxi: 'Vom bürgerlichen Trauerspiele', § 3. Reprinted in K. Eibl (ed.), *Lessing: Miß Sara Sampson. Ein bürgerliches Trauerspiel* (Commentatio, ii, Frankfurt, 1971), pp. 173–201, esp. pp. 175 f.

[11] G iv. 12 f.

Another contribution to the *Theatralische Bibliothek* turns upon the essence of the problem: the adaptation of traditional tragic themes and subject-matter to the requirements of different ages and nations. This is the unfinished and rather scrappy, but nevertheless very important essay *Von den lateinischen Trauerspielen, welche unter dem Namen des Seneca bekannt sind,* which appeared in the second number of the *Bibliothek* in 1755 (but dated 1754). Lessing undertook to discuss all the ten tragedies attributed to Seneca, but this plan foundered like so many others and the essay of 1754 deals with only two, *Hercules furens (The Madness of Hercules)* and *Thyestes.* Seneca's treatment of these themes is compared with that of Euripides — the first instance in Lessing's work of the unfavourable comparison of the arts of Rome with those of Greece which is so important, for example, in the *Laokoon.* The Senecan *Thyestes* is further compared with a modern French play on the same subject-matter, Crébillon's *Atrée et Thyeste* of 1707, 'so . . . daß man ohngefähr die Art und Weise sieht, mit welcher ein neuer Dichter einen alten und von den Sitten unsrer Zeit so abweichenden Stoff habe bearbeiten können';[12] and as there is no comparable modern treatment of the madness of Hercules, Lessing offers his own suggestions as to how a modern writer might present it.[13] He lays the stress firmly on the moral effect of the play, and although he does not attribute to the playwright a primarily didactic intention as Gottsched had done, his view of dramatic morality at this stage is still fairly crude. The ancients, Lessing observes, did not follow the Gottschedian recipe of first deciding what moral lesson they wished to inculcate and then devising a plot to fit it. They started from the event they wished to portray, knowing that a dramatist could interpret events as he wished and that a single event could be interpreted in a multiplicity of ways. But, Lessing alleges, the fact that the ancients were tied to the supposed historical or religious truth of their received plots did sometimes constitute a handicap. It prevented some of their plays from expressing satisfactory morals as a whole, although they might still contain isolated nuggets of useful moral truth. The modern poet

[12] Ibid., p. 138.   [13] Ibid., pp. 87 ff.

however has not the same excuse ('Entschuldigung'): he must choose his subject matter and dispose his moral accents appropriately.

It appears that Lessing at one time considered making an adaptation of the *Hercules furens* himself, in doing so following a similar procedure to that he had adopted in *Samuel Henzi*: choosing a modern character whose actions and fate resembled those of a classical tragic hero. Unlike Henzi, his modern Brutus, his modern Hercules was not a contemporary, but a seventeenth-century figure: Massaniello, leader of the Neapolitan rebellion against the Spaniards in 1647. Once again the figure and the theme appear to be political, but here Lessing deliberately selected other aspects for emphasis. On 14 July 1773 he wrote to his brother Karl, who was himself planning to write a tragedy on the figure of Massaniello, that his interest in this character had been a psychological one: that what had attracted him to Massaniello had been not his political role, but

die endliche Zerrüttung seines Verstandes, die ich mir aus ganz natürlichen Ursachen in ihm selbst erklären zu können glaubte . . . Ich glaubte sonach den Mann in ihm zu finden, an welchem sich der alte Rasende Herkules modernisieren ließe, über dessen aus ähnlichen Gründen entstandene Raserei ich mich erinnere, einige Anmerkungen in der Theatralischen Bibliothek gemacht zu haben.

We note that this letter dates from after the completion of *Emilia Galotti* and closely reflects the procedures adopted by Lessing in the psychological engineering of that play, and we cannot be certain of the date of the plan referred to here; but it seems reasonable to assume that the idea had occurred to him at the time when he was writing about Seneca in the *Theatralische Bibliothek*. If this is so, then we can legitimately describe it as a further step towards the writing of the first really 'modern' tragedy.

(ii)

Even so, *Miß Sara Sampson* comes as a surprise. It was written in a few weeks, in Potsdam in 1755. Unlike *Giangir* or *Samuel Henzi*, it is in prose, and its characters are not real historical or even real contemporary persons, but *fictional* ones — an important innovation. The setting is an England which one assumes to be contemporary, and the personages members of the lower fringe of the nobility rather than of the middle class: they are all of independent means, and do not have to think of earning their living. Mellefont's story of his cousin's will, which he tells to Sara (I, 7), as he had told it, years before, to Marwood (cf. IV, 8), is nothing but a mechanical motivating device: there is no real sense of social and economic realities. The play is enacted in exactly the same kind of social vacuum as the early comedies, and there is nothing to attach it to any known world of real experience except the characters' names. These are English — or ostensibly so; but they are fictional English rather than real. The kind father Sir William Sampson suggests such idealizations of the English squirearchy as Addison's Sir Roger de Coverley, a figure familiar to the German middle-class public from the numerous translations and imitations of the *Spectator* and other English 'moral weeklies' which were current in Germany at this time.[14] The virtuous heroine would recall those of Richardson's novels — the German translation of which had received a brief but enthusiastic review from Lessing in the *Berlinische privilegierte Zeitung* in 1754.[15] The names of the other protagonists are taken from Congreve — Mellefont from *The Double-Dealer*, Marwood from *The Way of the World*: curious names which are inherently fictional. They are the equivalents in English Restoration comedy of the Adrastes and Orontes of continental neo-classicism — and oddly enough, at a time when these conventional names were giving way to native ones in German comedy, the pseudo-English names introduced by Lessing in *Miß Sara Sampson* were to become just as much a convention of the German 'bürgerliches Trauerspiel', as exemplified by the heroine of Pfeil's *Lucie Woodvil* (1756), the Clerdon, Granville, and Henley of Brawe's *Freigeist*, the Lady Milford of Schiller's *Kabale und Liebe*. The name of the servant Waitwell (also to be found in *The Way of the World*) is of course a 'humour' name denoting his role: a conspicuous if minor illus-

---

[14] Cf. W. Martens, *Die Botschaft der Tugend. Die Aufklärung im Spiegel der deutschen moralischen Wochenschriften* (Stuttgart, 1968).

[15] G iii. 202 f.

tration of the fact that many features of *Miß Sara Sampson* recall comic rather than tragic traditions.[16]

There is a curious apocryphal anecdote recounting the origin of *Miß Sara Sampson*. According to this, Lessing went to the theatre one day with Moses Mendelssohn to see a sentimental French play. After the performance Lessing dismissed the work, saying that anyone could write tear-jerkers of that kind: 'Es ist keine Kunst, alte Weiber zum Heulen zu bringen.' Mendelssohn replied that that was easier said than done; upon which Lessing wagered that he could write one in six weeks. The next day he left Berlin for Potsdam and reappeared six weeks later − with *Miß Sara Sampson* completed.[17] It appears from accounts of the first performance that as a tear-jerker it was extremely successful; but it claims to be something more. It is, of course, not supposed to be a sentimental *comedy* (as was, presumably, the play Lessing and Mendelssohn went to see), but a tragedy. We know that Lessing was becoming increasingly interested in tragedy in the mid-fifties, having stopped writing comedies some years previously; we know that he was observing new developments in tragedy such as the 'bürgerliches Trauerspiel' − which designation *Sara* proudly carries on its title-page. We know from the Seneca essay and from the projected tragedies on the figures of Henzi and, possibly, Massaniello that he had been thinking about the problem of modern tragedy and attempting to assimilate modern subject-matter to tragic archetypes taken over from classical antiquity, to fit modern subject-matter into the traditional form. The inspiration for *Sara* − whether our anecdote is true or not − must have been the sudden realization of a way in which a number of disparate elements could be successfully combined. Sentimental comedy is undoubtedly one of those elements, and Lessing's early apprenticeship in comedy stood him in good stead when it came to the rapid execution of his design. (The play was, incidentally, completed at an appropriate moment to fill up volume six of his *Schriften*.)

It is often said that Lessing's play is an actual imitation of

---

[16] Cf. H. Rempel, *Tragödie und Komödie im dramatischen Schaffen Lessings* (Berlin, 1935).

[17] D 81 f. Cf. also R. Daunicht, *Die Entstehung des bürgerlichen Trauerspiels in Deutschland* (Berlin, 1963), pp. 277 ff.

Lillo's *London Merchant*, but the evidence for this is very slight. Both plays feature a female villain, a temptress — a common figure on the eighteenth-century stage and one by no means confined to the domestic drama — and in the scenes where this figure appears there are one or two incidental resemblances of situation and phrase, which again are little more than stock-in-trade: the use of the standard figure produces standard situations and corresponding dialogue. Lillo's play too betrays its comic ancestry in the use of names like Thorowgood and Trueman, and the Congrevian Millwood for its villainess. But there is no real resemblance of substance between *Sara* and *The London Merchant*: despite the importance of the temptress-figure, their basic plots are quite different. Lessing's play also, despite its subtitle, completely lacks the explicit bourgeois ethos and class feeling of Lillo's, and the latter's characterization of his play, in the prologue, as 'a Tale of private woe', is more completely true of Lessing's. Both plays are highly moral, but Lillo's much more crudely so; Lessing's is not without a touch of genuinely tragic moral ambiguity, though, as we shall see, he seems to have done what he could to expunge it. The remarks in the *Theatralische Bibliothek* show that English plays of this type had come to his attention as a possible solution to the problem of modern tragedy, but Lessing does not mention *The London Merchant* by name here or anywhere else before 1756,[18] and it seems unjustifiable to claim it as a direct influence. Other English plays have been suggested as sources for *Sara* — Shadwell's *The Squire of Alsatia* (again a comedy), Charles Johnson's *Caelia*, Mrs Susanna Centlivre's *The Perjur'd Husband*;[19] but there is still no real explanation of Lessing's sudden, unheralded venture into the English domestic manner.

We might perhaps look for a classical prototype for *Miß Sara Sampson*, bearing in mind the insistence in the Seneca essay on the modern dramatist's right, indeed duty, to alter details and to reinterpret events in a modern way, in particular in accordance with modern ideas of morality. And indeed we do not have far to look. Lessing did not continue his

[18] Cf. below, p. 89.
[19] Cf. P. P. Kies, 'The Sources and Basic Model of Lessing's *Miß Sara Sampson*', *Modern Philology*, xxiv (1927), 65–90.

Senecan studies in the *Theatralische Bibliothek*, but Seneca's
Medea would have lent itself admirably to the procedures
adopted there.[20] It could be compared again with Euripides
and with a modern French playwright: in this case none other
than Corneille himself, whose *Médée*, Lessing subsequently
wrote to Ramler (11 December 1755) 'taugt nichts' — his first
outright condemnation of the master. The story of Medea,
the Colchian princess, has the bloodthirstiness characteristic
of so many Greek legends. Having by her magic helped Jason
to steal the Golden Fleece, Medea becomes his wife. They
return to Greece, but here Jason tires of her: as a barbarian
enchantress, she brings him dishonour in the eyes of his
countrymen. He longs to recover his integrity and self-respect
and re-enter decent society. Admitted to the household of
King Creon, he falls in love with the king's daughter, and this
love is what finally decides him to cast off Medea. But she
will not allow him to enjoy the fruits of his desertion of her:
she kills her rival, murders the children she has born to Jason,
and is magically spirited away. The basic plot of Lessing's
play closely corresponds: Mellefont represents Jason, Sir William and Sara King Creon and his daughter, and Marwood
herself declares 'Sieh in mir eine neue Medea!' (II, 7). The
situation is in essential outline the same: Mellefont has been
moved by his love for Sara to mend his ways, to leave his life
of dissipation, and to abandon his wicked mistress, Marwood;
Marwood exacts her revenge. Lessing has made one or two
changes in the story (perhaps prompted by one or other of
his supposed English models). He has made Mellefont and Sara
elope, fearing Sir William's opposition to their union; he
makes Marwood eventually spare the life of her and Mellefont's child, Arabella — perhaps the death of this innocent,
like that of Cordelia, would have been too unrelievedly horrific
for an eighteenth-century audience; and he makes Mellefont
kill himself at the end of the play, whereas Jason had to live

---

[20] Cf. my essay, 'Lessing and the "Bürgerliches Trauerspiel"', in P. F. Ganz
(ed.), *The Discontinuous Tradition. Studies in German Literature in Honour of
Ernest Ludwig Stahl* (Oxford, 1970), 14–28. See also W. Barner, *Produktive Rezeption. Lessing und die Tragödien Senecas* (Munich, 1973); W. Woesler, 'Lessings
Miß Sara Sampson and Seneca's *Medea', LYB* x (1978), 75–93.

on in shame and despair. But these changes do not really affect the core of the play.

What does however alter the basic 'Senecan' model almost beyond recognition, and also seriously jeopardizes its tragic effect, is that Lessing has, in full accord with his theory, interpreted the events of the story from the point of view of eighteenth-century morality, and has asked his audience to do the same and to bestow its sympathies accordingly. This involves a massive shift in the centre of gravity of the play. To the ancients, Medea was a barbarian and a figure of horror; but that did not prevent her from being the protagonist of a tragedy. Ten or twenty years later, Lessing might have realized this; he might have attempted to engage our pity for his Medea-figure by probing, as Grillparzer was to do in his trilogy *Das goldene Vlies*, the complex sequence of events that led to her doing such terrible deeds, by showing us, in the words of the *Hamburgische Dramaturgie*, 'eine Reihe von Ursachen und Wirkungen . . . nach welcher jene unwahrscheinliche Verbrechen nicht wohl anders, als geschehen müssen' (No. 32). But in 1755 he could not, or at any rate did not, do so. Looking at the events from an exclusively and uncompromisingly moral point of view, he apportions responsibility and pity in inverse proportion to one another. Marwood is wholly wicked, and so deserves no sympathy whatever; Sara is virtuous and is the one who suffers most, and so she must have all our pity and be advanced to the status of tragic heroine. But can she really fill this role? Aristotle had held that the undeserved suffering of a virtuous person was not a tragic but an odious spectacle — and in accordance with this view we are not encouraged, in other dramatic treatments of the Medea legend, to take too close or personal an interest in the fate of King Creon's daughter. We are interested in a sequence of events, and the natural focus of our attention is the active party in those events: their purely passive victim remains a peripheral figure. In Euripides' *Medea* King Creon's daughter does not appear on stage at all; Seneca and Corneille introduce her in a scene or two; Grillparzer was to give her greater prominence, but still to keep her role an essentially subordinate one; Lessing makes her the heroine of his play.

A vital point in Aristotle's definition of tragedy, but one

which the majority of his commentators, including Lessing, have either misunderstood or simply ignored, is his repeated insistence that tragedy is an imitation of action and not of persons, and that it only includes the characters for the sake of the action.[21] He also speaks of the *incidents* of tragedy as arousing pity and terror. His basic meaning is not difficult to grasp, but accords with our everyday experience: there is a crucial difference between the recognition of certain *events* as archetypally tragic or terrible, and feeling sorry *for someone*; although the latter, more particular reaction may well accompany or constitute a part of the former, larger and more general one. Lessing, however, held that *pity for the protagonist* was the cardinal emotion which tragedy should seek to arouse; and although his theory of tragedy, first developed in the years following the composition of *Miß Sara Sampson*, was subsequently refined and modified in a number of important details, pity remains its corner-stone. In the *Hamburgische Dramaturgie* he asserts that the simple definition, 'ein Gedicht, welches Mitleid erreget', conveys the one essential feature of tragedy, all its other elements being deducible from this (No. 77). In *Miß Sara Sampson* he has, it would seem quite deliberately, sacrificed the greater effect for the lesser: instead of tragedy he has given us pathos. This is in full accord with his later theories; with the preference he shared with his contemporaries for subjects they could comprehend on their own level, rather than those which exacted a recognition of forces in the universe larger than themselves; and with the moralistic presupposition that only a virtuous person could serve as a tragic protagonist.

Many readers of *Miß Sara Sampson* find themselves thinking, whether or not they are aware of the classical prototype, that Marwood ought to have been the heroine of the play, and that only when she is on stage does it begin to come to life. Partly, this is simply because the scenes in which she appears seem more convincingly written: they contain a certain amount of real dialogue, rather than the exchanges of sentimental pathos which are all too frequent elsewhere in the text. This is true above all of the scenes between Marwood and

---

[21]   Cf. J. Jones, *On Aristotle and Greek Tragedy* (London, 1962).

Mellefont — we note how, for example, in II, 3, she switches, appropriately and convincingly, from the formal 'Sie' to the contemptuously intimate 'du' and back — and those between Marwood and Sara, particularly IV, 8, where even Sara is provoked to vigorous reaction. For, of course, what really disqualifies Sara as a tragic heroine is her almost total passivity and disengagement from the events which lead to her death. She is hardly faced with a single serious decision in the whole play. Marwood, on the other hand, is very much an active character, indeed the only active character in the work. The others remain static, supremely exemplified by Sara, who, eight weeks after her elopement with Mellefont, 'bleibt den ganzen Tag in ihrer Stube eingeschlossen und weint' (I, 2). They do not even give the impression, as do, say, Racine's characters even at their most passive-seeming, that they are waiting for something terrible and inevitable to *happen* to them: the situation of the protagonists is static until Marwood arrives and begins her intrigues. Furthermore, these intrigues do not serve to bring about the resolution of any tension there might be between Sara and Mellefont — the motif is hinted at (II, 3), but not developed — but merely fulfil her own private purposes of revenge. The play's intrigue is in this sense external to the situation of the protagonists, and in consequence the catastrophe seems arbitrary rather than inevitable.[22]

Given his radical transformation of the legend, Lessing had the twofold task of minimizing the audience's sympathy for Marwood — who might still, if he were not careful, steal the show — and maximizing the dramatic interest of Sara, even though pity for her is at least assured. Marwood is painted as black as possible by conventional means which the audience would immediately recognize and respond to: she is an obvious melodramatic villain. In the course of Act I she is repeatedly alluded to as a wicked and dangerous figure, and when we meet her in the opening scene of Act II she is shown coldly calculating how best she can achieve her ends, prepared to use even her own child as a weapon in her struggle. The virtuous characters in this play do not think of ends and means, but only of right and wrong. Sara longs to be married

[22] Cf. G. Fricke, 'Bemerkungen zu Lessings *Freygeist* und *Miß Sara Sampson*', in H. Moser, etc. (eds.), *Festschrift Josef Quint* (Bonn, 1964), 83–120.

to Mellefont because she loves him, and is prepared to endure
the shame of a secret union provided only that it be legitimized
in the sight of God and her conscience (I, 7); Marwood wants
Mellefont back for no such unworldly reason, but only to
restore her good name in the sight of the world, and for this
she is quite prepared to marry a man she despises and addresses
as 'Ungeheuer' and 'Scheusal' (II, 7).[23]

The play does distinguish, then, and sharply, between the
substance and the appearance of virtue, between 'Tugend'
and 'guter Name'. Marwood is a mother; but she is prepared
to torture her own child to death for the sake of her revenge
— 'Ich will es nicht gestorben sehen; sterben will ich es sehen!'
she cries out (II, 7), echoing, incidentally, Atreus in Seneca's
Thyestes.[24] Sara, on the other hand, is prepared to extend
true maternal love even to the illicit fruit of Mellefont's union
with this monster (V, 5). The wicked are constantly deceiving,
dissimulating, concealing their true feelings. Marwood awaiting
Mellefont (II, 2), like Lillo's Millwood awaiting Barnwell
(*The London Merchant*, I, 4), wonders what tactics to adopt.
Her face is a mask which can take on any expression that
may seem expedient. Only when she is alone can she momen-
tarily drop the mask and reveal her true self — which is not a
pretty sight (IV, 5). The virtuous, on the other hand, give the
expression of their emotions free rein, regularly through the
medium of tears. The opening exchanges of the first scene set
a tone of lachrymosity. Sir William and Waitwell weep; Sara,
we learn, weeps all day long; Mellefont weeps, for the first
time since his childhood (I, 5); and the text is full of references
to 'Tränen' and 'weinen'.[25] Even Marwood weeps (II, 3); but
this is presumably part of her arsenal of deceit, for at a moment
of violent stress, when she sees her purposes thwarted, her
emotions find a characteristically different form of physical
expression, as Sara observes:

— Ich erschrecke, Lady; wie verändern sich auf einmal die Züge Ihres

[23] Cf. above, p. 32.
[24] Riedel, op. cit., p. 105, sees the *Thyestes* rather than the *Medea* as the true
Senecan prototype of *Miß Sara Sampson*.
[25] These references are in fact largely confined to Acts I and III, but they establish a pervading atmosphere for the whole play: the average reader of *Miß Sara
Sampson* is left with the impression that 'everyone' is 'always' weeping.

Gesichts? Sie glühen; aus dem starren Auge schreckt Wut, und des
Mundes knirschende Bewegung — (IV, 8)

Genuine tears are a prerogative of the virtuous.

The cult of lachrymosity in eighteenth-century Europe is
an interesting subject for the social psychologist. The disposition to weep is taken as evidence of an emotional sincerity
which is the necessary pre-condition of virtue. Sometimes indeed one wonders just what is so virtuous about those characters in eighteenth-century novels and plays who weep so freely.
The device is frequently used, in the literature of the period,
of using the ability or inability to weep as an indicator of virtuous and vicious characters respectively, but the former
seem often, apart from weeping, actually to *do* very little to
demonstrate their virtue. The concept of virtue is an extremely
passive, defensive one which often seems to exhaust itself in
the mere possession of a virtuous disposition, without the
necessity for the performance of good deeds.[26] Some social
historians have seen this concept of virtue as essentially bourgeois: whereas the powerful enjoy freedom of action and can
see virtue in the exercise of this freedom, their social inferiors
are constrained to adopt an ethic of passivity and submission.[27]
It is also, of course, often strongly and explicitly associated
with Christianity, and the Christian love and forgiveness exercised by Sara and Sir William emerges as the strongest positive
ethical note of the play; but while recognizing this genuine,
positive strength we may observe that it consists in the exemplification of an attitude rather than in the performance of
specific actions. Finally, this passive concept of virtue may
possibly be more specifically associated with a predestinarian
form of religion, which holds that individuals simply belong
to the category either of the elect or of the damned; and although the former will presumably be naturally predisposed
to lead virtuous and the latter wicked lives, what they actually
do will in no way affect their ultimate destination.

Divine Providence is frequently invoked in this play, as it is
throughout Lessing's work; but although some interpreters

[26] Cf. G. Sauder, *Empfindsamkeit: I. Voraussetzungen und Elemente* (Stuttgart, 1974), esp. pp. 207 ff.
[27] A similar distinction is developed, with great rhetorical panache (and strong
preference for the allegedly aristocratic values), by Nietzsche in *Zur Genealogie
der Moral.*

have argued theological subtleties into *Miß Sara Sampson,*[28] it seems to me rather that Lessing is working here with a very simple, indeed elementary, moral categorization of his characters. The fact that Sara has — before the curtain rises, be it noted — disobeyed and run away from her father (a not inconsiderable transgression by the standards of the time) and eloped, if nothing worse, with Mellefont is not intended to detract substantially from our acceptance of her as a paragon of virtue: as Waitwell says, 'Ein Kind kann wohl einmal fehlen, es bleibt deswegen doch ein gutes Kind' (III, 3). On the other hand, the fact that Marwood has suffered what we may well regard as some injustice, having been deserted by Mellefont after an association lasting many years, is not intended by Lessing to attract any sympathy towards her. It is of course precisely Jason's desertion that makes the classical Medea a tragic figure: she is a criminal, but her crimes are not without a comprehensible motivation. In Lessing's play, however, Marwood is wholly evil, and Mellefont's desertion of her is to be seen as nothing more than the justly merited reward of vice — as Sara tells her, unknowingly, to her face:

> Wenn zum Exempel, ein Mellefont eine Marwood liebt, und sie endlich verläßt: so ist dieses Verlassen, in Vergleichung mit der Liebe selbst, etwas sehr Gutes. Es wäre ein Unglück, wenn er eine Lasterhafte deswegen, weil er sie einmal geliebt hat, ewig lieben müßte. (IV, 8)

And Marwood disappears from the scene boasting of her crime:

> Rache und Wut haben mich zu einer Mörderin gemacht; ich will aber keine von den gemeinen Mörderinnen sein, die sich ihrer Tat nicht zu rühmen wagen. (V, 10)

Thus Lessing has disposed his audience to pity Sara and reject Marwood; but there remains the problem of making Sara dramatically interesting enough for a tragic heroine. Two things can be done with such a figure of virtuous passivity. She can be made less wholly virtuous: she can be made to bear some measure of guilt, so that in some sense or some degree we feel she deserves the fate which strikes her down. Or she can be made to react in some positive way to her fate: to

---

[28] Notably H. Bornkamm, 'Die innere Handlung in Lessings *Miß Sara Sampson'*, *Euph.* li (1957), 385–96.

struggle against it, or at least to bear it with some dignity and fortitude. Tragic dramatists have usually taken care both to make their protagonists guilty and to make them meet their fate with dignity, and Lessing is no exception. The trouble, from his point of view, is that both these modifications compromise the purity of what he felt to be the only true tragic effect, pity. When the protagonist is guilty, our pity for his fate is tempered by the thought that he deserves it. If he has the courage to face it with equanimity, then we realize that he does not need our pity, that he has risen above it and that so in a sense we have not the right to pity him: in a word, our pity is tempered with admiration.

Lessing was aware of these difficulties, though perhaps not, at the time of writing *Sara*, with theoretical clarity. Guilt posed the lesser problem. Aristotle had said that the tragic protagonist ought to bring about his own fall by some *hamartia*, some error of judgement or conduct; Lessing and his contemporaries also found wholly undeserved suffering offensive to their sense of an ordered and harmonious universe and a benevolent Providence; Sara herself interprets her sufferings as a punishment for her desertion of her father, her failing in filial affection and loyalty. Admiration was much more of a stumbling-block to Lessing. There can be no doubt that we admire virtue; indeed, there can be no doubt that we are intended in some sense to admire Sara as she rises transfigured above her sufferings, reconciled to her father and forgiving the agents of her death. Without this transfiguration she would not be a tragic heroine; we note again that most dramatists who have treated the Medea legend, from Euripides to Anouilh, have not allowed us to witness the death of King Creon's daughter at all. Yet in his theoretical writings, as we shall see, Lessing constantly maintained that admiration is not a proper effect of tragedy, marshalling a number of highly suspect arguments to prove this. He associated admiration with the heroic form of tragedy, of which he came strongly to disapprove. He realized that we can admire even a wicked person who meets his destiny with fortitude, but he felt that this endangered the essential morality of tragedy, even though in such a case our admiration is tempered with moral satisfaction at the punishment of evil. The tragic effect is compounded of

such elements as recognition of the mutability of human
fortune; pity for a fellow human being; admiration, perhaps
for the essential goodness of a man brought low by a single
mistake, perhaps for the dignity with which he faces his death;
and satisfaction at the punishment of guilt and the vindication
of divine, or at least poetic, justice. Lessing's shortcomings
both as a tragic playwright (at any rate in *Miß Sara Sampson*)
and as a tragic theorist spring from his attempt to simplify
this complex: to reduce a subtle blending of aesthetic and
ethical values to a simple equation of them, and in particular
to reduce the complex blend and balance of emotions which
tragedy arouses to a single cardinal one, pity for a virtuous
protagonist, to which all other effects are merely ancillary.

   Jason occupies a curious position in the Medea legend: the
conquest of the Golden Fleece is his story, but what happens
afterwards is Medea's. Jason at the end of the story is the
man who was once a hero, but is one no longer. The modern
mind can find a characteristic interest in such a figure: Grillparzer's Jason, for example, is a fascinating study in the
demolition of a heroic identity. Lessing has certainly perceived
the modern possibilities of the figure of Jason, and his Mellefont is the most interesting character in the play, indeed the
only one of the *dramatis personae* who is really interesting *as*
a character at all. Lessing might perhaps have chosen to make
him his protagonist, and a modern producer of *Miß Sara
Sampson* — for the play is occasionally seen on the stage even
today — is very likely to make Mellefont, the 'anti-hero', the
centre of his interpretation. Lessing however does not intend
Mellefont for this role, for precisely the reason which in fact
makes him a more interesting and potentially a more genuinely
tragic figure than Sara: he wishes to dispose the accents of his
play in accordance with moral judgements, to attract the
greatest sympathy for the most virtuous of the characters.
For this purpose Mellefont will not do. He is a sinner, even if
a repentant one; and his repentance is, as it turns out, none
too secure. Throughout Act V his chief desire is for revenge,
and at Sara's death he cannot weep: she sees in his features
'stumme Verzweiflung' (V, 10) — itself a sin, for it is tanta-
mount to doubting the designs of Providence. It is such despair,
and not simply contrition and remorse, that prompts his

suicide. Despite Sir William's 'Er war mehr unglücklich, als
lasterhaft', our pity for him is too heavily diluted with moral
condemnation for him to serve as Lessing's hero.

In the black-and-white moral scheme of this play, he is the
only grey figure, but even he is not portrayed with any genuine
psychological probing: the alternatives between which he
vacillates are presented in simple moral terms. He has led, as
his servant Norton sourly reminds him (I, 3), a dissolute life;
he has fallen in love with Sara, and renounced his former
ways — 'Sie, liebste Sara, sehen, und alle Marwoods vergessen,
war eins' (I, 7). His conversion to the path of virtue is attested
by his weeping (I, 5). But he is weak, and his delay in marrying
Sara exposes him to temptations which his new-found virtue
is not yet able to resist. For this delay there is a material
reason: the necessity, since he has squandered his own money,
of making a settlement to secure a share in an inheritance
(I, 7). But in his soliloquy in the fourth act, he reveals an
inner reluctance to surrender his freedom, to bow his neck to
the yoke of matrimony:

> Warum muß ich eingeschmiedet werden, und auch so gar den elenden
> Schatten der Freiheit entbehren? — Eingeschmiedet? Nichts anders! —
> Sara Sampson, meine Geliebte! Wie viel Seligkeiten liegen in diesen
> Worten! — Sara Sampson, meine Ehegattin! — Die Hälfte dieser Selig-
> keiten ist verschwunden! und die andre Hälfte — wird verschwinden. —
> Ich Ungeheuer!
> (IV, 2)

Norton arrives, and observes his master's displeasure at 'die
Aussicht in einen Stand, der sich so wenig zu Ihrer Denkungs-
art schickt'; Mellefont confesses to a prejudice which he describes as a 'närrische Grille' (IV, 3). The monologue is the
only occasion in the play on which any of the characters
reveals what is going on in his mind in anything other than
purely conventional terms, or indeed reveals that there is anything going on in his mind which is not simply a matter of
black-and-white moral choice. Lessing had already shown in
Der Freigeist that he realized that the moral quality of life
was not a matter of simple black and white, and he seems
here to be revealing, or at least hinting at, possible depths of
real complex human feeling beneath the sentimental stereotypes which occupy the surface of *Miß Sara Sampson.*

But I think that critics who have pinned their interpretation of the play on Mellefont have over-estimated the subtlety of the work. It has been read, for example, as the tragedy of a conflict between the legitimate demands of individual, sub-jective feeling and the restrictions of a social morality which is not yet ready to grant them.[29] This is a reading coloured by seeing the play across the years of 'Sturm und Drang', by seeing in it what Schiller was to make of a similar conflict in *Kabale und Liebe* thirty years later. In 1755 the monologue would have been understood, and I believe was intended to be understood, in simple moral terms: Mellefont, recent con-vert to virtue, threatens to relapse into vice. The play has also been interpreted as a tragic variation on the traditional comic theme of the monomaniac fool, whose single obsessive folly — in Mellefont's case, his prejudice against marriage — is here not thwarted as it would be in comedy, but allowed to bring misery upon himself and those about him.[30] It is certainly true that *Miß Sara Sampson* owes a great deal to the forms and techniques of comedy; but the relationship is much more complex than this — and the play much simpler. It is basically a rather crude moral melodrama — a tear-jerker, in fact. True, Lessing was only twenty-five when he wrote it; but he had al-ready shown in *Der Freigeist* that he was capable of conceiving a more complex and mature moral vision than this. Rather than seeking out imagined subtleties in *Miß Sara Sampson*, we should ask why he should have regressed in this way.

Partly the answer may lie simply in the speed with which, for whatever reason, *Miß Sara Sampson* was written. But a further element which I believe entered into Lessing's calcul-ations was a deliberate decision to appeal to a certain kind of audience. Lessing fully shared Gottsched's concern for the cultural prestige of the German nation, though he disagreed with Gottsched as to the means by which this was to be ad-vanced, and hotly disputed Gottsched's personal claim to be the supreme arbiter in these matters. He realized that much more extensive concessions must be made to actual contem-

[29] Cf. F. Brüggemann, 'Lessings Bürgerdramen und der Subjektivismus als Problem', B 82-126 (originally in *Jahrbuch des freien deutschen Hochstifts*, 1926).
[30] Cf. R. R. Heitner, 'Lessing's Manipulation of a Single Comic Theme', *MLQ* xviii (1957), 183-98.

porary taste than Gottsched was prepared to grant. Why should he not then try, as least as an experiment, the middle-class domestic tragedy which had been so successful in England, to see whether this would not attract German middle-class audiences too? If the public was ever to be educated in matters of literary and theatrical taste, then first of all the serious dramatist must get the public into the theatre by giving it something he knew it would like. Accordingly, I believe, Lessing in *Miß Sara Sampson* is deliberately writing down to his public — anticipating the advice of the 'Theaterdirektor' in the 'Vorspiel' to Goethe's *Faust*:

> Bedenkt, ihr habt weiches Holz zu spalten,
> Und seht nur hin, für wen ihr schreibt —

by choosing to clothe the 'serious' skeleton of his tragedy in forms of flesh and blood which his audience would recognize from the familiar contemporary novels, moral weeklies, and sentimental comedies, and to which they would respond in the accustomed manner. This meant taking over from those sources the familiar figures of the virtuous heroine, the father who objects to his daughter's marriage — though this traditionally comic figure is here portrayed in a wholly serious light — and the wicked assailants of her virtue,[31] painting these figures almost exclusively in plain, strong black and white and going for plain, strong emotional responses of a kind the audience would willingly give. The result might not be the highest form of tragedy, but it would do as a beginning, and in his subsequent theoretical writings Lessing was prepared both in public and, more significantly, in private to defend the legitimacy of this kind of tragedy, or something like it. However, he never committed himself exclusively to the 'bürgerliches Trauerspiel', and, as we shall see, he tried in a number of sketches and plans to discover alternative and better forms of tragic drama suitable for the modern age.

Miß Sara Sampson is thus to be seen, I suggest, as a deliberate experiment on Lessing's part in writing a tragedy which makes the maximum possible concession to the taste of a not very sophisticated audience, who none the less had a fairly

[31] On the metamorphoses of these figures in eighteenth-century literature see H. Petriconi, *Die verführte Unschuld* (Hamburg, 1953).

high opinion of themselves and their own aesthetic and, in particular, moral sensibilities; who were not interested in the fates of princes or of mythological heroes, but preferred to confine their attention to their own domestic sphere; who wished to see vice punished, virtue, if not rewarded, then at least exemplified in worthy and sympathetic form, and the designs of Providence vindicated; who wished, not least, to have a good cry and to flatter themselves that their tears were the badge of true virtue. Lessing knew these attitudes well, being himself a member of this class of society and sharing these attitudes in many respects, and I do not believe that the moral poses of the characters in *Miß Sara Sampson* are being in any way questioned or ironized.[32] Nor do I believe that Lessing intends the play to be taken one way by an unsophisticated audience while a sophisticated one would see what he really meant.[33] Indeed, I do not believe that in this play he really *means* anything at all, in the sense of message or expressive content. *Miß Sara Sampson* was not written because Lessing had something to say and found this particular form to say it in; form is not here the servant of content, but the reverse. Lessing wanted first and foremost to *write a tragedy*, and tragedy was for him a dramatic genre defined by the evocation of certain emotional responses — which he over-simplified, and too readily equated with moral ones. Secondly, he wanted to write a *modern* tragedy, and so chose, almost as it might be at random, a modern subject-matter which would fit into the traditional form; but the content is only there for the sake of the form, rather as Aristotle says the characters in tragedy are there for the sake of the action. Lessing, as we shall see, held domestic misfortunes — the disruption of familial relationships, irrespective of any repercussions beyond the domestic circle — to be more truly tragic than 'heroic' disasters and affairs of state; but he chose domestic subjects for tragedies because he wanted to write tragedies and was not interested in heroic subjects, rather than because he wanted to

[32] The arguments on this point are admirably summed up by F. van Ingen, 'Tugend bei Lessing. Bemerkungen zu *Miß Sara Sampson*', *ABNG* i (1972), 43–73.

[33] As suggested by, for example, W. Mauser, 'Lessings *Miß Sara Sampson*: Bürgerliches Trauerspiel als Ausdruck innerbürgerlichen Konflikts', *LYB* vii (1975), 7–27.

convey a tragic vision of family relationships.[34] In *Miß Sara Sampson* the topics of virtue, family loyalties and affections, repentance and forgiveness, and submission to the decrees of Providence, together with their opposites, vice, hatred, revenge, and despair, recur again and again, and so can be called the play's themes; but they are only the ingredients with which Lessing is hoping to engender the tragic effect, and the play can really be said to be 'about' them only in the sense that a musical composition is 'about' the thematic material on which it is constructed. But while this is perfectly satisfactory in a non-representational art such as music, literature demands that its thematic material be meaningful in its own right; and the whole point of writing a tragedy with recognizably contemporary characters and setting was, one would have thought, precisely to increase the representational element in the genre at the expense of its traditional formal abstraction.

Miß Sara Sampson was in 1755 a work of radical innovation; for us today it has dated badly. A modern production can only succeed by playing down what Lessing chose to play up: by reversing the shift of tragic gravity which Lessing made in adapting his Senecan prototype, pushing Sara out of the limelight back to the periphery of the action where she belongs, and (since he has made such a melodramatic villain of Marwood, with her curses, grimaces, and asides, that she is not acceptable as a tragic protagonist) focusing attention on Mellefont. That Mellefont can be made to carry the play in this way does perhaps indicate that Lessing had realized some of the depths and complexities which might lurk inside him, at any rate to the extent of creating a viable dramatic character; but if the play can still be made to work in some way, that is a tribute more to the resilience of the archetypal tragic story than to Lessing's skill in adaptation. In the mechanics of its construction — the disposition and contrast of characters and scenes, the arrangement of climaxes, the shifts of fortune which make now a happy, now an unhappy outcome seem more probable — the play does manifest a high degree of competent craftsmanship. It is principally interesting, however (and as such, it is fascinating), as a document of literary and

[34] For a different view, see P. H. Neumann, *Der Preis der Mündigkeit: Über Lessings Dramen* (Stuttgart, 1977).

social history: for the very features of it which the modern
reader or spectator finds hardest to accept are the characteristic mid-eighteenth-century middle-class moral attitudes
which constitute (in the sense defined above) its thematic
content, and the sentimental rhetoric in which those attitudes
find their natural expression.

The terms 'middle-class' and 'sentimental' still call for
further elucidation. Lessing calls his play a 'bürgerliches
Trauerspiel'. In the *Theatralische Bibliothek* he had given a
very simple working definition of the new genre by saying
that it chooses 'Helden aus dem Mittelstande', protagonists
whose social class would hitherto have barred them from the
tragic stage. 'Ein bürgerliches Trauerspiel!' he wrote, in an
(anonymous) notice of his own play in the *Berlinische privilegierte Zeitung*, 'Findet man in Gottscheds Kritischer Dichtkunst ein Wort von so einem Ding?'[35] There was some discussion at the time as to what exactly the term meant, and this
has continued, inconclusively, to the present day.[36] We have
noted that in the *Theatralische Bibliothek* Lessing identifies
as 'das Volk' his own intended public, in fact predominantly
middle-class, conscious of its own distinctness from the more
remote and snobbish members of the aristocracy on the one
hand as from the 'Pöbel' on the other. A similarly vague de-
limitation will have to do for the 'middle-class' character of
Miß Sara Sampson. We should not attribute to Lessing any
very precise knowledge of English social structures and dif-
ferentiations, or seek to draw conclusions from the characters'
use of titles like 'Ritter' and 'Lady'.[37]

The play is not concerned to depict social structures. There
is certainly no element whatever of class conflict — such as is
already present in Martini's *Rhynsolt und Sapphira* of the
same year, with its aristocratic seducer and middle-class victim.
There are no significant differences of social class between
Lessing's protagonists: all are of good family and independent

[35] G iii. 246.

[36] The critical literature on this subject is summarized in K. S. Guthke, *Das
deutsche bürgerliche Trauerspiel* (Sammlung Metzler, cxvi, Stuttgart, 1972).

[37] In the first edition of the play (reprinted by Eibl, ed. cit.). Lessing makes
the common foreigner's mistake of calling Sara's father 'Sir Sampson'. This was
corrected in the edition of 1772: cf. Lessing's letter to his brother Karl of 1 December 1771.

means. Sara is the inferior of Mellefont and Marwood in social sophistication — Marwood refers to her disdainfully as a 'Landmädchen' (II, 3); and the sophisticated social world is given a different name by Norton: a 'nichtswürdigst[e] Gesellschaft von Spielern und Landstreichern — ich nenne sie, was sie waren, und kehre mich an ihre Titel, Ritter und dergleichen, nicht — ' (I, 3). There is perhaps here a hint of an equation of social inferiority with moral superiority — the glimmerings of what Nietzsche was to call the 'Sklavenaufstand in der Moral';[38] and there is a stronger hint in a later scene, also between Mellefont and Norton:

MELLEFONT. Nur der Pöbel wird gleich außer sich gebracht, wenn ihn das Glück einmal anlächelt.

NORTON. Vielleicht, weil der Pöbel noch sein Gefühl hat, das bei Vornehmern durch tausend unnatürliche Vorstellungen verderbt und geschwächt wird. (IV, 3)

But just as psychological differentiation between the characters is subordinated to their placement on a moral scale, so too is any social differentiation between them. The point of this exchange is not Norton's rudimentary class pride, but the moral aspect of Mellefont's social attitude: he despises his inferiors, and this, like his vacillation at the prospect of marriage, is intended to place his moral reformation in doubt. And just as the moral attitudes of Sara and Marwood to marriage are contrasted, so Mellefont's contempt for Norton and the 'Pöbel' is contrasted with Sir William's generosity towards Waitwell, whose long and faithful service he rewards by conferring social equality upon him (III, 7). Here too the moral attitude is more important than the egalitarian gesture in which it finds expression. In Act III events have taken a turn for the better, and it looks as if virtue may yet be triumphant; Lessing therefore ends the act with a crowning example of the virtue and nobility of Sir William. If one takes the scene at all seriously in social terms, then one notices that Sir William's gesture is immediately suspended: 'Nur dasmal sei noch der alte Diener, auf den ich mich nie umsonst verlassen habe.' (One might also mischievously wonder what Sir William

---

[38] Nietzsche, *Werke*, ed. Schlechta (Munich, 1955), ii. 653, 780 ff.

would say if Waitwell were to take him at his word.) Again,
though Marwood's pride and arrogance may be seen as aristocratic characteristics, Lessing does not in fact make or imply
any social comment on her. Just as Medea was a foreigner to
the civilized world of Greece, so Marwood is a foreigner to
the *moral* world of the Sampson family, to which Mellefont
seeks admission.

Strangely enough, since the aristocratic villains of eighteenth-century 'bourgeois' literature are so often characterized
as selfish, what most strikes the modern reader about this
moral world is the self-absorption of its occupants. The
characters have no concern but themselves and their own
immediate kin. They are purely private persons with no obli-
gations to anyone else; the concept of public duty, whose
conflicts with private inclination occupy such a central position
in the tragedies of, for example, Corneille, is here completely
lacking. Sir William is in no way concerned with public affairs;
he does not even have to dispense local justice, like Sir Roger
de Coverley; his fortunes and misfortunes and those of his
family are of import to no one but themselves. It was for this
very reason that Lessing's audience found them so touching;
not so much because the play illustrated that archetypal misfortune could befall anyone, irrespective of rank, but because
it gave the spectators the opportunity for a communal indulgence in private emotion, a kind of 'spiritual orgasm',[39] just
such as they saw exhibited on the stage. We hear a great deal
about virtue, but the virtues we see displayed are largely passive; forgiveness and generosity seem, moreover, to be practised
with as much view to the righteousness of the practitioner as
to the benefit of the recipient; in a word, the virtuous characters seem complacent and self-righteous, even self-indulgent
in their virtue. We hear a great deal about love, but gain little
sense of genuine relationships. In her penultimate dying
speech, Sara speaks of her father's love not so much as a personal bond of affection but as a commodity at her disposal,
and goes on to ask that Arabella be brought up in suspicion
of all love:

[39] Cf. L. Pikulik, *'Bürgerliches Trauerspiel' und Empfindsamkeit* (Cologne
and Graz, 1966), p. 85.

Da mich mein Vater liebt, warum soll es mir nicht erlaubt sein, mit seiner Liebe, als mit einem Erbteile umzugehen? Ich vermache diese väterliche Liebe Ihnen [Mellefont], und Arabellen. Reden Sie dann und wann mit ihr von einer Freundin, aus deren Beispiele sie gegen alle Liebe auf ihrer Hut zu sein lerne. — (V, 10)

We hear a great deal of contrition, of repentance; a virtue which can be exercised by the individual conscience in complete self-containment and self-sufficiency. It seems rarely, in this play, to involve a looking forward and a resolution to act rightly in the future, but all too often only a looking back at previous errors — and not even in genuine humility and appraisal of imperfection, but rather in self-indulgent enjoyment of the emotional experience of repentance in itself. In the third scene of the third act Waitwell, bringing Sara her father's letter of forgiveness and conciliation, actually reproaches Sara for just such a self-lacerating excess of contrition — 'Es ist, Miß, als ob Sie nur immer an Ihren Fehler dächten . . . ' — only to go on in his very next speech to work Sara up to yet another climax of moral ecstasy: 'Ach!' she replies, ' — Rede weiter, Waitwell, rede weiter!' And so it continues. The scene is the centre of the play and one of its principal climaxes; in the working up of moral emotion it is surpassed, if at all, only by the final scenes; in ecstatic lachrymosity it exceeds them. It casts a dubious light upon Lessing's view that pity was the cardinal tragic emotion: here the tears of sympathetic identification flow most freely at the play's *happiest* moment.[40] Only Mellefont's last speeches, again, appear to reveal anything beneath the conventions of sentimental repentance, a genuine recognition of genuine responsibility; here too the modern audience will readily sympathize with Mellefont, but for Lessing and his contemporaries Mellefont's sentiments are too profoundly flawed by his cosmic despair, his failure to recognize and accept the designs of Providence.

When we say that *Miß Sara Sampson* is a sentimental play, we are referring to the emotional self-indulgence uncritically

[40] Bornkamm, op. cit., regards this scene as the turning-point of the 'inner action', but it surely turns the play away from rather than towards a tragic conclusion. Fricke, op. cit., p. 110 also regards this scene as the climax of the play, but observes (p. 108) 'Tatsächlich geht es Lessing gar nicht um die *tragische*, sondern um die *moralische* Erschütterung.'

portrayed in its protagonists; but we are also referring to the
self-indulgent language which Lessing puts into their mouths
to express those emotions. The play is in prose, but seems far
from everyday speech. Language is not used as a means of
differentiating between the characters: they all speak in the
same manner, masters and servants, parents and children. Even
the nine-year-old Arabella speaks the same elaborate rhetorical
prose. It is in fact principally the lack of any such differentiation, rather than any particular syntactic features, which
entitles us to call the language of the play unrealistic; but it is
certainly more elaborate than the language of ordinary conversation. In the *Hamburgische Dramaturgie* Lessing was to
criticize Frau Gottsched's translation of comic dialogue on
the grounds of her clumsy and over-complicated syntax: 'dieses
Alsdenn, mit seinem Schwanze von Wenn; dieses Erst; dieses
Recht; diese Dadurch . . . ' (No. 20). But in *Sara* we find him
still using exactly the same kind of highly formal syntax himself. Characters indulge in balanced antithesis, in word-play,
in riddles, in set-pieces of rhetorical exchange, cluttered with
subjunctives:

MARWOOD. Ich muß um Vergebung bitten, Miß, daß ich so frei bin,
mich mit meinen eignen Augen von dem Glücke eines Vetters zu über-
führen, dem ich das vollkommenste Frauenzimmer wünschen würde,
wenn mich nicht gleich der erste Augenblick uberzeugt hätte, daß er es
in Ihnen bereits gefunden habe.

SARA. Sie erzeigen mir allzuviel Ehre, Lady. Eine Schmeichelei, wie
diese, würde mich zu allen Zeiten beschämt haben: itzt aber, sollte ich
sie fast für einen verstecken Vorwurf annehmen, wenn ich Lady Solmes
nicht für viel zu großmütig hielte, ihre Überlegenheit an Tugend und
Klugheit eine Unglückliche fühlen zu lassen.   (III, 5)

Much of this recalls the traditional rhetoric of high tragedy —
but also, paradoxically, the linguistic techniques of comedy.
In comedy what is said is often intended not to serve any
purpose of exposition or development of character or situation,
but simply to be funny, to make the audience laugh. Much of
the dialogue of *Miß Sara Sampson* seems similarly intended
simply to be tragic, to make the audience weep.[41] In tragedy,
however, it is vital that the emotional charge of the dialogue

---

[41] Cf. Rempel, op. cit., p. 39.

should be appropriate, that it should have a proper objective correlative in situation and action: the gratuitous working up of tragic emotion is merely embarrassing. Often the characters of *Miß Sara Sampson* seem to be not so much expressing their feelings, or exchanging information, or even seeking to influence each other, as scoring debating points off each other.[42] One would call this wit if it were supposed to be funny; indeed the word was often used at this time in the disparaging sense of superficial cleverness, and is so used in the play itself when Mellefont assures Marwood that 'Ein tugendhafter Entschluß sichert mich gegen Ihre Zärtlichkeit und gegen Ihren Witz' (II, 3). It should however be noted that formal wit of this kind is often encountered in the letters of the period – including Lessing's own. The characters' stylized utterances should therefore perhaps be taken as a faithful representation, if not of the way people spoke, then of the way they wrote, perhaps of the way they thought they spoke – Lessing himself, like Gellert, held that the best epistolary style was 'eine freie Nachahmung des guten Gesprächs'[43] – or of the way they would like to believe they spoke.

Lessing is not simply holding up a mirror to his middle-class public. He is painting a highly idealized, or perhaps one should say flattering, portrait. The vestiges of *éloignement* – the English setting and the formal rhetoric – contribute to this effect. The German bourgeoisie saw themselves not as they were, but as they would like to be, and as the example of the more emancipated English middle classes showed them they might be. At the same time the setting and the mere fact that the characters in a tragedy did not speak in measured lines was a revolutionary innovation, a great step in the direction of realism. For the curtain to rise on a tragedy and reveal not buskined antique heroes in some palace ante-room, but travellers in ordinary eighteenth-century clothes in a miserable inn,

---

[42] One reason why Marwood often seems a more convincing character than the others is that this kind of rhetoric is more appropriate to her scheming and dissembling than it is to their supposed emotional sincerity. On the rhetoric of the play cf. J. Schröder, *G. E. Lessing: Sprache und Drama* (Munich, 1972), notably the analysis of IV, 8 on pp. 169 ff.

[43] Gellert, *Briefe, nebst einer praktischen Abhandlung von dem guten Geschmack in Briefen* (Leipzig, 1751), p. 3 (reprinted in Gellert, *Die epistolographischen Schriften* (Stuttgart, 1971)): cf. Lessing's review of Gellert's work, G iii. 55–7.

who address each other not in alexandrines, but in broken,
elliptical prose — 'Hier meine Tochter? Hier in diesem elenden
Wirtshause?' — must have caused a considerable shock. It is,
however, rather as in *Minna von Barnhelm* but here to a
much greater extent, precisely these gestures in the direction
of realism which make us object to the unreality of most of
what follows. In its form the play keeps pretty closely to the
classical 'rules', and the infringement of the unity of place, to
which Lessing drew attention,[44] is in fact very timid: if the
stage direction at the beginning of Act II did not tell us us,
we should hardly realize that Marwood's room is 'in einem
anderen Gasthofe'. Place is not a vital dimension in the action,
as it is, for example, in *Götz von Berlichingen* or *Kabale und
Liebe*, or even in Lessing's own *Emilia Galotti*, where the different stage settings symbolically convey essential information
about the characters and what they stand for. The landlord's
opening question in I, 2, 'So früh, meine Herren, so früh?',
reminds us of the play's academic compliance with the rule
of the unity of time. The servants are not really so much
servants as confidants, employed to support the protagonists
just as in French classical tragedy: Lessing disguises their conventional role in a would-be realistic costume which is in fact
itself a convention. The apparent abandonment of the trappings of high tragedy, those trappings which in *Macbeth* can
make us accept 'a lot of stuff like that' as poetic stylization
wholly appropriate to the tragic events, makes us object in
Miß Sara Sampson to the way in which characters seem not so
much to express their emotions as to describe them at arm's
length, as something almost alien to themselves: such phrases
as Mellefont's 'Welcher plötzliche Übergang von Bewunderung
zum Schrecken!' (V, 4) sound more like quotations from
Lessing's theory of tragedy than the utterances of actual
tragic characters, let alone of real eighteenth-century middle-
class people.[45]

(iii)

Though *Miß Sara Sampson* may have been written to win a

[44] G iii. 246.
[45] Cf. E. Staiger, *Stilwandel* (Zurich, 1963), p. 49.

bet, it was not written to prove a theory. Its appearance is however followed by a number of important pronouncements on the essential nature of tragedy. Lessing's theoretical discussions of the genre begin and end with the assertion that pity is the cardinal tragic emotion, the one indispensable effect which the tragic playwright must produce in the spectator. Aristotle, in a famous passage over whose meaning controversy has raged since the Renaissance, states that tragedy, by arousing pity (*eleos*) and fear (*phobos*), accomplishes a purgation (*katharsis*) of these emotions. In the seventeenth century it had been suggested that tragedy also (or perhaps alternatively) aroused admiration for noble and remarkable deeds; and so Gottsched continued to maintain. But already in 1756 Lessing singles out pity, manifested in the audience's tears, as the only effect that really matters. He also asserts that all the 'rules' of tragedy, valid though they are, are superfluous, and their observance useless, if the poet fails in this one effect. The occasion for these observations is, rather surprisingly, the preface to a German translation of the tragedies of James Thomson — neo-classically 'correct' works remembered today, if at all, in the parodies of Fielding's *Tragedy of Tragedies*. Lessing however praises Thomson's regularity and — following the argument of the Seneca essay — his successful 'modernizations' of Greek subjects, compared favourably to those by French dramatists. But most importantly, Lessing here invokes for the first time Lillo's *London Merchant* and proclaims its essential superiority to Gottsched's *Sterbender Cato*:

Bei einer einzigen Vorstellung des erstern sind, auch von den Unempfindlichsten, mehr Tränen vergossen worden, als bei allen möglichen Vorstellungen des andern, auch von den Empfindlichsten, nicht können vergossen werden. Und nur diese Tränen des Mitleids, und der sich fühlenden Menschlichkeit, sind die Absicht des Trauerspiels, oder es kann gar keine haben.[46]

The elucidation of this doctrine is Lessing's main concern in what, though it was never intended for publication, is nevertheless generally and rightly regarded as one of the most important documents of his dramatic theory: the correspondence which he conducted with his friends Nicolai and

---

[46] G iv. 144.

Mendelssohn during his absence from Berlin (on the abortive
grand tour with Winkler) between August 1756 and the
summer of 1757.[47]

Like so many of his contemporaries, Nicolai wished to
encourage the growth of German literary culture and the
improvement of public taste. To this end he launched in 1757
a competition for the best German tragedy, and composed an
Abhandlung vom Trauerspiele for the guidance of intending
entrants. The main points of the *Abhandlung* are summarized
in a letter from Nicolai to Lessing dated 31 August 1756, and
had probably already been discussed by the three friends
before Lessing had left Berlin. The subsequent correspondence
touches upon a number of different aspects of tragedy, but
the central issues are its moral purpose and, dependent upon
this, the emotions it should seek to arouse and the moral
character of the tragic hero.

Refreshingly, as it seems to the modern reader, Nicolai
roundly asserts that it is precisely because of the assumption
that tragedy must have a moral purpose that most German
tragedies are so bad. For this assumption Nicolai blames the
Aristotelian doctrine of 'catharsis': rather than seeking to
purge passions, Nicolai says, tragic dramatists should *arouse*
them ('Leidenschaften erregen'). These passions are pity, fear
(or rather terror, 'Schrecken': Lessing suggests at a later stage
in the discussion that 'Furcht' would be a better translation),
and admiration. Tragedies may be classified according to the
passions they arouse: tragedies of sentiment — Nicolai suggests
provisionally the term 'rührende Trauerspiele' — evoke pity
and fear, heroic tragedies admiration, and there are also 'com-
posite' tragedies ('vermischte Trauerspiele') arousing both in
equal measure. The first category includes 'alle bürgerliche
Trauerspiele, ferner alle die, in welchen bürgerliches Interesse
herrschet, als Merope, Medea [!] usw'. (We note that Nicolai
does not define the term 'bürgerlich', but in the second instance it plainly means no more than 'private' or 'domestic',

---

[47] G iv. 155–227. See also the editions by R. Petsch (*Lessings Briefwechsel
mit Mendelssohn und Nicolai über das Trauerspiel* (Leipzig, 1910; reprinted Darmstadt, 1967)) and J. Schulte-Sasse (*Lessing, Mendelssohn, Nicolai: Briefwechsel
über das Trauerspiel* (Munich, 1972)); and cf. P. Michelsen, 'Die Erregung des Mitleids durch die Tragödie. Zu Lessings Ansichten über das Trauerspiel im Briefwechsel mit Mendelssohn und Nicolai', *DVJS* xl (1966), 548–66.

while 'bürgerliche Trauerspiele' in the first and stricter sense
are presumably tragedies of the new type with 'Helden aus
dem Mittelstande' which Lessing had so recently introduced
to Germany.) Tragedy may have a moral effect, but this is
secondary and not essential. Tragic guilt is not the same as
moral guilt; from this Nicolai goes on to argue that the tragic
hero does not have to be morally good.

From these propositions however Lessing fundamentally
(though amicably) dissents. Tragedy must have a moral purpose, though this is not a matter of simple didacticism. Heroic
tragedy is rejected: the tragic poet should not seek to arouse
admiration, but only pity; and the characters we are invited
to pity must be as virtuous as possible. This much is firmly
stated in his first reply to Nicolai, written in November 1756
(Nicolai's letter had only just caught up with him on his
travels). The moral element in tragedy is not an accidental but
an essential, though the nature of its moral effect is open to
investigation. Lessing is prepared to assent to Nicolai's view
that the precept 'Das Trauerspiel soll bessern' has produced
bad tragedy, but if so, then because it is unhelpful rather
than false: it sets the playwright a vague and distant goal
without any intimation of the means by which it is to be at-
tained. Lessing agrees that Nicolai's suggested alternative,
'Das Trauerspiel soll Leidenschaften erregen', might be more
expedient, for 'Wenn ich die Mittel habe, so habe ich den
Endzweck, aber nicht umgekehrt'. But he insists on narrowing
down the range of passions which it is proper for tragedy to
arouse. True tragedy arouses one passion only, namely pity:
terror and admiration are only stages in the emotional process
which tragedy sets in motion, terror marking the sudden on-
set of pity ('die plötzliche Überraschung des Mitleides') and
admiration the point at which, in the sense I have already suggested,[48] we perceive our pity to be no longer needed ('das
entbehrlich gewordene Mitleiden'); they are thus not 'tragic
passions' in their own right at all. Pity is the only one: 'so
sage ich nunmehr, die Bestimmung der Tragödie[49] ist diese:

---

[48] Cf. above, p. 75.
[49] It is perhaps worth pointing out that, *pace* the attempts of Walter Benjamin
(*Ursprung des deutschen Trauerspiels* (Berlin, 1928)) and others to distinguish be-

sie soll *unsre Fähigkeit, Mitleid zu fühlen*, erweitern.' And
the justification for this singling out of pity is an unequivocally moral one:

Der mitleidigste Mensch ist der beste Mensch [Lessing's emphasis], zu
allen gesellschaftlichen Tugenden, zu allen Arten der Großmut der auf-
gelegteste. Wer uns also mitleidig macht, macht uns besser und tugendhafter, und das Trauerspiel, das jenes tut, tut auch dieses, oder — es tut
jenes, um dieses tun zu können.

From this it follows that 'das Trauerspiel soll so viel Mitleid
erwecken, als es nur immer kann'; further that, in accordance
with the practice Lessing had followed in *Sara*, the victims of
tragic suffering should be as virtuous as possible, 'und Verdienst und Unglück in beständigem Verhältnisse bleiben'; and
finally that Nicolai's classification of different types of tragedy
can be dispensed with ('fällt mit Ihrer Erlaubnis ganz weg'),
for on Lessing's account there can be only one valid form —
that categorized by Nicolai as 'rührend'. The place for the
heroic mode is not tragedy, but epic.

Lessing never abandons this position, despite vigorous
counter-attacks from Nicolai and, in particular, Mendelssohn.
Mendelssohn defends the legitimacy of heroic tragedy, and
suggests that the portrayal of admirable deeds on the tragic
stage may awaken in the spectator the desire to emulate them:
'dem bewunderten Held [*sic*], wo es möglich ist, nachzuei-
fern'. But he points out that such moral effects are secondary,
and are only brought about through the mediation of reason.
The prime and essential effect is, as Nicolai had suggested,
aesthetic and emotional; tragedy *may* have a moral effect but
need not. Moreover it can perfectly legitimately arouse aesthetic admiration for characters and actions which are morally
questionable, again 'weil nach geendigter Illusion die Vernunft
wieder das Steuer ergreift': if anyone seeks to emulate such
deeds in real life — Mendelssohn cites the example of an
Englishman who had committed suicide after a performance
of Addison's *Cato*, leaving a note reading 'What Cato does
and Addison approves cannot be wrong' — then he is incapable

---

tween them, the terms 'Trauerspiel' and 'Tragödie' are in ordinary German usage
synonymous, and are used interchangeably by Lessing and his contemporaries.

of distinguishing between life and aesthetic illusion. Nor are such morally deplorable after-effects confined to admiration: 'Auch das Mitleiden kann uns zu Untugenden bringen, wenn es nicht von der Vernunft regiert wird, von der kalten symbolischen Vernunft, die man gänzlich von dem Theater verbannen muß, wenn man gefallen will.'[50]

Lessing musters a variety of arguments for his point of view.[51] Admiration is subordinate to pity, providing moments of relief ('Ruhepunkte'). Admiration is only part of a mixture of emotions which together go to make up pity ('Bewunderung und Schmerz'). Admiration has been confused with mere astonishment or surprise ('Verwunderung').[52] Admiration is evoked by characters who are larger than life, more than human, even inhuman, 'schöne Ungeheuer' whom we do not and cannot wish to emulate. Admiration is perhaps not even aroused by moral qualities at all, but only by physical prowess, and it is this which distinguishes the heroes of epic. The moral effects of pity are 'ungleich besser und sicherer'. Far from being, as Mendelssohn avers, the 'Mutter der Tugend', admiration is a vulgar habit, characteristic of the 'Pöbel', and not a propensity of the virtuous disposition: 'Ich glaube, der ist der größte Geck, der die größte Fertigkeit im Bewundern hat; so wie ohne Zweifel derjenige der beste Mensch ist, der die größte Fertigkeit im Mitleiden hat.' Of course the tragic hero must deserve our moral approbation, but that is not the same thing at all. The murder of Barnwell's uncle in the *London Merchant* provides Lessing with an illustration of what he does *not* understand by admiration:

wenn ihn Barnwell ersticht, entsetzen sich die Zuschauer, ohne mitleidig zu sein, weil der gute Charakter des Alten gar nichts enthält, was den Grund zu diesem Unglück abgeben könnte. Sobald man ihn aber für seinen Mörder und Vetter noch zu Gott beten hört, verwandelt sich das Entsetzen in ein recht *entzückendes Mitleiden* [my italics], und zwar ganz natürlich, weil diese großmütige Tat aus seinem Unglücke fließet und ihren Grund in demselben hat.[53]

[50] Mendelssohn to Lessing, first half of December 1756 (G iv. 179–84).
[51] Lessing to Mendelssohn, 28 November and 18 December 1756 (ibid., 170–6 and 185–95).
[52] Gottsched in fact uses both 'Be-' and 'Verwunderung': cf. *Dichtkunst*, ed. cit., p. 164 and p. 606.
[53] Cf. van Ingen, op. cit., p. 65 f.

There are contradictions and shifts of ground here, such as we should expect in an exploratory discussion of this kind; and Mendelssohn is right to describe some of Lessing's arguments as 'spitzfindig'.[54] But the over-all tendency is consistent and clear. Lessing will not have heroics on the tragic stage; like so many of his European contemporaries, he feels that the characters of heroic tragedy are 'bullies glorified by toadies'.[55] He wants to see the tragic poet portraying not figures whom the spectators are invited to look up to in this morally dubious or even pernicious sense, but characters evoking feelings of common humanity. Lessing's 'Mitleid' is a compassionate self-identification, highly charged with moral esteem, springing from, bearing witness to, and in turn intensifying what an earlier English writer, the Earl of Shaftesbury, had called our 'social Feeling or *Sense of Partnership* with Human Kind'.[56] The phrase is strongly echoed in Lessing's 'sich fühlende Menschlichkeit' and 'gesellschaftliche Tugenden'.

What we have here is plainly a vindication of the 'bürgerliches Trauerspiel' as exemplified by Lessing's own *Miß Sara Sampson*: a play which, though it teaches no specific 'moralischer Lehrsatz' in the Gottschedian sense, unmistakably invites us to dispose our sympathies according to a moral viewpoint, and to pity the sufferings of virtue rather than admire great deeds. Lessing however in the course of this correspondence never mentions his own play, nor even uses the term 'bürgerliches Trauerspiel' himself. Nor does he advocate the use of contemporary or middle-class characters. He continued to experiment with 'bürgerliches Trauerspiel' in *Tonsine* and *Emilia Galotti*, but the former — the only work, apart from *Miß Sara Sampson*, actually given the subtitle 'bürgerliches Trauerspiel' by Lessing himself — remained a fragment, and the latter was not completed until fourteen years later; and other experiments of Lessing's at this time appear to lead in different directions.

        [54] Mendelssohn to Lessing, 23 November 1756 (G iv. 169) and January 1757 (ibid., 197).
        [55] W. Empson, *Some Versions of Pastoral* (London, 1935), p. 200, on the similar reaction against the 'Tragedy of Admiration' in mid-eighteenth-century England.
        [56] Shaftesbury, *Characteristicks*, vol. i (London, 1737), p. 106 f.: quoted by Sauder, op. cit., p. 76.

IV

Alternatives

(i)

Nicolai's competition was not a great success, for it attracted only three entries. Not surprisingly, in view of the positions adopted in the correspondence by Nicolai and Mendelssohn on the one hand, Lessing on the other, the prize was awarded to a heroic tragedy, in alexandrines, on a subject from Greek history, J. F. von Cronegk's *Codrus*, while Lessing urged the merits of J. W. von Brawe's *Der Freigeist*, a domestic tragedy in prose with, like *Miß Sara Sampson*, an English setting. (Both dramatists, incidentally, died young: Cronegk was carried off by the smallpox at the age of twenty-six, before he could collect the prize, and Brawe died the following year aged only twenty.) The third play, *Der Renegat*, by Karl Theodor Breithaupt, was something of a hybrid, sharing with Brawe's play the theme of religious apostasy and the use of English (or pseudo-English) characters, but employing alexandrines like Cronegk's and an exotic (Turkish) setting. In their diversity the three plays reflect something of what was, despite the poor response to Nicolai's challenge, in fact a period of keen experimentation in German tragic writing.[1] Tragedies were being written in a great variety of forms. We find examples of all three of Nicolai's categories, 'rührend', 'heroisch', and 'vermischt'; we find contemporary, legendary, historical, and Biblical subject-matter, and settings familiar and exotic. Some writers keep the traditional rules of French neo-classical drama, some indeed insisting upon a literal identity between the time-scale of the action portrayed and the actual time of representation, while others adopt the freer treatment of time and place characteristic of the English and

---

[1]   Cf. R. R. Heitner, *German Tragedy in the Age of Enlightenment* (Berkeley and Los Angeles, 1963).

Spanish theatres. Some retain alexandrines, but this form was now beginning to be generally regarded as out of date. Most dramatists now preferred prose; but a few were already experimenting with unrhymed iambic pentameter or blank verse, again in the English manner. There are even experiments in length and formal division: beside the traditional five-act form we find tragedies in three acts and even in one, the last mentioned a particularly unusual variant which however found some favour at this time. In a series of plans and sketches, some of them extremely fragmentary, and most of which appear to date from the period between his return to Berlin and his departure for Breslau, Lessing experimented with a number of these possibilities.[2]

The common factor in all this experimentation is the attempt to revitalize the tradition: to appeal specifically to the sensibilities of an eighteenth-century audience while yet exhibiting a pedigree of classical or other legitimacy. Settings tried by Lessing range from Spain (*Tonsine*), through classical Greece (*Kleonnis*) and Rome (*Das befreite Rom*), the Near East in ancient times (*Alcibiades in Persien*) and more modern (*Fatime*), to sixteenth-century Poland (*Der Horoscop*). Other sketches, made in Breslau, record possible tragic themes in Bohemian history and Nordic legend, and there is even a suggestion for transposing the story of the execution of Charles I of England to Siam. But there is at least one plan for a tragedy with a German setting, though not, evidently, a modern one (*D. Faust*). Nearly all the characters Lessing proposes for tragic treatment, despite his later repudiation of the need for 'Fürsten und Helden', are of elevated rank. But apart from a solitary attempt at political tragedy in *Das befreite Rom* — and even there, as in the case of Massaniello to which we have already referred, the main interest seems ultimately to lie in the psychology of the protagonist[3] — the emphasis is generally on domestic catastrophe, on families destroyed by external or internal conflict, and on the 'private woe'[4] which this oc-

---

[2]   All the plans and fragments referred to here will be found in G ii.

[3]   Cf. above, p. 64. In *Das befreite Rom* Brutus feigns madness to further his aim of liberating Rome from the despotism of the Tarquins, but at the end, when that aim has been achieved, he refuses high republican office 'weil ihn seine Verstellung dazu untüchtig gemacht' (G ii. 467).   [4]   Cf. above, p. 67.

casions, while attempts to give this a greater, more public resonance remain fragmentary and inconclusive. However, although he had maintained so boldly that 'Nur diese Tränen des Mitleids . . . sind die Absicht des Trauerspiels', Lessing's practice shows that he recognized the need for something more. Like Brawe, Breithaupt, and others, Lessing saw in religious conflict — a subject of profound concern to him, and one which, as we know, he had already treated on the comic stage — a possible substitute for politics in providing modern tragedy with some greater intellectual weight, some appeal at a different level from that of simple 'Rührung' which, as the example of *Miß Sara Sampson* shows, could so easily degenerate into mere sentimentality. Religious conflict appears to be the mainspring of the tragedy in *Tonsine* and possibly in *Alcibiades in Persien*. *Der Horoscop*, which both in its Polish setting and its theme of prophecy and parricide recalls Calderón's *La vida es sueño*, raises in a 'modern' form the ancient tragic and religious question of free will and determinism, and of man's response to the decrees of fate or Providence;[5] *D. Faust*, of course, treats of salvation or damnation in the pursuit of knowledge. History, however, which in the hands of Schiller and his successors was to furnish the characteristic subject-matter of the classical German drama, seems to have had little appeal for Lessing as a possible source of tragedy, except where combined with the theme of religious conflict as in *Der Horoscop* and a couple of the later sketches, those on Mathildis, Queen of Scotland, and Drahomira, Queen of Bohemia.[6]

Formally the plans and fragments are equally varied, but just as the majority retain the traditional tragic *éloignement* rather than attempting more familiar or 'realistic' settings or characters of humbler rank, so the majority retain the traditional unities and proprieties of the tragic form. Lessing wrote to Nicolai on 21 January 1758 that the projected *Emilia Galotti* 'braucht ohne Bedenken alle Freiheiten der englischen Bühne', but such departures are not much in evidence elsewhere — or indeed in *Emilia Galotti* as it was completed four-

---

[5] Cf. C. Enders, 'Der geistesgeschichtliche Standort von Lessings "Horoskop"', *Euph.* 1 (1956), 208–16.
[6] G ii. 760 f. ('Drahomira' is the correct spelling).

teen years later. Evidently Lessing felt happiest within the traditional limits. Even *D. Faust* was to keep the unity of time![7] *Der Horoscop* is perhaps furthest from the classical norm, with half a dozen scene-changes and a complex structure apparently involving an important sub-plot; while in *Das befreite Rom* 'English' influence is suggested by crowd scenes and two violent deaths on stage. Many of these works are mere sketches — the last named, for example, exists in a complete scenario, but with no dialogue executed; but a number have fragments of scenes. Most are in prose; but in *Kleonnis*, *Der Horoscop*, and *Fatime* Lessing tries his hand at blank verse, in which even at this early stage he strikes the distinctive tone, stylized and yet at the same time colloquial and familiar, which was to come to full fruition in *Nathan der Weise*.

Clearly, having tried his hand at 'bürgerliches Trauerspiel', and produced a work of whose shortcomings (despite its success) he can hardly have been unaware, Lessing was anxious to explore other possibilities. Indeed, despite the implicit defence of 'bürgerliches Trauerspiel' in the correspondence, the experiments strongly suggest a reaction against the 'realism' and emotionalism of *Miß Sara Sampson* in the direction of more complex and demanding subject-matter and of various kinds of stylization in manner. Even in *Sara* Lessing had reminded his audience, through Marwood, of his play's Greek and Senecan pedigree; plainly the classical tradition still exerted a powerful attraction for him. In view of this it is not so surprising as it might at first seem that the only one of these tragic experiments to reach completion, *Philotas*, is classical in character, style, and theme. It is however unusual in its combination of a setting in classical antiquity with an invented plot, one-act form (with rigorously literal unity of time and place), and prose dialogue. Of all Lessing's finished dramatic works it is the most enigmatic.

(ii)

Lessing professed a low opinion of Cronegk's *Codrus*: writing to Mendelssohn on 22 October 1757, he characteristically

---

[7]   Cf. below, p. 114.

declares that he could write a better play on the subject himself. More details follow in a letter of 18 February 1758. But on 27 February Mendelssohn pointed out in reply that the plan ran completely counter to the views Lessing had been advancing in their earlier correspondence, for it was calculated to arouse not pity but admiration. We hear no more of *Codrus*, but the fragment *Kleonnis* of 1758 plainly represents an attempt to combine the theme of patriotic self-sacrifice, which is the mainspring of *Codrus*, with a more characteristically Lessingian 'domestic' element, the concern of a father for his children. A humane king (Euphaes), in whom devotion to his country and paternal affection are combined, is contrasted with a ruthless, fanatical patriot (Aristodemus), willing to sacrifice even his own daughter in the cause of victory.

The work however remained a mere fragment — a few sketches and notes, and an opening sequence of 180 lines of blank verse. Instead of completing it, Lessing devised a new, invented situation and a new, invented set of characters, though retaining Greek names and setting. *Philotas* was written in the latter part of 1758 and published early the following year. In it the same themes reappear, notably the conflict between heroic patriotism and 'jen[e] zärtern, bessern, menschlichern Empfindungen', as Euphaes calls them (*Kleonnis*, 1. 156 f.), and similar dramatic constellations[8] and motifs, notably the concern of father for son; but all is drastically compressed. The humane King Euphaes reappears in Aridäus, captor of the young Prince Philotas, his enemy's son. The name Aristodemus also recurs, as that of the general who persuaded Philotas's father to allow the Prince to accompany him into battle (sc. 2), but neither Aristodemus nor Philotas's (unnamed) father appear on stage. The representative of fanatical patriotic zeal in the play is the young prince himself. Captured on his very first day of active campaigning, as he tells us in the play's opening words —

So bin ich wirklich gefangen? — Gefangen! — Ein würdiger Anfang meiner kriegerischen Lehrjahre!

[8] It evidently occurred to Lessing's contemporaries that *Philotas* could be interpreted purely formally as a tragic counterpart to the Plautine comedies: the suggestion is denied by Karl Lessing, *G. E. Lessings Leben*, i. 205 f. Cf. Riedel, op. cit., p. 81.

— he feels disgraced and dishonoured. He feels too, as he tells Aridäus's general Strato (sc. 2), that his father will submit to yet further dishonour, and destroy the fruits of victory, for the sake of his recovery. But in the next scene he learns from Aridäus himself that 'das wunderliche Kriegesglück' has decreed the same fate for Aridäus's son as for himself: he has been captured by Philotas's father. Aridäus immediately perceives this as a providential opportunity for the two kings to sit down as equals at the negotiating table, conclude peace, and enjoy its fruits, for

Die Götter — ich bin es überzeugt — wachen für unsere Tugend, wie sie für unser Leben wachen. Die so lang als mögliche Erhaltung beider, ist ihr geheimes, ewiges Geschäft.   (sc. 3)

Philotas however thinks otherwise. In a long monologue (sc. 4) he argues that it is his duty to die for his country. The old soldier Parmenio, the fourth and last character to appear on the stage, warns him of the dangers of immature enthusiasm:

Mein lieber frühzeitiger Held, laß dir das sagen: Du bist noch Kind! Gib nicht zu, daß der rauhe Soldat das zärtliche Kind so bald in dir ersticke.
                                                       (sc. 5)

And Aridäus fears that Philotas's sentiments bode ill for his subjects when he comes to the throne:

Du wirst dein Volk mit Lorbeern und mit Elend überhäufen. Du wirst mehr Siege, als glückliche Untertanen zählen. — Wohl mir, daß meine Tage in die deinigen nicht reichen werden!   (sc. 7)

But finally the Prince, having tricked his captors into giving him a sword, acts out with it a pantomime of heroic resistance in battle, culminating in his — no longer merely mimed — self-immolation. Aridäus cries out in horror: 'Prinz, welche wütende Schwermut —'.

The phrase seems a curious one; but not if we think of that other soldier and man of honour, Tellheim, and the misanthropic melancholy to which he succumbs when he loses his faith in 'Tugend und Vorsicht'.[9] Aridäus expresses such faith in the words from scene 3 quoted above. Lessing, it seems, does not approve of Philotas's suicide. We shall find a some-

---

[9]   Cf. above, p. 37 f.

what similar treatment of violent and fatal action in *Emilia Galotti*, where Lessing seems to be trying to conserve our pity for the doer of a deed of which we cannot morally approve by showing it to be in some way beyond his rational control. Here however Philotas is not acting, like Odoardo Galotti, under unbearable provocation and psychological stress: he has quite coldly and deliberately resolved to kill himself, and the frenzy which precedes the fatal stroke is only play-acting. Both internal and external evidence — the play itself, and the views advanced by Lessing in the correspondence — lead us to conclude that Lessing cannot have intended us to admire Philotas; but it is very hard to pity him either. We feel more pity for Aridäus, who suffers however only vicariously. The true tragic loss is suffered by Philotas's father — in this sense it is he who takes over the (presumed) role of Euphaes in *Kleonnis* — but he does not appear. The feeling of this is indirectly strengthened in that the play's two other characters, Strato and Parmenio, are both also fathers with sons to care for: with this emphasis on the father-role Lessing was perhaps seeking, even unconsciously, to offset the lack of properly pitiable qualities in his protagonist.[10]

What of the political consequences of Philotas's death? It has destroyed the design for peace which 'das wunderliche Kriegesglück' had brought about. At first it seems that Aridäus will follow his example and sacrifice his own son to put himself once more on an equal footing with Philotas's father:

Der Krieg ist nicht aus, Prinz! — Stirb nur! stirb! Aber nimm das mit, nimm den quälenden Gedanken mit: Als ein wahrer unerfahrner Knabe hast du geglaubt, daß die Väter alle von einer Art, alle von der weichlichen, weibischen Art deines Vaters sind. — Sie sind es nicht alle! Ich bin es nicht! Was liegt mir an meinem Sohne? Und denkst du, daß er nicht eben sowohl zum Besten seines Vaters sterben kann, als du zum Besten des deinigen? — Er sterbe! Auch sein Tod erspare mir das schimpfliche Lösegeld!

(sc. 8)

As Mendelssohn had suggested, heroic action provokes to emulation! But Aridäus soon thinks better of this: to use Mendelssohn's phrase again, we see how 'die Vernunft wieder

---

[10] For a different view, see Neumann, op. cit., pp. 29 ff.

das Steuer ergreift',[11] and Aridäus returns to a tone which we recognize as more characteristic of him and of his creator:

Komm! Ich muß meinen Sohn wieder haben! Aber rede mir nicht ein, wenn ich ihn zu teuer erkaufe! — Umsonst haben wir Ströme Bluts vergossen; umsonst Länder erobert. Da zieht er mit unserer Beute davon, der größere Sieger! — Komm! Schaffe mir meinen Sohn! Und wenn ich ihn habe, will ich nicht mehr König sein. Glaubt ihr Menschen, daß man es nicht satt wird? —   (ibid.)

With these words the play ends. What are we to make of them? Philotas has sacrificed his life to the advantage of his country; an action of a kind which in *Codrus* is presented as tragically admirable. Lessing however strongly suggests that flesh and blood and human relations are worth more than one's country, and should not be sacrificed to it; and that peace is worth more than victory. The political conclusion to draw from this would be that a ruler should be concerned with the welfare of his subjects rather than with military glory. But Aridäus is not merely willing to sacrifice his country's cause for the recovery of his son; he seeks to renounce his responsibilities as king entirely and to withdraw into the sphere of private life. If everything that Aridäus has done is 'umsonst', if Philotas really is 'der größere Sieger', then the play depicts the helpless abdication of decent humanity in the face of barbaric militarism.[12]

This strange work has received a great diversity of interpretation. Some critics have seen it as a wholly serious attempt on Lessing's part to write a heroic tragedy: to depict, despite the very decided preference expressed in the correspondence, a hero and an action which arouse not so much pity as admiration, and to express the enthusiasm for patriotic self-sacrifice which had been generated, particularly in Prussia, by the outbreak of the Seven Years' War. Some of Lessing's contemporaries interpreted it in this way — and some were accordingly shocked by it, Bodmer for example, who countered it with his *Polytimet*.[13] Such enthusiasm had indeed affected the most

---

[11] Mendelssohn to Lessing, December 1756. Cf. above, p. 92.

[12] Cf. Seeba, op. cit., p. 63 f.; for a more conciliatory view see Neumann, op. cit., p. 34 ff.

[13] Cf. W. Grosse (ed.), *Lessing: Philotas, ein Trauerspiel* (Studienausgabe, Stuttgart, 1979 (Reclams Universalbibliothek, 5755)), which includes *Polytimet* and other contemporary material. Cf. also Seeba, op. cit., p. 56 f. and note.

unlikely people, such as the poet Gleim, who abandoned the decorous frivolities of anacreontic verse for which he was, and remains, better known ('Rosen pflücken, Rosen blühn, flüchtig ist die Zeit') for the more robust tones of his *Preußische Kriegslieder*. But a majority of readers have found it impossible to believe that Lessing could have intended anything so far removed from his expressed opinions both on the nature of true tragedy and on the sentiments of patriotism. We have already noted his reactions to the outbreak of the war. He wrote to Gleim that the *Kriegslieder* were too bloodthirsty and that 'der Patriot überschreiet den Dichter zu sehr', and later declared — this in the year in which *Philotas* appeared! — that 'Ich habe überhaupt von der Liebe des Vaterlandes ... keinen Begriff, und sie scheint mir aufs höchste eine heroische Schwachheit, die ich recht gern entbehre.'[14] Those who have tried to reconcile *Philotas* with such views as these have seen it not as a heroic but as an anti-heroic tragedy, a kind of tragic satire on patriotic heroism, indeed hardly a tragedy at all so much as 'a very unfunny comedy':[15] its protagonist a fool, his patriotic devotion a misguided fantasy, and his heroic rhetoric a sham whose hollowness we are intended plainly to perceive:

Jedes Ding, sagte der Weltweise, der mich erzog, ist vollkommen, wenn es seinen Zweck erfüllen kann. Ich kann meinen Zweck erfüllen, ich kann zum Besten des Staats sterben: ich bin vollkommen also, ich bin ein Mann.   (sc. 4)

On such a reading, this self-persuasion of Philotas's[16] is on a level with Damis's resolving (*Der junge Gelehrte*, II. 11) to marry on the grounds that 'Ich will die Zahl der unglücklich scheinenden Gelehrten, die sich mit bösen Weibern vermählt haben, vermehren'.

Patriotic self-sacrifice was certainly not, in real life, one of the 'gesellschaftliche Tugenden' of which Lessing approved. But *Philotas* has less to do with real life than *Miß Sara Sampson*, even if the outbreak of the war did suggest heroic patriotism as a theme on which a tragedy with contemporary

---

[14] Lessing to Gleim, 16 December 1758 and 14 February 1759.
[15] R. R. Heitner, 'Lessing's Manipulation of a Single Comic Theme', p. 191.
[16] Steinmetz ('Aufklärung und Tragödie', p. 23) calls it an 'intellektueller Kraftakt'.

relevance might be written: once again the overriding aim is
not to express or convey a view or attitude about certain
matters, but simply to *write a tragedy* about them. For this
purpose Lessing had to take seriously sentiments of which he
had, as he said, 'überhaupt . . . keinen Begriff'. This makes
Philotas far more abstract and remote than *Miß Sara Sampson*,
where at least the moral sentiments are drawn from a world
familiar and meaningful to him. It suffers too from the abandonment of the historical subject-matter of *Kleonnis*. Lessing's
notes for that work suggest that, while plainly regarding himself as under no obligation to follow his historical sources in
detail, he was trying to understand, and would have made us
try to understand, what the war between Messenia and Sparta
was about. In *Philotas* there are no such intimations; and in
their absence there can be no genuine conflict between patriotism and 'jene zärtern . . . Empfindungen'. Even an arbitrary
choice of names would have given at least the illusion of substance: Sparta and Messenia, Athens and the Dorians (as in
Codrus), Rome and Alba (as in Corneille's *Horace*). The kings
and princes and nations of *Philotas* are mere shadows. But
that, it seems, is what Lessing thought kings and princes and
nations were. He was evidently not capable, at this stage of
his career at any rate, of conceiving *any* legitimate causes for
war or patriotism or political action. The conception of a
dramatic situation as a providential design, in response to
which men are called upon to take moral decisions and moral
actions, is an immensely fruitful one for Lessing: it recurs in
all three of his mature dramas. But he cannot relate a public
theme like patriotism to it (except negatively) because his
notions of morality are still, as in *Miß Sara Sampson*, exclusively private. Partly this is simply the result of inexperience.
We have seen how his decision 'mehr unter Menschen als
unter Büchern zu leben' bore eventual fruit in *Minna von
Barnhelm*. But that is a play of peace rather than war; it celebrates the triumph of humanity, of 'gesellschaftliche Tugenden', of 'jene zärtern . . . Empfindungen', over politics and
over abstractions such as military honour. Only in *Emilia
Galotti* does Lessing admit that private lives, even under the
tutelage of a benevolent Providence, may not always escape
the influence of public matters.

The language of *Philotas* also reflects its abstraction. Despite the rigorous paring down and the evident desire to avoid the emotionalism of *Miß Sara Sampson* — which still tinges the words of Euphaes in *Kleonnis* — it still strikes the reader as unduly rhetorical; indeed, the concentration of the action within Aridäus's tent makes it exclusively a play of argument rather than event. The dialogue is marred again by 'Einfälle des Witzes', which disturbed, or at least puzzled, one contemporary critic.[17] Much of it is simply embarrassing, particularly the fifth scene, where once again techniques of comic dialogue are being used to very unfunny effect. (Similar exchanges occur more appropriately between Raina and Bluntschli in Shaw's *Arms and the Man*.) The play appeared anonymously, and Gleim promptly set to work to versify it — thereby earning the approbation, albeit somewhat ironic, of its author, who wrote to him on 31 March 1759 that the original lacked 'eine edle tragische Sprache'. I have already suggested that stylistic appropriateness was one of the major problems confronting the would-be tragic dramatist of the eighteenth century; it is one to which Lessing returns a number of times in his later critical writings.

Miß Sara Sampson was an experiment which had in some measure succeeded, if not to its author's entire satisfaction (or that of posterity); *Philotas* is one which fails. The one had made perhaps too many concessions to the taste of the theatre-going middle-class public; the other makes none at all, and pays the price of this rigour. (It was not in fact performed until 1774, two years after its reprinting in Lessing's collected *Trauerspiele*.) The one attempts to adapt for tragedy the contemporary bourgeois realism which had proved successful in comedy; the other to return to something closer to the traditional form of tragedy, purged of its more undesirable elements — 'admirable' heroism and alexandrine verse. But in the *Literaturbriefe* of 1759, if not so much in his own experimental practice, Lessing drew his countrymen's attention to a third possibility, as different from either of these as could be imagined.

[17] D 153.

(iii)

As early as 1750, in the preface to the *Beiträge zur Historie und Aufnahme des Theaters*, Lessing had declared that 'wollte der Deutsche in der dramatischen Poesie seinem eignen Naturelle folgen, so würde unsre Schaubühne mehr der englischen als französischen gleichen.'[18] But in the sixteenth and, most notably, in the seventeenth of the *Literaturbriefe* this casual assertion is developed into a violent attack on Gottsched for his wilful ignorance of German national taste and his consequent frustration of the natural development of the German theatre.[19]

'Niemand,' sagen die Verfasser der Bibliothek, 'wird leugnen, daß die deutsche Schaubühne einen großen Teil ihrer ersten Verbesserung dem Herrn Professor Gottsched zu danken habe.'

Ich bin dieser Niemand; ich leugne es gerade zu. Es wäre zu wünschen, daß sich Herr Gottsched niemals mit dem Theater vermengt hätte. Seine vermeinten Verbesserungen betreffen entweder entbehrliche Kleinigkeiten, oder sind wahre Verschlimmerungen.

Lessing concedes that the German theatre was, in Gottsched's heyday, in dire need of reform; indeed, his remarks on this point closely echo Gottsched's own in the preface to *Der sterbende Cato*.[20] But, so he argues, Gottsched had not been content with reform: 'er wollte nicht sowohl unser altes Theater verbessern, als der Schöpfer eines ganz neuen sein.' He had swept away what native growth there was on the German stage and substituted a Frenchified ('französierend') drama of his own which, as he ought to have realized, was quite alien to the German public:

Er hätte aus unsern alten dramatischen Stücken, welche er vertrieb, hinlänglich abmerken können, daß wir mehr in den Geschmack der Engländer, als der Franzosen einschlagen; daß wir in unsern Trauerspielen mehr sehen und denken wollen, als uns das furchtsame französische Trauerspiel zu sehen und zu denken gibt; daß das Große, das Schreckliche, das Melancholische, besser auf uns wirkt als das Artige, das Zärtliche, das Verliebte; daß uns die zu große Einfalt mehr ermüde, als die zu große Verwickelung etc. Er hätte also auf dieser Spur bleiben sollen,

---

[18] G iii. 359.   [19] G v. 70 ff.   [20] Cf. above, p. 3 and note.

und sie würde ihn geraden Weges auf das englische Theater geführet haben.

And to demonstrate 'daß . . . unsre alten Stücke wirklich sehr viel Englisches gehabt haben', he cites the example of the best-known of them, *Faust*,[21] and quotes what he claims to be a scene from one of the numerous traditional German plays on this subject. It is in fact as it stands his own work, though its basic motif, a trial of speed between spirits competing to be chosen as Faust's familiar, is indeed one traditionally associated with the legend, and probably did appear in some of the popular dramatic versions.[22] It is treated with characteristically Lessingian wit, which makes it not in the least 'groß, schrecklich, und melancholisch', but rather confirms, if anything, that these qualities lie beyond his dramatic range. But this does not invalidate his argument, nor discredit the identification of the Faust story as a genuinely German tragic theme. What is under attack here is no longer (as, for example, in the Seneca essay) Gottsched's moralism, but a different aspect of the patronizing, paternalistic way in which he went about his self-appointed task. Moreover, this patronizing attitude was one shared by many would-be reformers, including Lessing's own friends. Typical of Enlightened attitudes to the traditional taste and culture of the people are the remarks of Mendelssohn in his letter to Lessing of 19 November 1755, commenting on Lessing's own Faust plan: 'Wo sind Sie, liebster Lessing! mit Ihrem bürgerlichen Trauerspiele? Ich möchte es nicht gern bei dem Namen nennen, denn ich zweifle, ob Sie ihm den Namen Faust lassen werden. Eine einzige Exklamation, o Faustus! Faustus! könnte das ganze Parterre lachen machen.'

Lessing did not wish to pander to the vulgar; he regarded 'Bewunderung', for example, as a characteristic of the 'Pöbel' (to Mendelssohn, 28 November 1756). But we have seen in his discussion of comedy that he sought to appeal to what he called 'das Volk'; he enthusiastically defends a playwright like Plautus who had been censured by Gottsched for

[21] Gottsched had referred dismissively to 'das Mährchen von D. Fausten' in his *Dichtkunst*, ed. cit. p. 185 f.

[22] On these see E. M. Butler, *The Fortunes of Faust* (Cambridge, 1952), pp. 69-110.

compromising with public taste; and many years later he pointed out to Nicolai, who was extremely hostile to the 'Sturm and Drang' enthusiasm for 'folk poetry', that one must be careful to distinguish between 'Volk' and 'Pöbel' (20 September 1777). There seems therefore no reason to doubt the genuineness of Lessing's endorsement of popular taste in the drama in the seventeenth *Literaturbrief*. It is very much of a piece with his desire to found his new drama on a traditional base, which was what Gottsched had failed to do.

It must however be said that, apart from the (as I have argued) deliberate condescension of *Miß Sara Sampson*, he makes little or no attempt to put this precept into practice. It is also not wholly consistent with the other crucial, and in this case startlingly new, assertion of the seventeenth *Literaturbrief*:

Auch nach den Mustern der Alten die Sache zu entscheiden, ist Shakespeare ein weit größerer tragischer Dichter als Corneille; obgleich dieser die Alten sehr wohl, und jener fast gar nicht gekannt hat. Corneille kömmt ihnen in der mechanischen Einrichtung, und Shakespeare in dem Wesentlichen näher. Der Engländer erreicht den Zweck der Tragödie fast immer, so sonderbare und ihm eigene Wege er auch wählet; und der Franzose erreicht ihn fast niemals, ob er gleich die gebahnten Wege der Alten betritt.

A positive evaluation of characteristically national and popular cultural forms must lead, as it does with the 'Stürmer und Dränger', to cultural relativism: to the acknowledgment of a multiplicity of possible forms, all equally valid; to the recognition that, in Herder's words, 'Sophokles Drama und Shakespeares Drama sind zwei Dinge, die in gewissem Betracht kaum den Namen gemein haben.'[23] Lessing however asserts that Shakespearian drama is in the direct line of descent from that of ancient Greece; he accepts in principle the Gottschedian assumption that Shakespeare and Corneille are both to be judged 'nach den Mustern der Alten', and merely reverses its application.[24] This is the stance which Lessing continues to

[23] Herder, 'Shakespeare', in H. Nicolai (ed.), *Sturm und Drang* (Munich, n.d.), i. 302.

[24] Cf. Gundolf's formulation, 'Lessing rechtfertigt Shakespeare vor den Griechen, indem er sagt: Shakespeare ist *auch Kunst*, und Herder, indem er sagt: die Greichen sind *auch Natur*' (F. Gundolf, *Shakespeare und der deutsche Geist* (2nd edn., Berlin, 1914), p. 203).

maintain in the *Hamburgische Dramaturgie*; the seventeenth *Literaturbrief* marks the point at which he comes out in open and indeed fierce opposition not merely to feeble German imitations of the French classics but to the French drama itself, and to Corneille in particular. This is of course in itself a logical development from the opposition to heroic tragedy expressed in the correspondence, where the Cornelian type of tragic hero comes very much to mind; now Shakespeare is pressed into service as the supreme example of a 'national' dramatist who is as unlike Corneille as can be imagined, but Lessing does not stop to explain how 'der Engländer erreicht den Zweck der Tragödie'. The plays of Corneille can also hardly be intended as examples of 'das Artige, das Zärtliche, das Verliebte';[25] while later, in No. 30 of the *Dramaturgie*, Lessing attacks the complexity of a Cornelian plot on the grounds that 'Das Genie liebt Einfalt; der Witz, Verwicklung'.

The two arguments, that against heroic tragedy from general principles and that in favour of national and popular tradition in the drama, though they agree in condemning French classical tragedy, run on different lines; ultimately Lessing will attach more importance to the general argument and the appeal to the authority of the ancients, notably to Aristotelian theory. Lessing's critical thought remains at bottom essentially normative, and in this respect he is closer to Gottsched than to the 'Stürmer und Dranger'. But the seventeenth *Literaturbrief* undoubtedly played an important part in encouraging the next generation of German dramatists to follow the Shakespearian example.

How well Lessing actually knew Shakespeare at this stage is uncertain. He is mentioned in the *Beiträge* of 1750, but the discussion there follows closely that of Voltaire in Nos. 18–19 of the *Lettres sur les anglais*; Lessing acknowledges the debt quite frankly, though one does wonder why he did not bother to check Voltaire's (again, admittedly) very free rendering of

---

[25] The terms rather suggest, at least from an eighteenth-century point of view, Racine, to whom they were frequently applied at this period by both admirers and detractors. Cf. Charlotte von Dach, *Racine in der deutschen Literatur des 18. Jahrhunderts* (Bern, 1941), pp. 55–83, esp. p. 66. On Lessing's ignorance or misrepresentation of Racine, cf. M. Kommerell, *Lessing und Aristoteles* (3rd edn., Frankfurt, 1960), p. 19 f.

'To be, or not to be' against the original.[26] In the seventeenth
Literaturbrief there are mentions of *Othello, Lear,* and
Hamlet, but nothing to indicate detailed study. There are indeed possible echoes of *Othello* in the fragment *Fatime,* just
as *Julius Caesar* may have suggested a number of elements of
theme and treatment for *Henzi* and *Das befreite Rom*; but
Lessing's acquaintance with other English dramatists is far
more extensively demonstrable.[27]

The *Literaturbriefe* are a fascinating collection of critical
observations on a wide range of literature and *belles-lettres,*
extending to such topics as translation and poetic language
on the one hand, education and religion on the other. They
take the form of fictitious letters addressed to an officer
wounded in the battle of Zorndorf, informing him of the
developments which have taken place in German literature
since the war came to distract his attention from the arts of
peace. These developments, the first letter tells him, are
modest enough; and amongst them the drama occupies a very
humble place. Apart from the attack on Gottsched in Nos.
16–17, only two further sections of the *Literaturbriefe* are
directly or principally concerned with the drama. It is however noteworthy that both of these deal with tragedies on
subjects from English history. Nos. 63–4 discuss Wieland's
Lady Johanna Gray and No. 81 Weisse's *Eduard III* [28] (not to
be confused with the *Richard III* discussed in the *Hamburgische Dramaturgie*) and so, it seems, we may say that the
drama appears in the *Literaturbriefe* exclusively under the
English flag. Neither play is however particularly Shakespearian
in manner. Wieland's is an adaptation — though not quite so
plagiaristically close as Lessing, who in the *Literaturbriefe* has
few kind words for Wieland, would have us believe — of
Nicholas Rowe's *Lady Jane Grey* of 1715, itself one of those
pale classicistic echoes, like Thomson's tragedies, of the
Shakespearian tradition in eighteenth-century England. With
Shakespeare it has practically nothing in common beyond its

[26] The translation is probably by Mylius, but it appeared under Lessing's editorial auspices. Cf. PO xii. 13 f.

[27] Cf. C. C. D. Vail, *Lessing's Relation to the English Language and Literature*
(New York, 1936).

[28] On these see Heitner, *German Tragedy in the Age of Enlightenment*, pp.
224–36.

use of blank verse. This however Wieland had also chosen to imitate: his play is in fact the first German tragedy in this metre to be completed and performed (it had been acted in Zurich on 20 July 1758) and for this it had already been commended by Mendelssohn and Nicolai in their periodical the *Bibliothek der schönen Wissenschaften und der freien Künste* — praise which Lessing laconically endorses, though he then goes on to criticize Wieland in some detail. Weisse's play is in alexandrines — though in *Richard III* he abandons this metre in favour of blank verse — and in the French classical manner, as Lessing, again very tersely, observes:

Die Ökonomie ist die gewöhnliche Ökonomie der französischen Trauerspiele, an welcher wenig auszusetzen, aber selten auch viel zu rühmen ist. Und eben daher kann ich mich in keine Zergliederung einlassen.[29]

Though the plays of Wieland and Weisse are evidence of a general turning of German dramatists towards England and English models, Lessing in his direct advocacy of Shakespeare, even if on slender acquaintance, is thus ahead of his contemporaries. It is presumably for their 'Englishness' that he singles out Wieland and Weisse to exemplify what is most interesting and promising in contemporary German dramatic writing, though he was little interested in historical drama as such. But what exactly he thought he was advocating is not clear.[30] In the seventeenth *Literaturbrief* the name of Shakespeare is uttered as a slogan of liberation from French influence, but the main intention seems to be simply to discredit Gottsched and his pretensions to literary and theatrical dictatorship. Lessing sought freedom of experimentation for German dramatists, but the results rarely aroused his enthusiasm. Introducing Weisse's play in the eighty-first *Literaturbrief* he comments gloomily on the general state of the German theatre: 'Wir haben kein Theater. Wir haben keine Schauspieler. Wir haben keine Zuhörer.'[31] Its most promising writers have, as Weisse says, died young — Cronegk and Brawe; and he might have added Schlegel (the one real German dramatic talent of

[29] G v. 264.
[30] On Lessing and Shakespeare cf. Gundolf, op. cit., pp. 105–59; R. Pascal, *Shakespeare in Germany 1740–1815* (Cambridge, 1937), pp. 5 ff.; E. M. Batley, 'Rational and Irrational Elements in Lessing's Shakespeare Criticism', *GR* xlv (1970), 5–25.
[31] G v. 259.

the first half of the eighteenth century[32]), whose tone, Lessing thinks, Weisse comes at his best moments near to capturing. Remarks such as these suggest that Lessing was becoming increasingly sceptical of the possibility of encouraging a national cultural revival through the drama.

One or two detailed critical observations in the *Literatur-briefe* do however suggest a further positive development in Lessing's thinking in this field, with practical consequences for his own plays. His strictures in No. 63 on Wieland's characterization in *Lady Johanna Gray* could apply equally well to the practice which he himself had followed in *Miß. Sara Sampson* and defended, even insisted upon, in the correspondence with Mendelssohn and Nicolai. Wieland's characters may be morally good — every one of them is 'lieb' and 'fromm' — but this makes them poetically bad.[33] Wieland will do better, Lessing says, when he has studied real life more closely, and recognized the 'innere Mischung des Guten und Bösen in dem Menschen': a lesson which Lessing had yet to learn himself, at least where tragedy was concerned. The plea for simplicity in dramatic language at the end of No. 51 (a letter concerned with poetic diction in general, and in particular that of Klopstock) could similarly be turned against his own example.[34] But it is interesting to note that Lessing in No. 81 defends the use of 'witty' language in tragedy — provided always that it is psychologically plausible in the particular dramatic situation.[35] Again we return to the question of stylistic appropriateness. It was surely failure to identify the correct style which prevented Lessing from ever completing his Faust drama.

(iv)

The figure of Dr. Faust occupied Lessing's dramatic imagination at intervals over a period of twenty years or more. Familiar in legend and in popular theatrical entertainment, he is alluded to in the first scene of *Der junge Gelehrte*; Lessing

---

[32] In a review of 1753 (G iii. 164) Lessing had referred to Schlegel as 'der einzige, welcher Deutschland einen Corneille zu versprechen schien'!

[33] G v. 206.   [34] Ibid., p. 184.   [35] Ibid., p. 261 f.

may well have seen performances of one or more of the popular Faust plays; but the first evidence we have of an intention to treat the subject himself is Mendelssohn's letter of 19 November 1755 which we have already quoted, evidently referring to a previous remark or communication of Lessing's. From Lessing's own hand we have two or three scattered references in letters between 1755 and 1767; the single scene published in the seventeenth *Literaturbrief* under the heading 'Dritte Szene des zweiten Aufzugs', though this designation seems quite arbitrary; the so-called 'Berlin scenario', a summary of an opening sequence of a prologue and four scenes, of uncertain, but possibly early, date, published by Karl Lessing in the *Theatralischer Nachlaß* in 1786; and a note in the *Collectaneen* made in Breslau in the sixties. The rest is apocryphal: various accounts of conversations with Lessing on the subject by a number of people.[36] The longest are the accounts published after Lessing's death by C. F. von Blankenburg and J. J. Engel, and these are in substantial agreement as to the projected course of the action – notably, on Faust's salvation: for, at least twenty years before Goethe composed his 'Prolog im Himmel', Lessing had evidently decided to make this radical alteration to the legend. Karl Lessing and Blankenburg also allege that the work, or one version of it, was actually completed, and the finished manuscript lost in a chest which Lessing, on his way to Vienna and Italy in 1775, had sent back from Dresden to Wolfenbüttel but which never arrived. This story has often been repeated; it must however be regarded with the greatest scepticism. The disappearance of the chest is recorded in a letter from Lessing to Karl of 16 June 1776, in which he laments the loss of forty fables and an essay on the principles of German lexicography, intended for publication by Voss in Berlin, and a manuscript from the Wolfenbüttel library on which he had been working, or planning to work, in Dresden: 'wenn ich an das denke', he says, 'möchte ich vollends aus der Haut fahren.' But there is no mention of *D. Faust*. Schubart's *Deutsche Chronik* an-

---

[36] Most of this material is reprinted in G ii. 487–91 and 774–83. Cf. also R. Petsch (ed.), *Lessings Faustdichtung* (Heidelberg, 1911); K. S. Guthke, 'Problem und Problematik von Lessings Faustdichtung', *ZfdPh* lxxix (1960), 141–9; A. Henkel, 'Anmerkungen zu Lessings Faust-Fragment', *Euph.* lxiv (1970), 75–84.

nounced on 15 May 1775 that Lessing had sold 'sein vortref-
liches Traurspiel D. Faust' to the theatre in Vienna;[37] but
Baron von Gebler wrote to Nicolai from Vienna on 9 December of that year that, in reply to his enquiries on that matter,
Lessing had told him that he had planned two different treatments of the subject, 'einmal nach der gemeinen Fabel, dann
wiederum ohne alle Teufelei, wo ein Erzbösewicht gegen einen
Unschuldigen die Rolle des schwarzen Verführers vertritt' —
this is indeed confirmed by Lessing's own note made in Breslau
— and that 'Beide Ausarbeitungen erwarten nur die letzte
Hand.' The 'Sturm und Drang' writer Friedrich 'Maler' Müller,
recording many years later (in a letter of September 1820) a
conversation with Lessing in 1777, again speaks of the two
versions, but says that Lessing told him 'daß er . . . beide aber
wieder gelassen habe'.[38] The evidence for completion is very
slight: it looks rather as though Lessing was attracted to the
theme at various times of his life, maybe for different reasons,
and made, perhaps even simultaneously, attempts to treat it
in a number of different ways, but was not able to finish any
of them.

One can see why the Faust theme might be particularly
likely to attract him: it is the story of a man consumed by
the desire for knowledge and wisdom. So at all events Lessing
interpreted it, though Faust can also be represented as seeking
more mundane goals, such as pleasure, power, or wealth. On
this the Berlin scenario is clear. It begins with a Pandemonium,
or assembly of devils, apparently a feature of many of the
traditional Faust plays (Goethe's prologue in heaven is a variation of this). The various devils report to Beelzebub their
successes in luring men to sin. Then,

Dieses gibt Gelegenheit von Fausten zu sprechen, der so leicht nicht zu
verführen sein möchte. Dieser dritte Teufel nimmt es auf sich, und zwar
ihn in vier und zwanzig Stunden der Hölle zu überliefern.

Itzt, sagt der eine Teufel, sitzt er noch bei der nächtlichen Lampe,
und forschet in den Tiefen der Wahrheit.

Zu viel Wißbegierde ist ein Fehler; und aus einem Fehler können alle
Laster entspringen, wenn man ihm zu sehr nachhänget.

[37] D 365.   [38] Ibid., p. 430.

Lessing devoted much of his own life to the quest for knowledge and truth. Indeed, in a famous passage in one of his late
theological essays, *Eine Duplik* (1778), he proclaimed devotion
to this quest to be the highest distinction of man, at the same
time acknowledging the goal to be unattainable:

> Wenn Gott in seiner Rechten alle Wahrheit, und in seiner Linken den
> einzigen immer regen Trieb nach Wahrheit, obschon mit dem Zusatze,
> mich immer und ewig zu irren, verschlossen hielte, und spräche zu mir:
> wähle! Ich fiele ihm mit Demut in seine Linke, und sagte: Vater, gib!
> die reine Wahrheit ist ja doch nur für dich allein![39]

Unceasing pursuit of an unattainable goal; Faust, the figure
of modern times (be he historical or legendary) who most
powerfully embodies the drive with which Lessing himself
could most strongly identify — a man, one might well say,
'mit ihm von gleichem Schrot und Korne'.[40] Yet Lessing
could not successfully dramatize such a figure. Part of the
difficulty seems to have been that, however close the theme
or the figure of Faust may have been to him — indeed, given
the faith in Providence of which I have already spoken,
perhaps *because* of their closeness — Lessing was unable or
unwilling to grasp the theme's essentially tragic nature. The
'Stürmer und Dränger' immediately identify even more closely
with Faust, and are able to express their community of feeling
with him, because he is a tragic figure: he embodies not merely
their boundless aspirations, but the finally inevitable frustration of those aspirations, of which his damnation and
descent to hell can by a generation which has passed beyond
literal Christianity be regarded as convenient symbols. Goethe's
decision to 'save' Faust — again, the Christian terminology is
symbolic, not literal — came only later, and was executed, in
deeply ironic and ambivalent manner, even later still, when
the concluding scenes of his *Faust II* were written. But already for Lessing the thought of Faust's damnation is intoler-
able. Blankenburg recounts how in the projected conclusion
an angel was to intervene to snatch Faust from the devils:

> 'Triumphiert nicht', ruft ihnen der Engel zu, 'ihr habt nicht über Mensch-
> heit und Wissenschaft gesiegt; die Gottheit hat dem Menschen nicht

---

[39] G viii. 33.   [40] Cf. below, p. 136.

den edelsten der Triebe gegeben, um ihn ewig unglücklich zu machen; was ihr sahet, und jetzt zu besitzen glaubt, war nichts als ein Phantom.'[41]

The idea of a 'phantom' Faust is explained more clearly by Engel. The temptation and all-but-damnation of Faust were to take place in a dream, from which the real Faust was to awaken 'fester in Wahrheit und Tugend, als jemals', to thank Providence for the 'warning' he had received.[42] (One wonders what exactly the effect of the warning could be, if it is not to *change* Faust's desire to pursue the truth; and the idea of miraculous intervention is in fact totally alien to Lessing's views on the workings of Providence.)[43]

Schemes such as this are common in the 'Besserungsstücke', popular didactic plays portraying the miraculous cure of a variety of follies and vices, which flourished in the Austrian theatre from the seventeenth to the mid-nineteenth century: the most distinguished example is Grillparzer's *Der Traum ein Leben*, a play which was hailed as 'der österreichische Faust'.[44] Lessing had however in the northern German theatre of his day no such tradition on which to lean. Indeed this was un- doubtedly the principal stumbling-block. The theme was in many ways well suited to him. The Faust story was also a pre-eminently German one: this itself was an important factor, given his concern for the revitalization of German national literary culture (though here too the more immediate, even naïve response of the 'Stürmer und Dränger' to national and patriotic themes and subjects told to their advantage). The problem was to find a way of treating it which would appeal not merely to the kind of audience who flocked to see the puppet-plays and the less sophisticated itinerant troupes, but also to the new, more cultivated middle-class public whom Lessing saw as the ground in which the revivified German drama would blossom.

Mendelssohn in his letter had put his finger squarely on the sore point: 'Eine einzige Exklamation, o Faustus! Faustus! könnte das ganze Parterre lachen machen.' The implication is

[41] G ii. 780.   [42] Ibid., p. 783.   [43] Cf. below, p. 214.

[44] Cf. A. Sauer, *Grillparzers Gespräche und die Charakteristiken seiner Persön- lichkeit durch die Zeitgenossen*, i (Vienna, 1904 (Schriften des literarischen Vereins in Wein, i)), p. 162. On *Der Traum ein Leben* and the 'Besserungsstücke' cf. W. E. Yates, *Grillparzer: A Critical Introduction* (Cambridge, 1972), pp. 114 ff.

clear. Whatever the attractions of the Faust theme for Lessing, its associations in the mid-eighteenth century were so 'low' that a cultivated audience could not be persuaded to take it seriously, at all events not if treated literally.[45] It would have to be disguised or transposed in some way. We have seen that Lessing was no stranger to the idea of such transposition in tragedy, and he may have mentioned the possibility of a modernized Faust to Mendelssohn at this early stage. The Berlin scenario, however, though its advertised compliance with the unity of time may be regarded as a classicizing feature, indicates a literal treatment of the legend, and the setting of the prologue — midnight 'in einem alten Dome' — is decidedly Gothic; and the seventeenth *Literaturbrief* unequivocally advocates a Faust drama of the traditional stamp, its attractions being declared to lie precisely in its popular qualities.

While the dry Lessingian wit of the *Literaturbrief* Faust scene does not seem terribly appropriate, the admixture of comic effects is in itself one of the features of traditional dramatic treatments of the legend: there is plenty of it in Marlowe's *Doctor Faustus*, in Goethe's *Faust* — and in 'Maler' Müller's too. Müller's seems to have been the only other 'serious' literary treatment that Lessing knew: when they met in Mannheim in 1777, the *Situation aus Fausts Leben* had already appeared and the first part of *Fausts Leben dramatisiert* was complete in manuscript (it was published the following year). Müller makes considerable use of the comic potential of the legendary material, and frequently adopts an ironic, even parodistic tone. In his account of their conversation, Müller claims that Lessing commended him for this approach.[46] The ironic, familiar ('populär') tone was the right one: it was 'die einzige Weise . . . wie man diesem gehaltreichen, doch fürchterlich-drolligen Ding einen schicklichen Schweif angewinnen und aus seinem Zeitalter in das unsrige bequem übertragen

---

[45] In *Der junge Gelehrte* the reference to 'Fausts Höllenzwang' is placed in the mouth of the servant Anton, as a mark of boorish ignorance and superstition. It has been suggested that Damis's speech in the same scene, 'Aber, o himmlische Gelehrsamkeit . . . ', is a parody of a Faust monologue, such as those which open both Marlowe's play and Goethe's and are presumed to have been a regular feature of the popular versions: cf. G i. 282 f. and the note on G ii. 640.

[46] D 429 f.

mag'. By this account Müller had in Lessing's eyes succeeded in his own aim of capturing both the serious theme, which ought to appeal to the finer intelligences of the day as a particularly meaningful one, and the popular tone which had ensured the enduring success of the Faust plays on the stage, but which had hitherto been an obstacle to its acceptance by superior critical taste. Lessing himself did not however manage to effect this difficult combination. He had not found the right style — or mixture of styles: though his completed tragedies owe so much to his apprenticeship in comedy, the deliberate use of comic effects in a 'serious' context, the deliberate mixture of tones and registers — strictly forbidden, of course, by the neo-classical rules of stylistic propriety — was still beyond his grasp, at least while he approached the problem from the angle of tragedy. And so he was driven back to the alternatives of, on the one hand, a straightforwardly traditional, on the other, a serious but radically modernized treatment:

das eine . . . mit Teufeln, das andere ohne solche, nur sollten in dem letzten die Ereignisse so sonderbar auf einander folgen, daß bei jeder Scene der Zuschauer würde genötigt gewesen sein, auszurufen: das hat der Satan so gefügt.[47]

(v)

The theories and experiments of the late fifties had thus taken Lessing hardly any further towards a solution of the problem of modern tragedy than the point which he had reached with *Miß Sara Sampson*. And indeed, despite his ventures in the directions of a purified classicism on the one hand, and national and popular themes and styles on the other, his last major piece of work in the dramatic field before the Breslau interlude leads strongly back towards that contemporary bourgeois realism which was perhaps after all the most promising of all the possibilities he had so far explored. This venture was of course the *Theater des Herrn Diderot*, the translation of Diderot's two plays and their accompanying

[47] Ibid., also quoted in G ii. 778.

theoretical essays, which has already been mentioned.[48] It is in fact, apart from those of the *Literaturbriefe* we have discussed, the only piece of dramatic or theatrical criticism actually published by Lessing between the Thomson preface of 1756 and the *Hamburgische Dramaturgie*. It appeared in 1760, anonymously; in the preface to the revised second edition of 1781 Lessing acknowledges his authorship, which had long been an open secret, and the influence which Diderot had exerted upon his own thought:

Denn es mag mit diesem auch beschaffen sein, wie es will: so bin ich mir doch zuwohl bewußt, daß er [mein Geschmack], ohne Diderots Muster und Lehren, eine ganz andere Richtung würde bekommen haben. Vielleicht eine eigenere: aber doch schwerlich eine, mit der am Ende mein Verstand zufriedener gewesen wäre.[49]

The precise nature and extent of this influence is a matter of critical controversy. Some, too readily assuming the cultural priority of France before Germany as a matter of course, have alleged[50] that even *Miß Sara Sampson* was influenced by the plays of Diderot — the first of which did not appear till two years later. (At least one French critic, as if to redress the balance, has stated that Diderot 'unscrupulously pillaged' Lessing's work.[51]) It seems however to be largely agreed that in general Lessing found in Diderot 'a French dramaturge with whom he could *agree*, not a teacher from whom he could *learn*'.[52] It seems likely that Lessing, discovering, in the midst of his own experimentations, the work of Diderot, was encouraged to find a kindred spirit grappling with the same problems and coming up with solutions very similar to his

---

[48] Cf. above, p. 27.   [49] G iv. 149.

[50] Most recently Hildebrandt, *Lessing*, p. 240.

[51] A. Nivelle, *Kunst- und Dichtungstheorien zwischen Aufklärung und Klassik* (Berlin, 1971), p. 118 (less pointedly in the French original, *Les Théories esthétiques en Allemagne de Baumgarten à Kant* (Paris, 1955), p. 189, note).

[52] R. R. Heitner, 'Concerning Lessing's Debt to Diderot', *MLN* lxv (1950), 82–8, esp. p. 87. Cf. also R. Mortier, *Diderot en Allemagne* (Paris, 1954), p. 58: 'Ce dont Lessing avait rêvé obscurément, sans oser le formuler, voilà qu'un Français le proclamait bien haut et bien fort.' On some of the social implications of Diderot's and Lessing's dramatic theory and practice, see P. Szondi, 'Tableau und coup de théâtre: Zur Sozialpsychologie des bürgerlichen Trauerspiels bei Diderot. Mit einem Exkurs über Lessing', in Szondi, *Lektüren und Lektionen* (Frankfurt, 1973), pp. 13–43.

own. Both men stand on the threshold of a new age; both are
present at, and, without fully realizing it, actively engaged in,
the breakdown of a received cultural and critical tradition.[53]
Both see themselves as reformers and purifiers rather than as
iconoclasts: both are classicists at heart (though both subsequently underwent a more radical evolution) and repeatedly
invoke the authority of the ancients (particularly the Greeks)
beside that of 'nature' and truth to life; both oppose the
mixture of tragedy and comedy in the name of the traditional
separation of genres, while actively working to create a new
middle genre lying *between* them (on this point Diderot is
theoretically more advanced than Lessing — but also more
contradictory[54]). Both recognize that a cultural gulf separates
them from their immediate predecessors, and attempt to
appeal to contemporary audiences in a way that those predecessors had failed to do; but, believing fundamentally in
the unique validity of the classical tradition, can only conclude
that their predecessors have perverted it and that their own
task is accordingly to return to it. So it comes about that
both of them introduce contemporary realism to the theatre
of their respective countries under the banner of Sophocles
and Aristotle.

Lessing indeed planned and embarked on a life of Sophocles,
but his departure for Breslau cut short work on this project.
Sophocles appears again in the *Laokoon*, where his *Philoctetes*
— a favourite example of Diderot's too[55] — is cited to disprove
Winckelmann's contention that the Greeks restrained their
physical expression of pain and suffering. The stoic repression
of suffering may arouse admiration, but hinders the tragic
dramatist in the arousal of pity: 'Alles Stoische ist untheatralisch; und unser Mitleiden ist allezeit dem Leiden gleichmäßig,
welches der interessierende Gegenstand äußert.'[56] The tragic
stage is not a gladiatorial arena — though the heroes of Senecan
tragedy are little better than gladiators, and the Romans' taste

---

[53] Cf. R. Wellek, *A History of Modern Criticism*, i (London, 1955), p. 1 and
passim.

[54] Cf. especially the 3e *Entretien sur le Fils naturel, in Œuvres esthétiques,*
pp. 135–75.

[55] Ibid., p. 120, and the earlier discussion in *Les Bijoux indiscrets* (1748),
translated by Lessing in No. 84 of the *Hamburgische Dramaturgie* (G iv. 622).

[56] G vi. 16.

for such spectacles may well, Lessing suggests, have been the reason for their failure to produce great tragedy. Philoctetes, Lessing argues, is a true hero, one capable both of noble deeds and the unrestrained expression of human feelings, for

Beide machen den menschlichen Helden, der weder weichlich noch verhärtet ist, sondern bald dieses bald jenes scheinet, so wie itzt Natur, itzt Grundsätze und Pflicht verlangen. Er ist das Höchste, was die Weisheit hervorbringen, und die Kunst nachahmen kann.[57]

But these human feelings are not, it seems, to include 'das Artige, das Zärtliche, das Verliebte', which Lessing had condemned in the seventeenth *Literaturbrief*. In the *Laokoon* he rounds upon the French dramatist Châteaubrun, who had thought to 'improve' on Sophocles by introducing a love-interest into his own *Philoctète*.[58] The true tragic dramatist will, like his comic counterpart, seek to strike a mean: in this case, between cold heroics and effeminate softness. In the same way Lessing suggests in his notes on the life of Sophocles that Sophocles is the greatest of the Greek tragedians, representing the mean from which Aeschylus and Euripides in different directions depart.[59]

Both these works are however contributions to antiquarian scholarship — and the *Laokoon* to general aesthetic theory — rather than to dramatic criticism. The latter indeed draws for its literary illustrations principally on epic poetry, a genre which at the time of the correspondence on tragedy with Mendelssohn and Nicolai had not appeared to interest Lessing very much. The promised continuation of the *Laokoon* never appeared, and the existing 'Part I' seems indeed as complete in itself as any of Lessing's works. In a letter to Nicolai of 26 May 1769 Lessing develops the theory of 'natural' and 'arbitrary signs', on which his distinction between poetry and the visual arts partly rests, in order to demonstrate the superiority of the drama over all other literary genres.[60] But whether this really represents a true summary of his intentions at the time of working on the *Lakoon* three or more years before must be doubtful. It seems more likely that it reflects the reawaken-

---

[57] Ibid., p. 38.   [58] Ibid., p. 35.   [59] G iv. 774 ff.
[60] Cf. V. A. Rudowski, *Lessing's Aesthetica in Nuce* (Chapel Hill, 1971 (University of North Carolina Studies in the Germanic Languages and Literatures, lxix)).

ing of Lessing's interest in the drama and its fundamental nature which we owe to his engagement with the 'National-theater' in Hamburg.

V

Hamburg and the *Dramaturgie*

(i)

The theatre built in Hamburg by Konrad Ackermann in 1765 was one of the first public buildings in Germany to be put up expressly for the performance of plays.[1] There were a number of court theatres, largely built for and still devoted to opera and ballet; but apart from these, the history of the German theatre in the eighteenth century is that of itinerant troupes, performing in converted, improvised, and temporary premises — even though they might establish themselves in one town or another for a longer period of time — under the leadership of actor-managers. Some of these were persons of considerable ability, notably Frau Neuber, Schönemann, Ackermann, Ekhof, Schröder. A good few sprang from respectable middle-class backgrounds and had some measure of education. But their profession took them out of that respectability to the fringes of society. In Frankfurt in 1751 an actor could still be refused communion; and though Lessing wrote of this incident, 'Wir hätten nimmermehr geglaubt, daß ein protestantischer Theologe einer solchen Päpstischen Tyrannei fähig sein könnte,'[2] his own parents had, as we have seen, been extremely hostile to his interest in the theatre during his early years in Leipzig.

A number of attempts were however made in the course of the century to bridge the gap between the theatre and respectable society and literature. In Leipzig, the moving spirit had been Professor Gottsched; in Hamburg, it was Johann Friedrich Löwen, a government secretary, who was married to the actor

---

[1]   Cf. J. G. Robertson, *Lessing's Dramatic Theory: being an introduction to and commentary on his Hamburgische Dramaturgie* (Cambridge, 1939, reprinted New York, 1965); Bruford, *Theatre, Drama and Audience in Goethe's Germany*; F. Kopitzsch, 'Lessing und Hamburg', *WSA* ii (1975), 47–120, esp. pp. 58–78.

[2]   Review in *Kritische Nachrichten aus dem Reiche der Gelehrsamkeit*, 1751: LM iv. 269.

Schönemann's daughter, and had been closely associated with
Ackermann when the latter had brought his troupe to Hamburg
in 1765. Very soon however he had begun to criticize Ackermann's running of the theatre, and in 1766, in his *Geschichte
des deutschen Theaters*, he called for a complete reform of its
organization, by which it would be taken out of the hands of
the actor-managers and subjected to some kind of public
control. In accordance with Löwen's ideas, a consortium of
Hamburg citizens was formed to take over the theatre management from Ackermann; and in October 1766 the consortium announced its intentions in a statement of policy,[3]
invoking the name of Diderot and possibly also echoing J. E.
Schlegel's *Gedanken zur Aufnahme des dänischen Theaters*,
which had been published posthumously in 1764. (Lessing
cites both writers in the 'Ankündigung' of the *Dramaturgie*.)
It was presumably Löwen who wrote this and who invited
Lessing to join the theatre as literary adviser, though on exactly
what terms is not clear. Lessing, disappointed in his hopes of
obtaining a permanent appointment in Berlin, laid aside classical scholarship and turned back to the drama.

It was however as critic rather than as playwright that
Lessing was to be principally active in Hamburg, even if we
do owe to his engagement there the completion of *Minna von
Barnhelm* — which indeed became the most successful
work in the repertory of the 'Nationaltheater'.[4] As the season
opened, he embarked on a kind of house journal, a twice-
weekly 'kritisches Register'[5] of the work of the theatre, commenting upon the plays themselves and on all aspects of their
production, as well as on the drama in general. Though he had
no say in the actual choice of plays to be performed, he
could point to gaps in the repertory and draw comparisons.
The *Hamburgische Dramaturgie* was in fact to be a miscellany
like his previous essays in journalistic dramatic criticism, the
Beiträge and the *Theatralische Bibliothek*, with the important
difference that it was to be intimately linked with the day-to-
day running of a particular theatre. And in a rather similar
spirit to that in which Löwen had aimed to wrest control of
the theatre from the traditional 'Principalschaft', Lessing

³ Robertson, op. cit. pp. 20 ff.   ⁴ Ibid., pp. 44 ff.
⁵ *Dramaturgie*, 'Ankündigung' (G iv. 233).

sought to protect his journal from the vagaries of the commercial market in books and periodicals by publishing it himself. He started his own publishing firm, in partnership with his friend J. J. C. Bode; to raise the necessary capital he auctioned (to the distress of his Berlin friends) the considerable library he had assembled in the course of the previous six years. 'Nationaltheater' and *Dramaturgie* opened in May 1767.

Things soon started to go wrong with both ventures. Despite the pretensions of Löwen and the consortium, the change in nominal control made no effective difference to the practical running of the theatre, which remained in Ackermann's hands. The finances of the enterprise were very shaky; the second season was a failure, the last performance under Löwen's auspices took place in November 1768, and in March 1769 the consortium was formally wound up and the theatre reverted to actor-management. Lessing soon perceived that all was not well, writing to his brother on 22 May 1767 that 'Keiner weiß, wer Koch oder Kellner ist.' His criticisms of production and performers were not well received, particularly, it seems, by the principal leading actress, Sophie Hensel; Susanna Mecour, the chief soubrette and the original Franziska in *Minna von Barnhelm*, refused from the start to allow Lessing to mention her name, even favourably. Very soon Lessing's critiques in the *Dramaturgie* begin to lag behind the productions they discuss, and after No. 25 discussion of the actual performances is altogether abandoned. In a letter of 4 August 1767 to Nicolai, accompanying copies of Nos. 1–26 for Nicolai's bookshop, Lessing writes, 'Daß ich ungern diesen Wisch schmiere, können Sie glauben; und Sie werden es ihm hoffentlich ansehen.' Soon after this, publication of the *Dramaturgie* was interrupted by just that kind of activity which Lessing and Bode had hoped to avoid. A pirate edition appeared in Leipzig: Lessing and Bode could no more escape the harsh realities of the book trade than Löwen could those of the theatre. Nos. 32–82 appeared in batches between December 1767 and June 1768; serial publication then ceased completely, and Nos. 83–104 appeared in book form at Easter 1769, after the 'Nationaltheater' had formally ceased to exist. Soon afterwards, 'J. J. C. Bode & Co.' followed the theatre consortium into liquidation, and Lessing lost his money. The

final pages of the *Dramaturgie* express his disillusionment at
the failure of the Hamburg experiment, in phrases recalling
No. 81 of the *Literaturbriefe*, but with an increased bitterness
proportionate to his greater personal involvement and the
high hopes he had initially entertained. Once again it had
seemingly proved impossible to establish a theatre which
would both appeal to the general public and satisfy serious
literary standards.

The *Dramaturgie* was never intended to be a systematic
treatise of dramatic theory; if anything, it finally turns
out to be rather more of one than was originally envisaged.
It retains to the end the external form of a twice-weekly
periodical: 104 numbers ('Stücke') in all, making up a full
year's run, save that Nos. 97–8 and 101–4 are combined.
It even retains what would have been the correct periodical
dating, but after No. 31 (14 August 1767) this is a fiction and
can be disregarded. The end of regular serial publication
coincided approximately with the end of comment on details
of performance, and from No. 29 onwards, where Lessing
uses the production of *Rodogune* as the excuse for another
ferocious attack on Corneille, the substance of the work is
taken up more and more by similar 'digressions' and Lessing
departs further and further from matters of theatrical
practice. A performance of Voltaire's *Mérope* occasions a
comparison, on the lines of the Seneca essay in the *Theatralische Bibliothek*, of Voltaire's treatment of the story with
those of Euripides and the Italian Maffei; a performance of
Thomas Corneille's *Comte d'Essex* similarly enables Lessing
to acquaint his readers with English and Spanish plays on the
same subject. Weisse's *Richard III* introduces a profound
investigation of Aristotle's definition of tragedy; Diderot's
Père de famille a discussion of Diderot's work which is,
notably, much more concerned with Diderot's theory than
with his plays. Lastly, *Die Brüder* by Romanus prompts yet
another classical-modern comparison, before the final sum-
ming-up of the state of the German theatre in the 1760s of
which the *Dramaturgie* as a whole has given us, as it were, a
patchwork picture.

Lessing finds the outlook deeply depressing. The classical
tradition, represented by the dramatic masterpieces of the

Greeks, its principles enshrined in the eternally valid critical pronouncements of Aristotle, has been lost. The blame for this lies largely if not entirely with the French — whose works still dominated the Hamburg repertory. Corneille had set a thoroughly bad example, both in practice and in theory; and the sorry tale had been continued in Lessing's own century by Voltaire, who with 41 productions of 10 plays was by far the most-performed dramatist of the 'Nationaltheater'. The few German plays which have appeared, such as Cronegk's *Olint und Sophronia*, which was chosen to open the season, are for the most part inferior copies of bad models. In spite of its faults, of which Lessing is now quite plainly aware, the most encouraging development of the eighteenth-century theatre was the bourgeois realism of such writers as Diderot, which he strives to invest with Aristotelian legitimacy. As for the playwright Lessing himself, despite the modest success of *Miß Sara Sampson* and the greater of *Minna von Barnhelm* on the Hamburg stage, we are left with the impression of a sceptical observer rather than of the enthusiastic participant in theatrical revival which he had no doubt originally hoped to be.

He does continue to indicate new directions for theatrical development, beyond those represented by the actual plays performed. His well-tried technique of expository comparison enables him to draw his readers' attention to examples of the classical, English, and Spanish theatres — none of which was represented in the Hamburg repertory. Following up the message of the seventeenth *Literaturbrief*, he urges his compatriots to make the acquaintance of Shakespeare, whom they could now at last read extensively in their own language thanks to Wieland's translation, which he recommends (No. 15). His opinion of Wieland has clearly risen since the *Literaturbriefe*; in No. 69 he even quotes from, and praises enthusiastically, Wieland's novel *Agathon* — once again, the occasion is furnished by Shakespeare. He quotes extensively from other critics too: a good deal from Voltaire, with whom, after initial approbation, he comes to disagree more and more sharply; from Corneille, from Aristotle, from Diderot, and numerous seventeenth- and eighteenth-century critics, French, German, and English, all presented as contributions to the general debate.[6] In No. 50 he apologizes for all these citations and allusions, which suggest that the general theatre-going public is being neglected in favour of a narrower and more learned readership. Sometimes he allows the contradictions between his various authorities to stand, and draws no conclusions of his own; as he says at the end of No. 95, he is not concerned to present 'ein dramatisches System', but only *fermenta cognitionis*, food for thought. And the value of such critical debate is stressed in a counter-attack on those commentators who would spurn it as unproductive pedantry (Nos. 96, 101–4).

Lessing himself pleads for the sovereignty of genius with such pronouncements as 'Das Genie lacht über alle Grenzscheidungen der Kritik' (No. 7). But he is much concerned to define the nature of true genius and its operations, and to distinguish it from the gratuitous and anarchic self-expression with which the cruder of his young contemporaries seemed all too often to identify it. The true genius is a writer with a purpose:

Mit Absicht handeln ist das, was den Menschen über geringere Geschöpfe erhebt; mit Absicht dichten, mit Absicht nachahmen, ist das, was das Genie von den kleinen Künstlern unterscheidet, die nur dichten um zu dichten, die nur nachahmen um nachzuahmen . . .   (No. 34)

This implies that the workings of genius are a deliberate conscious activity; and to such activity the understanding of rules and principles can only be a help. So it is that Lessing can acknowledge, with perhaps excessive self-deprecation, the role which critical consciousness has played in the creation of his own dramatic works (No. 101–4).[7] It was in this spirit that Lessing composed the *Dramaturgie*, for the benefit of himself and others working in the German theatre. It is however undeniable that as the *Dramaturgie* leaves day-to-day theatrical commentary behind, it becomes more and more literary, abstract, and theoretical in character.

---

[6]   His sources are exhaustively documented by Robertson, who fails however to do justice to the positive value of Lessing's eclecticism, seeing in it merely a lack of originality.

[7]   Cf. T. J. Reed, 'Critical Consciousness and Creation: The Concept *Kritik* from Lessing to Hegel', *OGS* iii (1968), 87–113.

(ii)

This is evident above all in what is probably the best-known, and is indeed the most substantial, of Lessing's critical undertakings in the *Dramaturgie*, the analysis of Aristotle's theory of tragedy. It may well be that Lessing misinterpreted Aristotle — though on this point more recent critics disagree[8] — and that his exegesis is chiefly of interest today as a contribution to the tragic theory of his own time, marked strongly as it is by the limitations and distortions of the eighteenth century's understanding of tragedy. But Lessing undoubtedly intends, and believes that he has achieved, a work of exact scholarship, stripping off the accretions of centuries, the misrepresentations of successive editors, commentators, and translators, to lay bare Aristotle's exact text and its true meaning.[9] He does this, of course, in the belief that the *Poetics* of Aristotle constitutes as infallible an authority in respect of the drama, especially tragedy, as does the work of Euclid in geometry (Nos. 101-4). The name of Aristotle is invoked in support of Lessing's own views on four principal topics: the relation of drama (in particular, tragedy) to history, the proper construction of a tragic plot, the character of the tragic hero, and the nature of the emotions which tragedy should seek to arouse.

History has long furnished subject-matter for the writers of tragedy. The reason generally given for such a choice is that it establishes probability: what has happened once, says Aristotle, can happen again, so that by choosing historically attested stories the tragedian can readily command belief in the characters and events of his play. But Aristotle is quite clear that the purposes of the historian and the poet are quite different, and the statements they make of radically different kinds:

The one tells of what has happened, the other of the kinds of things that might happen. For this reason poetry is something more philosophical

---

[8]   Cf. W. Schadewaldt, 'Furcht und Mitleid? Zu Lessings Deutung des Aristotelischen Tragödiensatzes', B 336-42, and the reply by W.-H. Friedrich, 'Sophokles, Aristoteles und Lessing', *Euph.* lvii (1963), 4-27. The fullest discussion is M. Kommerell, *Lessing und Aristoteles*.

[9]   Cf. D. Borchmeyer, 'Corneille, Lessing und das Problem der "Auslegung" der aristotelischen Poetik', *DVJS* li (1977), 208-21.

and more worthy of serious attention than history: for while poetry is concerned with universal truths, history treats of particular facts.[10]

For this reason, as Lessing argues, the playwright is under no obligation to follow slavishly the recorded course of historical events (No. 19), and it is accordingly irrelevant to criticize him for failing to do so (No. 23 f.) It is not his job to reproduce history, but to make constructive use of it: 'die unnützen Schätze des Gedächtnisses in Nahrung des Geistes zu verwandeln' (No. 30). For this reason, 'Dem Genie ist es vergönnt, tausend Dinge nicht zu wissen, die jeder Schulknabe weiß' (No. 34). And commenting on Diderot's reiteration of the traditional distinction that comedy portrays types, tragedy individuals, Lessing insists that both comedy and tragedy aspire to that generality ('Allgemeinheit') which makes poetry 'philosophischer und folglich lehrreicher . . . als die Geschichte' (No. 89).

All this seems authentically Aristotelian. Yet in a number of these passages Lessing reveals a subtle, doubtless unconscious, but yet profound difference of emphasis. He himself cites the traditional distinction that whereas in comedy the characters are the 'Hauptwerk', in tragedy 'die Charaktere weniger wesentlich sind und Schrecken und Mitleid vornehmlich aus den Situationen entspringt' (No. 51). And Aristotle himself had said that tragedy is an imitation of action and not of persons, and only includes the characters for the sake of the action. For Lessing's own theory of tragedy, however, character is of prime importance. So we find him insisting that while the tragedian can be indifferent to historical fact, 'die Charaktere sind ihm heilig' (No. 23); history as a source for the drama comprises 'ein Repertorium von Namen, mit denen wir gewisse Charaktere zu verbinden gewohnt sind' (No. 24). The point is repeated later: tragedy employs 'wahre Namen' only for the sake of the 'Begriff des Charakters, den wir mit den Namen . . . zu verbinden gewohnt sind' (No. 91). Lessing stresses character, and psychological motivation,

---

[10] *Poetics*, ch. 9. The translation is that of T. S. Dorsch, in *Aristotle, Horace, Longinus: Classical Literary Criticism* (Harmondsworth (Penguin Classics), 1965), p. 43 f. Cf. also the translation by M. E. Hubbard in D. A. Russell and M. Winterbottom (eds.), *Ancient Literary Criticism* (Oxford, 1972), pp. 85-132. For the present chapter I have relied largely on these two versions, modifying them where it seemed appropriate to my purpose.

because in his view the essential tragic effect depends, as we shall see, upon a close sympathetic identification between the audience and the tragic protagonist; here he departs from Aristotle, unaware of this though he may be.

Moreover, even faithfulness to historical character is subject to further qualification, as we see in the discussion of Corneille's *Rodogune* in Nos. 29 ff. What attracted Corneille was, it seems, the character of Cleopatra and the actions which proceeded logically from that character. Lessing however objects to Corneille's heroine, not because her character does not accord with that recorded in history, but because it does not accord with his (Lessing's) notions of femininity and his moral sense of human character in general. Corneille's Cléopâtre is 'ein Ungeheuer ihres Geschlechts' (No. 30), 'ein häßliches abscheuliches Weib, das . . . die erste Stelle im Tollhause verdienet' (No. 31); even if such a woman existed, even if more than one such woman has existed, 'sie ist dem ohngeachtet eine Ausnahme, und wer eine Ausnahme schildert, schildert ohnstreitig das minder Natürliche' (No. 30). The principle of fidelity to historically established character is here subordinated to a principle of higher generality. Certain kinds of character – the criterion is essentially moral – are not acceptable subjects for dramatic representation. They cannot even be invoked to motivate historically attested tragic events:

Der Poet findet in der Geschichte eine Frau, die Mann und Söhne mordet; eine solche Tat kann Schrecken und Mitleid erwecken, und er nimmt sich vor, sie in einer Tragödie zu behandeln. Aber die Geschichte sagt ihm weiter nichts, als das bloße Factum, und dieses ist eben so gräßlich als außerordentlich . . . -Was tut also der Poet?   (No. 32)

Lessing's answer, of course, is that the poet, if he is a true one, will seek to motivate these events plausibly: he will seek 'eine Reihe von Ursachen und Wirkungen zu erfinden, nach welcher jene unwahrscheinliche Verbrechen nicht wohl anders, als geschehen müssen' (ibid.). But his idea of psychological plausibility does not encompass the behaviour of Corneille's Cléopâtre, even if such behaviour is consistent with her historically attested character.

The admissibility of historical characters for the drama would thus appear to be drastically circumscribed. A character

such as Cleopatra (or, as we shall see, Richard III) is excluded
on the one hand, the admirably great — such as the paragons
of Christian heroism in *Olint und Sophronia* (Nos. 1 ff.) — on
the other. Lessing later argues in the name of Aristotle for an
'intermediate' kind of tragic hero, but not many such are
furnished by history. But in fact Lessing is concerned with
character only at the level of generality: that is, the names of
dramatic characters are entirely arbitrary and there is no
good reason for choosing 'wahre Namen' at all. This conclusion
is indeed drawn at the end of No. 33 (we have now moved on
from *Rodogune* to Favart's *Soliman II*, but the point at issue
is the same). Lessing reasserts that 'die Charaktere dem Dichter weit heiliger sein müssen, als die Facta.' He argues that
action is derived from character so that, as is intimated in No.
32, a convincing psychological portrayal will make even
unlikely events seem probable and even inevitable. But he
also recognizes that a single event ('Factum') can be motivated
in a number of different ways. The poet may choose to
follow the motivation suggested by the historical account and
the historically attested characters; or he may, if it suits his
purpose better, substitute his own. But in the latter case he
will be better advised to use his own names too, rather than
the historical ones: the 'Wesentliches und Eigentümliches' of
historical character (No. 33) can only inhibit the dramatist in
his pursuit of universality. The idea of truth to historical
character is really something of a red herring: in fact, Lessing
seeks to divorce tragedy from history more radically than
Aristotle had done.

Lessing's investigation of the topic of 'wahre Namen' has
an obvious relevance to his own dramatic practice. Both his
completed full-length tragedies are modernizations of classical
stories; and such ideas as the transposition of the *Hercules
furens* to seventeenth-century Naples or of the execution of
King Charles of England to Siam are evidence of the same
concern — to prevent the universal significance of tragedy
from being obscured by the associations of particular historical
facts. At the same time this reveals that despite the contrary
emphasis of his theory, Lessing in fact recognizes — perhaps
unconsciously — that the centre of tragedy, the aspect of
reality with which it is most essentially concerned, is, as

Aristotle had said, not character but action: 'eine solche *Tat* kann Schrecken und Mitleid erwecken.' (If the realization had been conscious, we might have expected to find him laying much more emphasis on Aristotle's own repeated insistence on the point.) The modern European mind, however, regards character as much more autonomous than did the Greeks. And for Lessing and his eighteenth-century contemporaries, the elaboration of psychology, the stress on identification between audience and dramatic character, was further necessary as a means of making accessible the events of tragedy, which for other ages seemed significant and moving *because* they were outsize, remarkable, and even monstrous. We have certainly to admit that Lessing's success in *Emilia Galotti*, as in *Minna von Barnhelm*, is largely due to his investing his characters, even if fictional, with a persuasive historical reality of their own.

Lessing's preoccupation with character means that he has relatively little to say about plot and dramatic structure, though the stress laid on motivation marks in this connection an important advance on the theory expounded in the earlier correspondence.[11] And in Nos. 37 ff. of the *Dramaturgie* he does explore Aristotle's discussion of the different elements of a tragic plot: 'reversal' and 'recognition' (*peripeteia* and *anagnorismos*) and various treatments of disaster or suffering (*pathos*). Here Lessing comes up against a notorious problem of the *Poetics*: an apparent contradiction between Chapter 13, where Aristotle says that the best kind of tragic plot embodies a change from good fortune to bad, and Chapter 14, where he says that the most moving kind of incident is that in which an impending disaster is avoided through a timely recognition (as in the story of Merope, the subject of Voltaire's tragedy which occasions Lessing's discussion). This discrepancy continues to vex commentators on the *Poetics* to the present day.[12] Lessing's argument is of little consequence either for the substance of his tragic theory as a whole, or for his dramatic practice; it is interesting chiefly as an illustration

[11] There is a brief discussion of *hamartia* (cf. above, p. 75) in the letter to Mendelssohn of 18 November 1756 (G iv. 192 f.).
[12] Cf. Russell and Winterbottom, op. cit., p. 109 and note; John Jones, *On Aristotle and Greek Tragedy*, p. 46 f.

of his method and of his attitude to Aristotle. Lessing accuses
the French commentator Dacier of being more concerned
with Aristotle's reputation for infallibility than with the substance of his doctrine; but he himself declares that while Aristotle may be wrong — though we hear no more of this — it is
unthinkable that he should contradict himself. The contradiction can be only apparent, and the reasons for it must be
explained. And the method is recourse to the original Greek
text and elucidation of the precise meaning of the particular
terms. To his own satisfaction, at any rate, Lessing proves
that the contradiction is indeed only apparent: there is
nothing to prevent a tragedy from containing both the 'best'
(according to Aristotle) kind of *peripeteia* and the best treatment of *pathos*, for each is a distinct 'Teil der Fabel' (No. 38).
But he does not state his own view on the best kind of tragic
ending, preserving an Aristotelian ambiguity on the question.
Such few pronouncements on this matter as can be found in
his writings suggest that he did not think a tragedy need end
unhappily,[13] but his three completed tragedies do all end in
death and disaster.

The question of what is the essential, indispensable defining
characteristic of the tragic genre is finally tackled in Nos. 73 ff.
The starting-point is afforded by Weisse's *Richard III* with its
archetypal villain-hero. Corneille's Cléopâtre had been condemned as an unacceptable tragic protagonist, on essentially
moral grounds, without recourse to Aristotle. But in Nos.
73 ff. Lessing undertakes to prove that the choice of such a
protagonist is contrary to Aristotelian writ. The argument
turns upon the same central issues as the correspondence of
1756/7: the question of the 'tragic passions', the true nature
of tragic fear, and the emotional and moral effect of tragedy
upon the spectator. It also touches, parenthetically, on the
difference between dramatic representation and narration.
And it very largely takes the form of a critical exposure of
the misinterpretation (according to Lessing) of Aristotle by
Corneille, who finally achieves a kind of negative apotheosis
as the great villain of dramatic history, perverting its course
by both example and precept (No. 81).

[13] Cf. Lessing to Nicolai, November 1756 (G iv. 164); *Dramaturgie*, No. 55;
Lessing to Gerstenberg, 25 February 1768 (on the subject of the latter's *Ugolino*).

As in Nos. 37 ff. Lessing presents us with a detailed analysis of key Aristotelïan terms, once again seeking to bring out a coherent meaning. The texts subjected to this analysis are the basic definition of tragedy in Chapter 6 of the *Poetics* as 'a representation of an action . . . by means of pity and fear bringing about the purgation of such emotions', and the characterization of the tragic hero[14] in Chapter 13, where it is stated that the misfortunes of an utterly wicked man may touch our human fellow-feeling (*philanthropia*) but cannot arouse pity or fear because pity is aroused by undeserved suffering and fear by the suffering of one like ourselves. Aristotle, says Lessing, would have condemned Weisse's Richard out of hand:

Die Tragödie, nimmt er an, soll Mitleid und Schrecken erregen: und daraus folgert er, daß der Held derselben weder ein ganz tugendhafter Mann, noch ein völliger Bösewicht sein müsse. Denn weder mit des einen noch mit des andern Unglücke, lasse sich jener Zweck erreichen.
(No. 74)

Lessing first disposes of the term 'Schrecken', even though he has himself used it unquestioningly earlier in the *Dramaturgie* (Nos. 32, 37-8, 49, 51). The terrors which Richard's actions arouse in us ('Erstaunen, Entsetzen, Schauder') are not what is meant by tragic fear: this should be rendered not 'Schrecken' but 'Furcht'. As perhaps Nicolai had reminded him, the suggestion had already been made in the correspondence (2 April 1757). But at that stage the definition of 'fear' was a point of subordinate interest: this is why it could be ignored until now. In 1756/7 Lessing, Mendelssohn, and Nicolai were agreed in ascribing to Aristotle a view of the effect of tragedy which they further agreed was wrong. This was that tragedy, through evoking pity for its protagonist, aroused in the spectator fear that he might suffer like misfortune, and thereby 'purged' him of the passions portrayed in the stage-figures — for so the text was generally construed up to Lessing's day: thus the portrayal of the tragic consequences of, say, jealousy purged

[14] There is no such term in Aristotle and modern commentators agree (John Jones going, I think, furthest in this respect) that its use distorts Aristotle's meaning, implying as it does the typically modern shift of emphasis from action to character; but it is convenient to follow Lessing in using it here.

the spectator of jealousy. This view of tragedy as didactic, that is, embodying specific moral lessons, was generally espoused by writers from Corneille to Gottsched. It had been challenged by Nicolai and Mendelssohn, who had argued that tragedy aroused passions (pity, fear, admiration) but did not 'purge' or 'purify' ('reinigen') them and was morally neutral; Lessing had however contended that tragedy aroused pity — all other emotional effects being subordinate — and that this arousal was itself a morally improving experience, without any 'purgation' and irrespective of whether a particular play embodied any specific moral lesson. In the *Dramaturgie* he still attaches central importance to pity, asserting indeed 'daß die Tragödie, mit einem Worte, ein Gedicht ist, welches Mitleid erreget' and that from this elemental definiton even its dramatic, as opposed to narrative, mode of presentation can be inferred, since our pity can be aroused only by something we actually see (No. 77). But around this centre the argument is radically reorganized, and fear takes on a new importance. In the supposedly 'Aristotelian' view maintained by Corneille and repudiated by Lessing and his friends in 1756/7, the arousal of fear was a secondary stage in the tragic process: fear came after pity. But in the *Dramaturgie* Lessing explains that without the fear provoked by the recognition of the tragic hero as 'one like ourselves', without the self-identification of spectator and hero, though we may feel 'mitleidige Regungen' — the *philanthropia* which even a wicked man's misfortunes may arouse — we shall not feel that intensity of emotion which alone deserves the name of tragic passion ('Affekt'). Only this is properly described as pity (No. 76). Pity and fear are interdependent: fear is 'das auf uns selbst bezogene Mitleid' (No. 75). Lessing thus stresses the self-identification of spectator and tragic hero. Aristotle says that we can feel *philanthropia* for a wicked man, but can only feel pity for undeserved suffering. But for Lessing even this is not enough: even undeserved suffering does not arouse pity unless the hero is 'mit uns von gleichem Schrot und Korne' (No. 75). In this he is going further than Aristotle, who merely says that fear is aroused 'by the [one] like' (*peri ton homoion*). He does not actually say like whom or what.

In fact Lessing too, despite his insistence on the point, is less than totally explicit. Aristotle says that while the misfortune of a blameless man is not tragic but odious, the misfortune of an utter villain does not arouse pity or fear: therefore there remains 'the man in between these. This is one not preeminent in virtue and justice, but who falls into misfortune not through depravity and vice, but through some error' (Ch. 13). That is, the 'likeness' is a moral one. The tragic hero is neither faultless nor depraved, but in between: a good man (Ch. 15), better than the ordinary (Ch. 2), but not perfect. Lessing however seems to demand the removal of any psychological distance between spectator and hero. Many readers, encouraged by Lessing's own dramatic practice, assume further that this means that the hero should be of the same social rank as the spectators — which Aristotle would probably have found beyond comprehension, let alone assent. In fact Lessing does not actually say this. Looking back over two hundred years, we can see in the efforts of Lessing and his contemporaries the beginnings of a sociological approach to literature; but the very fact that they are pioneers in this field means that often they fail to make, or appear only to be groping towards, distinctions and definitions which seem obvious to us. Defending his own *Miß Sara Sampson*, Lessing had declared the tragic effect to be independent of the rank of the characters portrayed:

Die Namen von Fürsten und Helden können einem Stücke Pomp und Majestät geben; aber zur Rührung tragen sie nichts bei. Das Unglück derjenigen, deren Umstände den unsrigen am nächsten kommen, muß natürlicherweise am tiefsten in unsere Seele dringen ...   (No. 14)

But this, while suggesting a preference, even a strong preference, for (to use his earlier phrase) 'Helden aus dem Mittelstande',[15] does not categorically exclude those of elevated rank. Elsewhere in the *Dramaturgie* we find examples of the latter with whom we can identify ourselves in the appropriate manner: Hamlet (No. 11), Merope (No. 47),[16] Queen Elizabeth (No. 57). We think of Lessing as the champion of 'bürgerliches Trauerspiel' both in example and in theory; but it is a curious

---

[15] Cf. above, p. 62.
[16] We recall that *Merope* is one of Nicolai's examples of tragedies 'in welchen bürgerliches Interesse herrschet': cf. above, p. 90.

fact that save in No. 14, where the reference is to his own
Miß Sara Sampson, Lessing does not use the term in the
Dramaturgie, any more than he had done in the correspondence of 1756/7. On both occasions, his aim is to define the
essential features of the tragic genre, and to exclude forms
which are not in his view properly tragic: he is not concerned
with accidentals or subdivisions within that genre. And on
both occasions the one essential feature is defined as the
arousal of 'Mitleid'.

Lessing's new interpretation of tragic fear gives this emotion
an importance which it did not have for him in 1756. But it
is still a subordinate even if an essential constituent of tragedy,
rather like 'Schrecken' in the correspondence, necessary only
because, according to his present argument, pity cannot be
aroused without it. This is open to the objection that Aristotle
uses the terms 'pity and fear' as an almost inseparable pair,
suggesting much more of an equal partnership than Lessing
allows. This objection he now however sets out himself to
counter: as in No. 38, Aristotle must be vindicated, not merely
in spirit, but to the letter. If pity is the only emotion which
tragedy seeks to arouse, and this necessarily implies fear, why
does Aristotle specifically mention fear as well? Lessing finds
the answer in the doctrine of 'catharsis' to which in 1756/7
he had been unable to attach any useful meaning. Tragedy
arouses pity and fear in order to purge (*kathairein*) or, as
Lessing rather differently interprets it, to purify ('reinigen')
pity and fear. Correcting the misrendering generally current
in his day, Lessing points out that Aristotle's phrase 'the purgation of such passions' (*tēn tōn toioutōn pathēmatōn kath-
arsin*) cannot possibly refer to the passions, jealousy or
whatever, portrayed on the stage, of which Aristotle makes
no mention. It must refer to the passions aroused in the
audience, pity and fear and the emotions related to them: so
the specific moral effect, the 'Absicht' of tragedy, is not contained in its 'message', is indeed independent of the content
of any particular tragedy, but is a direct consequence of the
emotional effect which defines the genre as a whole (No. 77).
Now, says Lessing, even such a critic as Dacier, who unlike
Corneille has at least construed the Greek correctly, has only
very imperfectly understood its meaning: he thinks that tragic

pity purges us of excessive fear, thereby helping us the better
to face our misfortunes, which are so much less terrible than
those of an Oedipus, a Philoctetes, or an Orestes. This is
indeed the traditional Stoic interpretation of the moral effect
of tragedy;[17] but for Lessing, as we know, 'alles Stoische ist
untheatralisch'.[18] Dacier may have shown how pity purifies
fear, but we need to see also how fear purifies pity, pity pity,
and fear fear; moreover even these make up only half the
possible permutations, for we are to understand by the 'puri-
fication' of a passion not merely the purging of an excess, but
also the making up of a deficiency. Invoking the Aristotelian
moral concept of the 'mean', Lessing defines the virtuous
man as one neither excessively, nor insufficiently, disposed to
pity and fear. The task of tragedy, the 'Reinigung der Leidenschaften', is therefore the attuning of these feelings to a
correct proportion in his soul: by doing this tragedy accomplishes a 'Verwandlung der Leidenschaften in tugendhafte
Fertigkeiten' (No. 78).

This argument is much more sophisticated than that of
1756/7, when Lessing had maintained that tragedy fulfilled
its moral aim wholly and sufficiently by arousing pity. But
ingenious though it is, with its mathematically symmetrical
'table of purifications', on closer examination it is not very
convincing. Lessing's scheme remains theoretical and abstract:
if Dacier did not explore the whole range of possibilities, he
at least explained how one of them was supposed to work. In
the correspondence Lessing had held, consistently enough,
that pity was an unqualified virtue, that tragedy ought therefore to arouse as much pity as possible,[19] that the word
'reinigen' was meaningless and that Aristotle's doctrine of
'catharsis' was false. Ten years later he admits that a man
may feel too much pity as well as too little — though this
concession seems artificially prompted by the desire to con-
struct a symmetrical argument — and devises an interpretation
of 'Reinigung' which enables him to 'save' the term 'catharsis'
and claim Aristotelian authority for his own views. This interpretation is however very dubious. For Aristotle, pity is not a

---

[17] Cf. above, p. 59.

[18] *Laokoon*, ch. 1 (G vi. 16): cf. above, p. 120.

[19] Lessing to Nicolai, November 1756 (G iv. 164). Diderot argues similarly:
cf. *Œuvres esthétiques*, p. 152.

virtue, but, like fear, a harmful passion which disturbs the
balance of the soul and needs to be driven out; tragedy accomplishes this by bringing these passions to a climax and a
resolution.[20] What the spectators feel after this resolution is
presumably the same as the 'cathartic' effect of 'orgiastic'
music described by Aristotle in his *Politics*: 'they are, as it
were, set on their feet, as if they had undergone a curative
and purifying treatment.'[21] Perfunctory though this may be,
it is both more enlightening and more persuasive than Lessing's
'Verwandlung der Leidenschaften in tugendhafte Fertigkeiten'.
No more than in 1756/7 can Lessing explain how the virtuous
disposition, schooled in pity, is to be translated into action.

Though his theory of *katharsis* is in part intended as an
answer to Plato's accusation that poetry was morally harmful
because of its arousal of the passions, Aristotle nowhere
asserts that it is of actual moral benefit. This however is for
Lessing axiomatic: 'Bessern sollen uns alle Gattungen der
Poesie: es ist kläglich, wenn man dieses erst beweisen muß'
(No. 77). Very early in the *Dramaturgie* he describes the
theatre as 'die Schule der moralischen Welt' (No. 2) and 'das
Supplement der Gesetze' (No. 7). His own critical intelligence
and, no doubt, his own experience of play-writing had taught
him that it was simply not true that the dramatic poet began
his work, as Gottsched had averred, by choosing 'einen moralischen Lehrsatz, den er seinen Zuschauern auf eine sinnliche
Art einprägen will'.[22] On the contrary, the poet began with a
story or a character which he sought to interpret. It was not
necessary for him to point a specific moral: the attempt to do
so was one of the faults of, for example, Voltaire's *Semiramis*
(No. 12). The tragic poet, above all, set out to move his
audience emotionally; Lessing is right to perceive this as the
essential defining characteristic of the genre. His belief in the

[20]   Lessing's nearest approach to this is the idea of a scale or 'ladder' of passions,
'Mitleid' induced by 'Schrecken' and resolved in 'Bewunderung', which is advanced
in the letter to Nicolai of November 1756 (G iv. 162) but never mentioned again.
It is once more significant that Lessing abandons this idea, which is intimately related to the form of a tragic *action*, to concentrate on the moral qualities of tragic
characters.
[21]   Aristotle, *Politics*, book viii, ch. 7: translated by T. A. Sinclair (Harmondsworth (Penguin Classics), 1962), p. 314. Cf. Russell and Winterbottom, op. cit.,
pp. 132 ff. Lessing alludes briefly to this passage at the beginning of No. 78 of the
Dramaturgie.   [22]   Cf. above, p. 59.

moral worth of emotions, especially pity, provides him with the starting-point for a theory of the tragic emotions which reconciles that perception with the moralistic assumptions of the age from which he was unable to emancipate himself completely.

Indeed, those assumptions sometimes appear in undisguisedly old-fashioned form. Shakespeare's treatment of jealousy in *Othello* is commended, it seems, on the basis of the very same didactic theory of tragedy which is later so elaborately repudiated: 'Othello hingegen ist das vollständigste Lehrbuch über diese traurige Raserei; da können wir alles lernen, was sie angeht, sie erwecken und sie vermeiden' (No. 15).

Nowhere are Lessing's assumptions more clearly set out than in No. 34, in his elaboration of that 'Absicht' which distinguishes the true genius from those lesser artists whose art is an end in itself. Serious art is neither merely decorative, as was that of many of Lessing's inferior contemporaries, nor merely expressive, as it is in large measure for the 'Stürmer und Dränger', but communicative: the artist sets out to say something to his fellow-men. And for the representational ('imitative') arts of literature and drama, the highest forms of art in Lessing's view, however important their emotional impact, their communicative function cannot be entirely divorced from their representational content. Drama must after all have some kind of moral message: it is a representation of good and evil and so must of necessity engage and, as it were, train our 'Begehrungs- und Verabscheuungskräfte' (No. 34). And underlying the moralism we perceive yet another, the most fundamental of all Lessing's assumptions: the wisdom, omnipotence, and benevolence of divine Providence, which it is the dramatist's ultimate task to reveal.

Earlier in the same number, Lessing suggests that genius is the creator of a world of its own, which is not simply a copy of the one we live in but a reflection of its inner truth:

[eine] Welt, deren Zufälligkeiten in einer andern Ordnung verbunden, aber doch ebenso genau verbunden sind, als in dieser; [eine] Welt, in welcher Ursachen und Wirkungen zwar in einer andern Reihe folgen, aber doch zu eben der allgemeinen Wirkung des Guten abzwecken.

(No. 34)

Now a comedy (such as Favart's *Soliman II*, the play under discussion here) can easily do this. But in the preceding numbers of the *Dramaturgie* the tragic poet has been set a very similar task: 'eine Reihe von Ursachen und Wirkungen zu erfinden, nach welcher jene unwahrscheinliche Verbrechen nicht wohl anders, als geschehen müssen' (No. 32). The tragic poet too must, even in the most apparently calamitous and meaningless events, exhibit and justify the workings of Providence; he must create a dramatic world in which all the parts are related in a meaningful design. Though his subject-matter is suffering and disaster, he must present it so as to make it intelligible, depict it in such a way that it no longer offends our moral sense. Aristotle had said that while tragedy had to depict undeserved suffering in order to arouse pity, the spectacle of misfortune befalling the totally blameless was not tragic but odious (*miaron*). And so Aristotelian authority can once again be invoked to condemn Weisse's *Richard III*. Not only can we not feel pity for Richard; we cannot even feel pity, properly understood, for his innocent victims, for in their case our pity is compromised by a 'fremde, herbe Empfindung', identified with Aristotle's *miaron*, which has no place in tragedy because it tempts us to the gravest of sins in Lessing's eyes, 'Murren wider die Vorsehung' and 'Verzweiflung' (No. 79). And here the distinction between poetic and historical truth is again made. Historical truth is no justification for the dramatist's presenting such an unedifying spectacle. He must not content himself with merely depicting a part of reality, but must present an image of the whole in which those partial dissonances are resolved: 'das Ganze dieses sterblichen Schöpfers sollte ein Schattenriß von dem Ganzen des ewigen Schöpfers sein' (No. 79). Tragedy is theodicy: it demonstrates in 'partial Evil, universal Good', and so should not depict radical, unresolved evil.[23] Some such thoughts as these undoubtedly underlie Aristotle's dictum that it is odious to behold misfortune afflicting a totally blameless man; on the other hand, Aristotle does not condemn as *miaron* the

---

[23] Cf. above, p. 54. For a recent account of this aspect of Lessing's dramatic theory from a theological point of view, cf. A. Schilson, *Geschichte im Horizont der Vorsehung: Lessings Beitrag zu einer Theologie der Geschichte* (Mainz, 1974), pp. 72–82.

slaughter of Medea's children, nor the even grislier fate of the sons of Thyestes. But again Lessing finds it necessary to cite Aristotelian chapter and verse in support of his own views.

'Zwar mit dem Ansehen des Aristoteles wollte ich bald fertig werden, wenn ich es nur auch mit seinen Gründen zu werden wüßte' (No. 74). But despite this and other, similar rhetorical disclaimers, the reader is left with the impression that Lessing is determined to prove Aristotle right and, what is more, right for all time. Now Aristotle's *Poetics* continues to claim the attention of scholars to this day not merely because its elliptical mode of expression and its contradictions and ambiguities make it a happy philological hunting-ground, but also because Aristotle possessed an extremely acute critical mind and a profound knowledge of the Greek tragic repertory. Nor are his views without relevance to modern European drama, for the major serious form of that drama was in fact based, however remotely, upon the Greek model: even Shakespeare is essentially a Renaissance dramatist rather than the Nordic bard whom the 'Stürmer und Dränger' wished to see in him. But Corneille had already observed that modern Europe had from its own experience and its own philosophy of life, so different from those of the Greeks, evolved its own characteristic new forms of drama, which had met with the approval of the theatre-going public; he therefore argues for a relaxation of the letter of Aristotelian law 'pour n'etre pas obligés de condamner beaucoup de poemes que nous avons vû réussir sur nos théâtres' (as Lessing quotes him in No. 81). And indeed Lessing's own practical dramatic efforts, like those of any serious playwright, were in fact aimed at this same goal, of evolving new forms to express new sensibilities and new perceptions of life. But for Lessing the theorist, any such relaxation is unthinkable. Weisse's *Richard* has indeed enjoyed great success on the stage; we cannot but admire 'das Zweckmäßige' of the hero's actions, however misdirected; the play 'vergnügt durch . . . Beschäftigung unserer Seelenkräfte'; but in calling itself a tragedy, it demands to be judged by the highest of standards, and by those standards — those of Aristotle as Lessing interprets them — it fails (No. 79). To relax those standards as Corneille proposes can have only one result: 'die Tragödie muß unter ihrer höchsten Wirkung

bleiben' (No. 81). Corneille's suggestion that there may be
legitimate possibilities of tragic drama other than those described by Aristotle is finally and categorically rejected (No.
82).

(iii)

Yet elsewhere in the *Dramaturgie* Lessing himself is still sympathetically investigating alternatives. That it is possible for
tragedy to attain the supreme goal is proved by the example
of Greek drama — and of English (No. 81). Shakespeare is invoked in comparison with Voltaire: *Hamlet* (No. 11 f.),
Romeo and Juliet and *Othello* (No. 15). And the Germans
are encouraged, even urged to read him (ibid.). But they are
not told to imitate him: 'Shakespeare will studiert, nicht ge-
plündert sein' (No. 73). There is no detailed examination of a
Shakespeare play in the *Dramaturgie*; Weisse's *Richard III* is
not compared with Shakespeare's — to which Lessing might
indeed have felt obliged to apply similar strictures.[24]

What Lessing praises in Shakespeare is his power of psychological penetration. Thus in *Hamlet* he can persuade us of the
ghost's reality, first by making us see it through the hero's
eyes and share his reaction to it, then by making the ghost itself a character capable of arousing 'Mitleid', and not just a
'poetische Maschine' like the ghost in Voltaire's *Semiramis*.
Romeo and Juliet and *Othello* show a profound understanding
of love and jealousy, whereas Voltaire only skims the surface
of these passions (No. 15). But Lessing does not commend
the form or style of Shakespearian drama. In fact what he has
to say about these aspects of English drama — generally,
perhaps deliberately, he does not mention Shakespeare by
name — is far from complimentary.

On one point in particular he seems to have changed his
mind completely since the seventeenth *Literaturbrief*. There,
we recall, Gottsched was censured for failing to see 'daß uns die
zu große Einfalt mehr ermüde, als die zu große Verwickelung',
and that in this respect the national taste of the Germans resembled that of the English. But in the *Dramaturgie* Lessing

---

[24] Shakespeare's Richard is cited as an example of 'das Schreckliche' in *Laokoon*, ch. 23 (G vi. 151 f.), but the point is not pursued.

insists from the very first number, where Cronegk's *Olint und Sophronia* is compared unfavourably with its source in Tasso in this respect, that simplicity is the hallmark of genius. Complication is, we are now told, a *fault* in the English dramatic style and a feature which does *not* appeal to German taste: 'die englische Manier in diesem Punkte, zerstreuet und ermüdet uns' (No. 12). Not that the French are any better — indeed, a climax is reached with the condemnation of *Rodogune* for its complexity: 'Das Genie liebt Einfalt; der Witz, Verwicklung' (No. 30). So the French have no right to criticize the English on this score (No. 46). Lessing is also opposed to the English habit of mixing tragedy and comedy in a single work, and comments critically on Wieland's defence of Shakespeare in this respect (No. 69 f.). The ground of Wieland's argument is truth to nature. But as we know, Lessing holds the dramatist's task to be not to imitate the surface of reality with all its contrasts and dissonances, but to resolve these in a higher truth; and this the 'komische Tragödie, gotischer Erfindung' (No. 70) does not do. As with the 'historical' atrocities of *Richard III*, mere truth to appearances, to our raw experience of the world, is not adequate to the 'more philosophical and more worthwhile' ends of tragedy. The poet must not simply reproduce his material, but select and organize.

The only English play to be discussed in any detail in the *Hamburgische Dramaturgie* is *The Earl of Essex, or the Unhappy Favourite*, by the Restoration dramatist John Banks. Thomas Corneille's *Comte d'Essex*, one of the most popular of historical tragedies in its day, was played twice at the 'Nationaltheater'; having said all that he has to say about it (largely following Voltaire) on the first occasion (Nos. 22 ff.), Lessing takes the opportunity of the second performance to discuss English and Spanish plays on the same subject (Nos. 54 ff.). After summarizing Banks's play, Lessing describes it as 'ein Stück von weit mehr Natur, Wahrheit und Übereinstimmung . . . , als sich in dem Essex des Corneille findet'. Banks is praised, like Shakespeare, for his psychology — though not so much in the portrayal of his protagonist as in that of Queen Elizabeth. Lessing quotes a fairly lengthy extract to illustrate this. But whereas Banks's play was in blank verse, Lessing's translation is in prose; and the change is made

quite deliberately. Lessing condemns Banks's florid and rhetorical style, for 'Bei einer gesuchten, kostbaren, schwülstigen
Sprache kann niemals Empfindung sein' (No. 59), and advocates, here as elsewhere in the *Hamburgische Dramaturgie*
(and, indeed, in the *Literaturbriefe*)[25] a simple, 'natural'
mode of expression as the appropriate corollary of realistic
psychological portrayal, both serving the dramatist's aim of
making his audience identify themselves with the characters
on stage.

Despite the occasional praise of English drama of the
Shakespearian type, the positive recommendations of the
Dramaturgie thus point rather in the direction of bourgeois
realism and of Lessing's old ally, Diderot. Indeed, some of
Lessing's highest praise is reserved for *Le Père de famille* (No.
84). There is however very little discussion of Diderot's play;
and the discussion of Diderot's dramatic theory which follows
concentrates largely on a single point — once again, character.
We should have welcomed some consideration of other aspects,
notably, in view of the sharp distinction between poetry and
the visual arts which Lessing draws in *Laokoon*, of Diderot's
theory of *tableaux*;[26] but it is interesting to see once more
the central importance which Lessing attaches to character in
drama. He also makes, or implies, comment on a matter of
great practical consequence, Diderot's advocacy of a *genre
sérieux* between tragedy and comedy. In both these matters,
despite Lessing's continuing praise for Diderot, his agreement
is not unqualified.

By way of introduction, and as a kind of supplement to
the works he had translated in *Das Theater des Herrn Diderot*,
Lessing gives us the dialogue from the novel *Les Bijoux indiscrets* in which, as early as 1748, Diderot had first voiced,
through the fashionable, transparent veil of Oriental fable, his
dissatisfaction with the theatrical tradition of his own country.
In the works of the ancients, all was nature, simplicity, and
truth; in the moderns, complication and artificiality, both in
dramatic construction and in dialogue. After quoting this
general plea for realism in the drama, Lessing goes on to

   [25] Cf. D. Droese, *Lessing und die Sprache* (Zurich, 1968), pp. 80 ff.; Schröder,
Lessing: Sprache und Drama, pp. 139 ff.
   [26] Cf. Szondi, op. cit.

consider Diderot's contribution to the theory of dramatic characters. Diderot's starting-point was the traditional distinction that the characters of tragedy were individuals — Regulus, Brutus, Cato; those of comedy, types — the miser, the hypocrite. Diderot argued that the possibilities of character-comedy had been virtually exhausted, and proposed therefore to substitute for character-types what he called *conditions*. The term (Lessing translates it 'Stände') can denote profession or social position or even, as in the case of the *fils naturel* or the *père de famille*, domestic relationship: once again, like Lessing's 'Volk' to whom true comedy is addressed, like Nicolai's 'bürgerliches Interesse', like Lessing's tragic hero 'mit uns von gleichem Schrot und Korne', it does not have the sociological precision which the reader of today expects it to have. These *conditions* were to be treated as types, like the traditional comic characters: Diderot says that while there is scarcely a play without a father in it, there is not one designed to portray the *condition* of father.[27] To this theory Lessing raises two objections. Firstly, the stage-figure will have to have a character of some sort — 'traurig oder lustig, ernsthaft oder leichtsinnig, leutselig oder stürmisch' — and the action of the play will flow from this: that is, it will be, in accordance with Lessing's familiar emphasis, motivated psychologically rather than by *condition*. Secondly, if the character is only such as accords with the type of the *condition* — the judge, for example, must be 'ernsthaft und leutselig' — the figure will be excessively abstract or idealized (No. 86). This leads to a lengthy discussion, including a substantial excerpt from the English critic Richard Hurd, on the nature of that universality which according to Aristotle all dramatic characters must have. For here (No. 89 f.) we return to the highest authority of all.

Diderot has, in Lessing's view, exaggerated and misunderstood the distinction between tragic and comic characters. The 'wahre Namen' of tragedy do not, as we have seen, denote individuals in the historical sense, for tragedy deals in universals: excessive particularization is a fault in the tragic poet, and Sophocles, who painted men as they should be, was in

---

[27] *Œuvres esthétiques*, p. 154.

this respect superior to Euripides, who painted them as they actually were (No. 94). Correspondingly, while comedy has traditionally portrayed typical characters, it should not overload its figures with 'characteristic' detail to the point at which they become caricatures and are no longer credible as individual human beings. In Hurd's terminology (No. 95, footnote), the 'draught of character' in both tragedy and comedy should be 'general', even though the former tends to be more 'particular', the latter more 'representative'. In adopting this argument Lessing seems himself to be drawing the traditional genres closer to one another. Now Diderot in the *Entretiens* had advocated the introduction of new intermediary genres, *comédie sérieuse* and *tragédie domestique et bourgeoise*. Lessing however suggests that this is unnecessary — 'Wird der Nutzen, den wir davon hoffen dürfen, groß genug sein, daß es sich der Mühe verlohnt, eine neue Gattung dafür fest zu setzen und für diese eine eigene Dichtkunst zu schreiben?' (No. 86) — even though he then adopts Diderot's terminology in pointing out that Dorval, the *fils naturel* of the play of that name, is, as befits the *genre sérieux*, less individual than a tragic, less typical than a comic character (No. 87–8). Lessing's point appears to be that it is superfluous to talk of new genres when the traditional, established ones, if their true nature is properly understood — hence the appeal to Aristotelian authority yet again — are fully adequate to any dramatist's purpose.[28] But he breaks off the discussion at the end of No. 95, disclaiming any intention of establishing a 'dramatisches System' of his own, and leaving his readers to draw their own conclusions. Beginning in No. 84 by praising Diderot's play and endorsing his rejection of the artificialities of French classicism, Lessing thus goes on to criticize Diderot's theory in the name of the infallible Aristotle, and ends with an unresolved difficulty. The whole sequence epitomizes Lessing's ambivalent attitude to traditon and innovation in the drama of his own day.

Though far more comedies than tragedies were performed by the 'Nationaltheater', tragedy dominates the *Dramaturgie*, particularly from No. 30 onwards, that is to say after the

[28] Cf. above, pp. 92, 138.

abandonment of comment on performance and production. This reinforces one's impression that, from its starting-point in a working relationship with the living theatre, the *Dramaturgie* soon becomes much more general and theoretical in nature. The early numbers of the *Dramaturgie* indicate a keen interest in the live theatre, in the technique of acting, in the visual aspect of drama — a 'transitorische Malerei' and a 'stumme Poesie', joining together what *Laokoon* had put asunder (No. 5).[29] But later, despite Lessing's continued insistence on the difference in effectiveness between drama and narration, his approach becomes more and more literary, even academic. There are no more appeals to popular taste or to the native theatrical tradition which he had invoked in the seventeenth *Literaturbrief*.[30] The gap between literary drama and theatrical practice, which he had seen the Hamburg experiment as a new opportunity to bridge, seemed to be widening again.

(iv)

Best of all accounts of the state of drama and theatre in eighteenth-century Germany is that provided by Goethe in his unfinished novel *Wilhelm Meisters theatralische Sendung*, written in his early years in Weimar, between 1775 and 1786. Within its pages are encapsulated the history of the literary drama in Germany from the dominance of French classicism to the proclamation of Shakespeare by the 'Stürmer and Dränger', with a running accompaniment furnished by popular forms of entertainment such as puppet-theatres, acrobats, ballad-singers, and jugglers. We hear discussions of the Three Unities and of the banishment of Harlequin. The idealistic hero dreams of becoming the 'Schöpfer eines großen National-

---

[29] There is no adequate treatment of this aspect of Lessing's dramatic criticism and theory. The best to date is U. Otto, *Lessings Verhältnis zur französischen Darstellungstheorie* (Frankfurt and Bern, 1976). Cf. also O. G. Graf, 'Lessing and the Art of Acting', *Papers of the Michigan Academy of Science, Arts and Letters*, xl (1955), 293–301, and T. Ziolkowski, 'Language and Mimetic Action in Lessing's *Miß Sara Sampson*', *GR* xl (1965), 261–76.

[30] Lessing however later criticized Sonnenfels, the reformer of the Viennese theatre, for taking too little account of public taste: cf. his letter to Eva König of 25 October 1770.

theaters . . . , nach dem er so vielfältig hatte seufzen hören';[31]
but he, and we, become fully acquainted with the obstacles
which stand in the way of the realization of this dream. In his
company we meet travelling theatrical troupes and see them
in all their doubtful glory, with their scandals artistic and
financial, erotic and social; we meet actors and actor-managers
modelled in many cases upon the major figures of real theatrical history; we follow Wilhelm's attempt to secure responsible
control of his troupe and free it from the professionals on the
one hand and from aristocratic patrons on the other.

The fragment ends with Wilhelm, after much doubt and
hesitation, confirming anew his commitment to the theatre.
But for the older Goethe it was the doubt and hesitation
which prevailed; work on the novel was broken off in 1786
and when in the nineties he took it up again and recast it into
the opening books of *Wilhelm Meisters Lehrjahre*, it took on
a new meaning. The theatre is no longer the main subject of
the novel, but only one element in a more general scheme of
'Bildung'; moreover that 'Bildung' is no longer conceived as a
'national' goal, but has fallen back within the confines of the
individual personality, in accordance with the precept of
Weimar classicism:

> Zur Nation euch zu bilden, ihr hoffet es, Deutsche, vergebens;
> Bildet, ihr könnt es, dafür freier zu Menschen euch aus![32]

Here, at least ostensibly, a positive message is drawn from disillusion. But in Lessing's similar words in the final section of
the *Dramaturgie* there is only disillusion and bitterness, so
different from the optimism of the 'Ankündigung':

> Über den gutherzigen Einfall, den Deutschen ein Nationaltheater zu ver-
> schaffen, da wir Deutsche noch keine Nation sind! Ich rede nicht von
> der politischen Verfassung, sondern bloß von dem sittlichen Charakter.
> Fast sollte man sagen, dieser sei: keinen eigenen haben zu wollen . . . Der
> süße Traum, ein Nationaltheater hier in Hamburg zu gründen, ist schon
> wieder verschwunden: und so viel ich diesen Ort nun habe kennen lernen,
> dürfte er auch wohl gerade der sein, wo ein solcher Traum am spätesten
> in Erfüllung gehen wird.   (No. 101-4)

---

[31] Book i, ch. 18: cf. *Lehrjahre*, i. 9 (Hamburger Ausgabe, vii. 35).
[32] Goethe/Schiller, *Xenien* (1797), 'Deutscher Nationalcharakter': Goethe,
ed. cit., i. 212.

In 1769 the Hamburg pastor, Johann Melchior Goeze, later Lessing's most famous theological adversary, attacked the theatre from the pulpit as a threat to religion and morality. A lively controversy broke out; but Lessing wrote to Nicolai on 11 October that he would not be sorry to see all the theatres closed, not only in Hamburg but in all Germany. 'In zwanzig Jahren würden sie doch wieder geöffnet; und vielleicht griffe man sodann die Sache von einer bessern Seite an.' Already in the summer of 1768 he had turned his attention once more to classical scholarship — indeed, the attention paid to Aristotle in the later numbers of the *Dramaturgie* itself reflects this; the first numbers of his new scholarly work, the *Briefe, antiquarischen Inhalts*, were completed in July of that year. In the autumn he was planning to sever his connections with Hamburg and go to Italy, but nothing came of this, and by the spring of 1769 he was once more standing idle in the market-place.[33] He considered going to Vienna, where it seems he was invited to be a founder-member of a new literary academy; but was then offered and accepted the post of librarian to the Duke of Brunswick, which he finally took up at the beginning of May 1770. Despite further offers from Vienna (1771) and Mannheim (1776) he remained in the ducal service for the rest of his life.

But for all its frustrations, Lessing's time in Hamburg was by no means fruitless. The *Dramaturgie*, wayward and unsystematic though it is, is still an impressive work, the first really substantial German contribution to dramatic theory. It embodies a coherent doctrine, although that doctrine has to be pieced together and sometimes inferred from its diverse and scattered observations. We may summarize that doctrine as follows. The drama, like all serious art, has a communicative purpose: to make us aware of the true nature of reality, to reveal the workings of its inner laws. It does this not by mere copying of the sometimes confusing and contradictory surface of reality, but by the creation of a stage-world in which the relationship of the parts to each other and to the whole can be seen and understood. Above all it peoples this stage-world with human beings like ourselves, characters who can command our

[33] *Dramaturgie*, No. 101–4 (cf. Matth. 20: 3).

sympathetic identification; neither paragons of virtue nor monsters of vice, but people whose flaws and errors we can comprehend without having to attribute them to radical, incorrigible evil. And our entering into these characters will obviously be rendered easier if they are made to speak in familiar, natural language; which does not mean descending into crudity and bathos, but avoiding affectation and rhetoric. It is not necessary for a play to teach a specific moral lesson — writing to Nicolai on Goeze's attack on the morality of the drama, Lessing observes 'Die elenden Verteidiger des Theaters, die es mit aller Gewalt zu einer Tugendschule machen wollen, tun ihm mehr Schaden, als zehn Goeze' — though it can hardly be a bad thing in Lessing's view if it does; but the main effect of drama is achieved through its appeal to the emotions. With this Lessing has in sum created a programme for the kind of realistic, largely middle-class drama which came to dominate the European stage in the nineteenth century and which indeed, despite the experiments of our own time, still seems of all the dramatic forms evolved in Europe after Shakespeare the one most capable of appealing, as Lessing desired, to a wide and in the best sense popular audience.

What seems old-fashioned in the *Dramaturgie* is Lessing's insistence on the traditional genre-divisions and on the infallibility of Aristotle. Indeed in these respects it was old-fashioned even by the more advanced standards of its own day: in his *Briefe über Merkwürdigkeiten der Literatur* of 1766, Gerstenberg had already demanded 'Weg mit der Classifikation des Drama!',[34] and within a few years the 'Stürmer und Dränger' were proclaiming, noisily and often incoherently, their emancipation from Aristotelian authority. The battles Lessing had fought to preserve the purity of tragedy no longer concerned them, and when Schiller twenty and more years later rediscovered the merits and the principles of classical drama, he did so by a very different route of his own. Yet the 'Stürmer und Dränger' continued to respect Lessing's work. What mattered to them was his message of liberation from purely mechanical rules, and perhaps above all the simple fact that a German critic had at last had the courage to condemn

---

[34] *Sturm und Drang*, ed. Nicolai, i. 59.

the French neo-classic style which, despite various attempts to break out in other directions, had dominated the German drama until that day and prevented it from discovering an identity of its own; to condemn it, moreover, in the name of that very authority of classical antiquity whom its practitioners most professed to revere. The 'Stürmer und Dränger' also admired Lessing for his championship of Shakespeare, even if on rather slender evidence; and though in their own experimentations it was to take a very different form, they shared his desire for a drama centred upon character and psychological realism.

The *Dramaturgie* was thus a critical work of immense importance. But nor had Lessing the playwright been idle in Hamburg. He had written for the Hamburg theatre his first mature dramatic masterpiece. He had also revised his earlier comedies for a new collected edition, extending *Der Misogyn* from one act to three. Strangely enough, while his critical attention was turning more and more to tragedy — there is in the *Dramaturgie* no elaboration of a theory of comedy comparable to that for tragedy[35] — his practical efforts were largely devoted to comedy. He seems to have worked both on *D. Faust* and *Emilia Galotti* in Hamburg, but we do not know how much progress he made; however, two new comedies reached a fairly advanced stage, though neither was completed. One is *Der Schlaftrunk*, in three acts, begun in Berlin in 1766 for a bet — as we are told by Karl Lessing — and somewhat inexplicably abandoned when more than half of it had actually been set up in type.[36] The work is a light-hearted comedy of intrigue in the old style; the first draft even uses neo-classical names, though in the final version, written no doubt after the move to Hamburg and the completion of *Minna von Barnhelm*, German ones are substituted. It may well be that Lessing abandoned it because he realized that in *Minna von Barnhelm* he had created a kind of comedy which left this earlier manner far behind. It is a light-weight piece, somewhat in the manner of *Der Misogyn*, but with rather more in the way of circumstantial realism and with neither the satirical nor the

---

[35] Some analogies are pursued by B. Duncan, 'The Implied Reader of Lessing's Theory of Comedy', *LYB* x (1978), 35-45.
[36] Cf. G ii. 785 f.

sentimental element so much developed. On the one hand, the forgetfulness of old Herr Richard and the litigiousness of Berthold are not aberrations of the order of Wumshäter's misogyny, and all the characters are essentially likeable; but on the other, there is no hint of the emotional depths present in Lelio and Laura in *Der Misogyn*, let alone in Tellheim and Minna. From Karl Lessing's account of the occasion which gave rise to the work, one might have expected something more interesting. Lessing was maintaining that any subject-matter could be turned into a tragedy or a comedy, all depending upon the dramatist's choice of treatment, and Ramler thereupon challenged him to write a comedy in which the plot hinged upon a sleeping-draught. There is nothing about *Der Schlaftrunk* that in the least suggests tragedy; but Ramler's subject (unless he was thinking of *Romeo and Juliet*) is hardly the stuff of which high tragedy is made.[37] He could well have picked one lying more obviously on the borderline between the genres.

Just such a challenge Lessing however set himself in the other comic fragment of the Hamburg years, *Die Matrone von Ephesus*: a comedy of love and death, whose setting is a tomb. The young widow Antiphila is so consumed with grief at her husband's death that she shuts herself up in the tomb with his coffin and vows to stay there till she dies. But a strange soldier appears and before very long has persuaded her to fall in love with him. In the story as told by the Roman satirist Petronius in his *Satyricon*, the couple even substitute the dead husband's body for that of a crucified captive which has been stolen while the soldier has left it unguarded. Lessing refers to the story in No. 36 of the *Dramaturgie* in connection not with the difference between tragedy and comedy, but with that between drama and narrative. This is a topic to which he returns a number of times. Drama, Lessing insists, acquires through its creation of illusion a much greater power to move us. 'Kalte Erzählung' is contrasted in No. 14 with 'theatralische Handlung'; in No. 48 it is allowed that a genius,

---

[37] In H. L. Wagner's *Kindermörderin* of 1776 (which Lessing admired: cf. below, p. 194) the heroine's downfall is sealed when she is raped while under the influence of a sleeping-draught. However, Wagner subsequently found it quite simple to rewrite his play with a happy ending: cf. *Sturm und Drang*, ed. cit., ii. 1908 ff.

such as Euripides, can mix drama and narrative for the sake of his 'höhere Absichten', but No. 77 insists that tragedy must be enacted, not narrated, if it is to achieve its proper emotional effect. Once again the point is related to the primacy of the psychological element in Lessing's view of the drama: a narrative can tell us what happens, but 'da die Illusion des Drama weit stärker ist, als einer bloßen Erzählung, so interessieren uns auch die Personen in jenem weit mehr, als in dieser' (No. 35). The converse of this is that we can tolerate or even enjoy in narration events the actual spectacle of which would be repugnant, such as the tale of the Ephesian widow, which Lessing describes as 'die bitterste Satyre, die jemals gegen den weiblichen Leichtsinn gemacht worden' (No. 36).[38] Popular though the story is, he claims that no dramatist has succeeded with it, for 'der Charakter der Matrone, der in der Erzählung ein nicht unangenehmes höhnisches Lächeln über die Vermessenheit der ehelichen Liebe erweckt, wird in dem Drama ekel und gräßlich' (ibid.).

There is undoubtedly some truth in Lessing's argument, but perhaps what is really needed for a successful dramatic treatment of the tale, with its cynical view of even the keenest human emotion and its appurtenances of coffins, corpses, and crucifixions, is simply a harsher sense of humour than Lessing's: it might work as black farce, in which we are not encouraged to take the characters seriously. For Lessing, with his strong preference for comedy with what I have called a positive affective bias and his general insistence upon convincing characterization and motivation, this is not a possible solution. The dramatist must change the story, while yet keeping it recognizable: 'Kurz, die petronische Fabel glücklich auf das Theater zu bringen, müßte sie den nämlichen Ausgang behalten, und auch nicht behalten; müßte die Matrone so weit gehen, und auch nicht so weit gehen' (No. 36). In the theatre we are bound to enter into the characters, and so they must not be shown behaving in a morally repugnant way. In fact the comic playwright's task with this subject is, we might say, the same as that of the tragic poet with that of

[38] Another example is the starving to death of Ugolino and his sons, in Dante's narrative and in Gerstenberg's play: cf. Lessing's letter to Gerstenberg of 25 February 1768.

Rodogune: faced with a story 'ebenso gräßlich als außerordentlich' (No. 32) he must strive, through his characterization, to
make moral sense of it.

How does Lessing set about this? Evidently we are to
understand Antiphila's grief at her husband's death as an
excess of which she needs to be cured, even if it is not the
kind of aberration which is usually depicted as comic: in this
it resembles Philotas's heroic patriotism. Sincere though it
may be, it is not a 'gesellschaftliche Tugend': it is morbid and
self-regarding, and in this it is also like Tellheim's self-drama-
tizing pride. As Minna rescues Tellheim (where Aridäus and
the others fail to rescue Philotas), so Philokrates the soldier
(the roles of *Minna* are reversed!) is to rescue Antiphila, to
bring her back from the tomb to life, sanity, and human
society. But perhaps Philokrates was to learn some kind of
lesson too: to come to Antiphila motivated by curiosity and
sexual desire, but to learn through the genuineness of her
emotion to recognize her worth as a person, so that between
them a love might grow which was neither exaggerated,
romantic passion nor casual, cynical sexual appetite, but a
mature affection between two rational human beings.

This we can only surmise, for we do not know how the
fragment (seven scenes) was to end. We do know from the
sketches that Lessing intended to change the grisliest feature
of Petronius' story. The substitution of the husband's body
was to be suggested by the maid Mysis, not by Antiphila
herself; and the body of the crucified captive was not to have
disappeared after all, so that the substitution would remain
merely an ingenious suggestion, in accordance with Lessing's
theory that 'bei der bloßen Möglichkeit ergötzte uns das Sinn-
reiche der Tat, bei ihrer Wirklichkeit sehen wir bloß ihre
Schwärze; der Einfall vergnügte unsern Witz, aber die Ausfüh-
rung des Einfalls empört unsere ganze Empfindlichkeit' (No.
36). But in the execution Lessing did not get as far as this;
and after the seriousness with which Antiphila and her grief
are portrayed it is hard to imagine her being convincingly
'cured' to the point even of agreeing to such a scheme. Lessing
seems here to be venturing on the dangerous path later trod-
den by Kleist in his re-working of Molière's *Amphitryon*,
where the introduction of intense emotion and serious psy-

chological probing into a comic, even farcical plot gravely threatens, indeed in the view of many readers completely destroys, the comic effect. *Die Matrone von Ephesus* is an unsuccessful experiment, its comic and serious elements unhappily juxtaposed, the result often embarrassing, much as in *Philotas* — to which, with its similar one-act form and classical décor, it bears a considerable resemblance. It marks another step, however, in Lessing's exploration of the boundaries between the genres and his evolution of a non-tragic form of serious drama.[39]

But the later numbers of the *Dramaturgie* had insisted on the maintenance of those boundaries and on the supreme excellence of the tragic form. It therefore remained for Lessing to make one more attempt at that highest of goals.

[39] The fullest discussion of *Die Matrone von Ephesus* is in M. M. Metzger, *Lessing and the Language of Comedy* (The Hague, 1966), pp. 162–87. Cf. also Schröder, *Lessing: Sprache und Drama*, pp. 292 ff.

VI

Tragedy (II): *Emilia Galotti*

(i)

Lessing arrived in Wolfenbüttel to take up his duties as ducal librarian at the beginning of May 1770. Though disillusionment was soon to set in here too, his first letters from Wolfenbüttel express pleasure and relief at the making of a new start. After the bitterness with which the venture of the 'Nationaltheater' had ended, he was particularly glad to leave the theatre behind him, and to concentrate on the antiquarian and theological studies which were increasingly claiming his attention. But the theatre would not leave him alone, as he complained to Eva König on 10 June: 'Können Sie glauben, daß Ackermann nun auch in Wolfenbüttel spielen will? . . . Mir ist es gar nicht gelegen, und ich glaube, der Teufel hat sein Spiel, daß mir die Komödie immer auf den Hacken bleibt.'

Yet even before leaving Hamburg, on 5 January of that year, he had taken the decisive step which was to lead to the completion of his last tragedy. He had written to his publisher Voss proposing a new edition of his works. It may have been Voss who suggested that the edition should include a complete volume of tragedies; certainly on 15 December 1770 he wrote encouraging Lessing to complete some of the plays which he had heard from Karl were nearly finished — *Der Schlaftrunk, Die Matrone von Ephesus*, and *D. Faust.* But from Lessing's correspondence with Ramler at the same time it appears that he had already, or possibly even earlier, conceived an idea for a new tragedy. It was to be on a subject from Roman history: the revolt of the slaves under the leadership of the gladiator Spartacus in 73–71 BC. The choice of such eminently political subject-matter, and of a historical setting, are surprising in the light of the views expressed on these matters in the *Hamburgische Dramaturgie*; but Spartacus was to be, as Lessing wrote to Ramler on 16 December 1770, a hero 'der aus andern Augen sieht, als der beste römische', and the projected play is described as an 'antityrannische Tragödie'.[1] It is another attempt, like *Philotas* and the unfinished *Kleonnis*, to combine the traditional décor of classical tragedy, and its elevated language (*Spartacus*, like *Kleonnis*, was to be in blank verse) with a more modern, humanitarian outlook or message. Unlike Philotas and unlike the traditional Roman hero, Spartacus was to be a hero inspired by 'Menschenliebe'. Lessing's model in this seems to have been the French dramatist Bernard-Joseph Saurin's *Spartacus* of 1760, in which the author, while trying to revive the Cornelian style of tragedy, sought also to imbue it with a spirit more acceptable to his own age, portraying 'un Héros humain et vertueux'.[2] Lessing asked Voss to send him a copy of Saurin's play and borrowed (without acknowledgment) an idea from it for the articulation of his plot: Spartacus was to hold captive the daughter of his chief enemy, the consul Crassus. But Lessing was unable to finish his play, and only the merest scraps survive.[3] Perhaps the devising of a suitable plot was the difficulty — or perhaps Lessing thought that Spartacus was after all an admirable rather than a pitiable character. At all events, if Voss was to have his volume of tragedies — on 1 December 1771 Lessing wrote assuring him 'daß es mir mit dem Bande Tragödien Ernst ist' — then something else would have to take its place.

The answer was indeed found in the completion of an earlier project, one which is first recorded in a letter to Nicolai of 21 January 1758. Like *Spartacus* and the earlier *Das befreite Rom*, it was on a subject from Roman history, but in this case transposed into modern dress. The letter to Nicolai dates from the aftermath of Nicolai's competition for the best German tragedy, when Lessing was still trying to persuade Nicolai not to give the prize to Cronegk's *Codrus*. A certain young

---

[1]   The latter phrase may have originated with Ramler rather than with Lessing: in a letter to Lessing of 15 December 1770, J. A. Ebert expresses puzzlement at the expression, occurring in a letter of Ramler's to Lessing which Lessing had forwarded to him (LM xix. 423).

[2]   Quoted by M. Mühle, *Bernard-Joseph Saurin. Sein Leben und seine Werke* (Dresden, 1913), p. 65. Cf. also H. C. Lancaster, *French Tragedy in the Time of Louis XIV and Voltaire* (Baltimore, 1950), pp. 317 ff.

[3]   G ii. 574-7.

tragedian of his acquaintance, Lessing writes, is working on
something which is sure to be better:

Sein jetziges Sujet ist eine bürgerliche Virginia, der er den Titel *Emilia
Galotti* gegeben. Er hat nämlich die Geschichte der römischen Virginia
von allem dem abgesondert, was sie für den ganzen Staat interessant
machte; er hat geglaubt, daß das Schicksal einer Tochter, die von ihrem
Vater umgebracht wird, dem ihre Tugend werter ist, als ihr Leben, für
sich schon tragisch genug, und fähig genug sei, die ganze Seele zu erschüttern, wenn auch gleich kein Umsturz der ganzen Staatsverfassung
darauf folgte. Seine Anlage ist nur von drei Akten, und er braucht ohne
Bedenken alle Freiheiten der englischen Bühne.

The story of Virginius (Verginius) and his daughter is to be
found in Book III, Chapters 14 ff. of Livy's history of Rome.
The decemvir Appius Claudius attempted to seduce the
daughter of the centurion Virginius, and when she resisted his
advances, got his henchman Marcus Claudius to claim her as
his slave, the claim being heard in court by Appius himself.
The girl's fiancé Icilius, then her father pleaded to no avail;
Appius pronounced in favour of Claudius. Then Virginius, obtaining leave for a few words with his daughter in private,
seized a butcher's knife and stabbed her to the heart, crying
out 'Thus, my daughter, in the only way I can, I maintain
your freedom!' and 'Upon you, Appius, and upon your head
be this blood!' Livy goes on to relate the subsequent upsurge
of popular feeling, the threatened mutiny of Virginius' fellow-
soldiers, and the Senate's response: the decemvirs were removed from power and the safeguards of liberty and of
plebeian rights which they had overridden were restored and
strengthened. Appius was thrown into prison, where rather
than await judgement he committed suicide; but Marcus
Claudius was spared at the instance of Virginius himself,
and went into exile.

The point of Livy's story is plainly political — the abuse of
power leading to its forfeiture — and the 'pathetic but honour-
able' (*miseram sed honestam*) death of Virginia is presented as
the occasion for the political revolution, just as are the rape
of Lucretia by Tarquin and her subsequent suicide in the very
similar story of *Das befreite Rom.* Earlier dramatizations of
the story which Lessing knew, by the Frenchman Campistron

(1683), the Spaniard Montiano (1750), the Englishman Crisp (1754), and the German Patzke (1755)[4] all stress the political element. Patzke in his preface, in an argument which seems to be echoed in Lessing's letter to Nicolai, points out that the story contains in fact two tragic actions ('Der Tod der Virginia, oder die durch das Laster unterdrückte Unschuld, und der Tod des Appius, oder das von der Tyranney befreyte Rom'), and says that he himself, having chosen 'die rührende Begebenheit der Virginia' for the tragic focus of his play, has therefore suppressed the political consequences of her death: 'Virginia stirbt hier, ohne daß Rom unmittelbar gerächet wird.'[5] But he retains the background of political unrest and the role of Icilius as an active political opponent of Appius. These elements Lessing completely removes; and of the finished *Emilia Galotti* he again declares, in a letter of 1 March 1772 to his brother Karl, 'Du siehst wohl, daß es weiter nichts, als eine modernisierte, von allem Staatsinteresse befreite Virginia sein soll.' It is however noteworthy that he does not refer to the completed play as a 'bürgerliches Trauerspiel'; indeed, in the *Trauerspiele* of 1772 *Miß Sara Sampson* is no longer so designated either., After his initial innovatory experiment with the earlier work, Lessing was, as we have seen, more concerned with the essentials of the tragic genre than with particular sub-forms or variants.

What sent Lessing back to *Emilia Galotti* rather than to any other of his hitherto unfinished projects we can only guess; he may have been reminded of it by the coincidence that Crassus' daughter, in Saurin's *Spartacus*, is called Émilie. Lessing's last attempt to write something approaching straight classical tragedy had failed; his critical explorations in the *Dramaturgie* had suggested that, whatever its shortcomings, contemporary

---

[4] Lessing published a lengthy synopsis of Montiano's play in the *Theatralische Bibliothek* (LM vi. 70–120), began a translation of Crisp's (G ii. 708), and reviewed Patzke's (G iii. 257). *Emilia Galotti* shares with Campistron's *Virginie* two substantial departures from the story as told by Livy and treated by the other dramatists: the heroine's mother is still alive (in Livy etc. Virginius is a widower) and her fiancé is a nobleman, not a plebeian. On the sources of *Emilia Galotti*, see G. Kettner, *Lessings Dramen im Lichte ihrer und unserer Zeit* (Berlin, 1904), pp. 185–93, but he does not mention Patzke.

[5] J. S. Patzke, *Virginia* (Frankfurt and Leipzig, 1755), p. 8 f. Cf. my article 'Patzke's *Virginia*', *NGS* viii (1980), 19–27.

domestic middle-class realism was perhaps after all the most satisfactory dramatic medium for his own age. The medium was one he knew he could handle, being that in which he had achieved his one real dramatic masterpiece to date — albeit a comedy rather than a tragedy; and as with *Miß Sara Sampson* the use of a story from classical antiquity provided a certain amount of pedigree. The work was speedily completed and dispatched to Berlin in instalments, the last section of the manuscript accompanying the corrected proofs of the first printed signatures. The volume of tragedies duly appeared, and *Emilia Galotti* was reprinted three times in the course of 1772. On 13 March of that year it received its first performance, by the Döbbelin troupe in Brunswick, to celebrate the birthday of the Duchess, consort of Lessing's employer. Lessing himself was absent, pleading toothache[6]; he never did attend a production of the play.

In a letter to Karl of 10 February 1772, Lessing stated that he had not been able to use the original plan because it was only in three acts, nor the version on which he had worked in Hamburg because it was intended for performance rather than publication. These comments suggest a desire that the play which was to complete the volume of tragedies should conform to rigorous and fairly conservative stylistic norms. In accordance with this, we note that the 'Freiheiten der englischen Bühne', proclaimed in the original letter to Nicolai with an enthusiasm adumbrating that of the seventeenth *Literaturbrief*, are largely absent from the finished work. But Nicolai, who had seen and discussed the earlier plan with Lessing in Berlin, claimed that its basic outline could still be discerned in the completed play.[7] And there seems no reason to doubt that in returning to the theme Lessing retained his original affective intention: to exclude the political element, dominant in *Codrus* but never congenial to him; perhaps to go one better than Patzke, and to present a domestic catastrophe which would arouse pity unmixed with admiration. As he had originally conceived *Emilia Galotti* in 1758 as a model tragedy exemplifying the theory of the genre which he had worked out in the correspondence with Mendelssohn and

---

[6]   Cf. his letter to Eva König, 15 March 1772.   [7]   D 194.

Nicolai, so the completed *Emilia Galotti* of 1772 may be regarded as a model tragedy exemplifying (even if not written
specifically in order to exemplify) that theory as it had been
further developed and refined — but not radically modified —
in the *Hamburgische Dramaturgie.*

We saw that in the *Dramaturgie* Lessing argues that the
playwright should create a coherent and comprehensible
stage-world as an image of the coherent world created by
divine Providence; should people that stage-world with characters who can command the sympathetic identification of the
spectators — neither paragons of virtue nor monsters of depravity; and should reinforce this identification by conveying
the characters' thoughts and feelings in simple, unaffected,
natural language. To all these matters he has in *Emilia Galotti*
devoted intense care.

The plot is constructed with masterly precision and
economy. The cast is the same size as in *Miß Sara Sampson,*
but there are no mere confidants: every character (with the
possible exception of Rota) plays a vital part in the action,
instigating, advancing, retarding, or deflecting its course. As
in a typical comic plot,[8] much of the mechanical intrigue is
left to the servants: Appiani is murdered by Marinelli's agent
Angelo acting on information extracted from the Galottis'
servant Pirro. But this is only a subordinate part of the action.
The killing-off of the fiancé is of course a departure of Lessing's
from the original story; nor is it found in any of the earlier
dramatizations.[9] Some have thought it dramatically a mistake,
introducing as it does a subsidiary climax in the middle of the
play after which the pace of the action slows appreciably.
Variation of pace is of course an important element in
dramatic effect; moreover, the shock of Appiani's death and
the subsequent slowing of the action contribute importantly
to the increasing psychological tension of the play's second
half. It is however true that the two halves have rather different theatrical styles. The first is more reminiscent of

[8]   K.-D. Müller, 'Das Erbe der Komödie im bürgerlichen Trauerspiel: Lessings
Emilia Galotti und die commedia dell' arte', *DVJS* xlvi (1972), 28–60, interprets
the whole play in terms of a systematic (though not necessarily conscious) inver-
sion of standard comic formulae.

[9]   Cf. F. O. Nolte, 'Voltaire's *Mahomet* as a source of Lessing's *Nathan der
Weise* and *Emilia Galotti*', *MLN* xlviii (1933), 152–6.

comedy, with its numerous subordinate figures and its two changes of scene, the second more typical of classical tragedy with its concentration on the principals (save for the *coup de théâtre* of Orsina's unexpected appearance) and its unchanging location.

The changes of scene are strictly functional: we can regard the play as keeping the unity of place, generously interpreted, as the whole action takes place within the Prince's domain; there is a world outside, represented by Sabionetta and beyond it Appiani's estates in Piedmont, but from that world the action is decisively and fatally isolated. We meet the Prince on his own ground, then Emilia on hers, then they are brought together in a third place, a place where the Prince is seen, so to speak, in his private rather than in his public capacity — his 'Lustschloß' — but in which princely power is still ultimately decisive. The unity of time is also fairly closely observed, and this too — the Prince's discovery that this very day his hopes regarding Emilia are to be confounded by her marriage and her removal from his dominions — makes an essential contribution to the play's psychological atmosphere and to the functioning of the plot: hasty, improvised, ill-considered action, generally with results other than those intended, is one of its most striking features, we may even say one of its themes.

In space and time and in other elements of Lessing's dramatic mechanism there are a good many of what may appear from the point of view of literal verisimilitude to be improbable coincidences: the fact that Dosalo is on the way to Sabionetta, the fact that Conti happens on this day of all days to bring Emilia Galotti's portrait to the palace with him, the fact that Marinelli's henchmen have an accomplice, albeit a reluctant one, in the Galotti household, the fact that the Prince hasn't read Orsina's letter and the consequent surprise of her arrival at Dosalo. But Orsina herself tells us that 'nichts unter der Sonne ist Zufall' (IV, 3). In Lessing's view it was the dramatist's business *not* to leave the kind of loose ends which are apparent to a partial or superficial view of reality: everything must be made to fit. Though the dramatist's work must be truthful, even realistic, he must not adopt crudely mimetic standards of plausibility, nor must he be judged by them.

The external mechanisms of Lessing's play are thus very carefully designed. But, in accordance with his theories, much more importance is to be attached to the psychological portrayal of the characters; and it is here that he has most significantly modified his source-material.

In the *Dramaturgie* Lessing tells us that the tragic protagonist should be 'mit uns von gleichem Schrot und Korne'. Though this is not necessarily to be taken socially, in fact the Galottis are of the middle class, albeit fairly elevated. Odoardo holds a high military rank, which was not very usual for a commoner at the time, and Emilia is to marry a nobleman, who is of course portrayed sympathetically. However, even the Prince is no villainous, bloodthirsty tyrant; the puritanical Odoardo's characterization of him as a 'Wollüstling' (II, 4) is an exaggeration. He is a sensitive, cultivated man, who would rather attend to his private inclinations (art, love) than his public duties — not in itself an unsympathetic trait in Lessing's eyes, as we saw in Aridäus — and whose attraction to Emilia is not merely sexual (though it would be foolish to deny its libidinous component) but, like Mellefont's attraction to Sara Sampson, betokens a potential preference for the simple, natural and uncorrupted way of life of the bourgeoisie over the artificial constraints of court life, the affectations of the 'Zirkel der ersten Häuser', and the conversation of an Orsina (I, 6).[10] Orsina herself is deserving of our pity: she is not a moral monster like Marwood, and if she is a shade mad, that in itself, as Odoardo observes, makes her worthy of 'Mitleid' and even 'Hochachtung' (IV, 7). And Marinelli, even if the Prince in the play's closing words does rhetorically describe him as a devil, is not really an 'Erzbösewicht' like the 'schwarzer Verführer' of Lessing's modernized Faust drama. True, there is not much we can sympathize with in Marinelli (though his dry wit often amuses and therefore in some measure attracts); but he is not a figure of gratuitous evil, for his conduct and motivation are perfectly comprehensible. His livelihood depends upon his serving the Prince, and indeed on making his services indispensable (one reason for his insistence

---

[10] Some critics have regarded the Prince as the real protagonist of the play: cf. J. Schmidt, 'Lessing', in R. von Gottschall (ed.), *Der neue Plutarch*, xi (Leipzig, 1885), p. 315. Brüggemann (B 108) describes him as a 'tragische Figur'.

on the Prince's taking no initiatives of his own); he seeks to
turn the situation to his own advantage as best he can, but he
is not simply a melodramatic villain.

If the play's basically unsympathetic characters are not
presented as all black, nor are the sympathetic characters all
white: all have their flaws. Claudia, with her social ambitions,
is the most obvious example. Appiani, noble and worthy
young man that he is, full of lofty sentiments, is in danger of
being paralysed by the brooding introspection so strikingly
portrayed in II, 7, even in the gait with which he enters. He is
the kind of man who is only capable of resolute action when
his 'Blut ist in Wallung geraten', as it is after the quarrel with
Marinelli (II, 11).The same is even truer of Odoardo: a man
of high moral principles (and, unlike the melancholic Appiani,
all too prone to outbursts of moral indignation) but incapable
at the critical moment of translating them into action. Emilia
herself, innocent, loyal, and virtuous as she is, is not without
her failings. Too readily she gives in to her mother's advice in
II, 6 not·to tell her father or Appiani of the incident with the
Prince in church. And though, as Claudia says, 'die Furcht-
samste und Entschlossenste unsers Geschlechts', though able
in the short term to deal with the Prince's advances (IV, 8),
she knows that she has a sensual side to her own nature and
that she will not be able indefinitely to resist its promptings:
'Ich habe Blut, mein Vater; so jugendliches, so warmes Blut,
als eine. Auch meine Sinne, sind Sinne. Ich stehe für nichts.
Ich bin für nichts gut . . .' (V, 7).

The characters of the play are thus all imperfect human
beings, with good and bad qualities in varying proportion,
with whom the spectators can in varying measure identify
themselves. They are perceived and drawn with a high degree
of psychological realism, and Lessing has taken great pains to
make the action proceed inevitably from the interrelation of
these characters within the closed system of space, time, and
causality which he has created. He has also been at great pains
to ensure that the pity we feel for them is unmixed with the
admiration evoked by heroic tragedy.

The Roman Virginius is plainly the victim of a tragic
necessity: he is forced to choose between two equally repugnant alternatives, his daughter's death and her otherwise inevit-

able degradation. In this situation, he deserves our pity: in his ability to make the choice and do the deed, he demonstrates his moral autonomy and thereby earns our admiration. The tragic paradox is well summed up in the words of Virginius in Campistron's play:

> Et que tout l'Univers, sachant que je suis père,
> Admire mon courage, et plaigne ma misère. (V, 7)

But for Lessing this will not do: we are not to be permitted to admire the tragic hero, but only to pity him. The deed remains, like Cléopâtre's in *Rodogune*, an 'unwahrscheinliches Verbrechen', and this judgement could only be reinforced if it were seen as the outcome of a free moral choice. Whatever supposed moral imperative had dictated his action, Odoardo would appear a 'kalter Mörder seiner Tochter' like Aristodemus (*Kleonnis*, l. 159). His killing of his daughter must rather be seen, like Lucas's killing of his father in *Der Horoscop*, as an act of unwilled necessity.[11]

The role of Emilia has also been rendered more complex than that of the totally innocent Virginia. As we have noted, her latent sensuality renders her vulnerable to attack (this is much more precisely articulated than Sara's falling for Mellefont), and she herself compounds the danger by following her mother's unwise advice in II, 6. But this is not all. At the climax of the play it is she who takes over the active role: Lessing makes her actually provoke her hesitant, unwilling, and helpless father into killing her.[12] In the completed play it is not so much Odoardo as Emilia herself to whom 'ihre Tugend werter ist als ihr Leben'. But if this is so, does this not make *her* an unacceptable tragic protagonist, a 'schönes Ungeheuer' like Philotas? In the *Hamburgische Dramaturgie* (No. 1) Lessing had condemned the eagerness for death of Christian martyrs like the protagonists of Cronegk's *Olint und Sophronia*; and he reminded Karl in his letter of 10 February 1772 that he did not care for 'die jungfräulichen Heroinen und Philoso-

---

[11] Cf. Enders, op. cit., esp. p. 213.

[12] This is to some extent anticipated in Crisp's play, where Virginius hesitates, but is confirmed in his original intention by Virginia's resolve to die; more strongly in Campistron's, where Virginius fails to strike and his daughter actually guides his hand.

phinnen' — an apt description of the eloquently stoical
Virginias of Campistron, Montiano, Crisp, and Patzke. (In Livy,
of course, Virginia herself says not a word.) If Emilia's death
is the result of her free moral choice rather than Odoardo's,
that makes it no less an 'unwahrscheinliches Verbrechen'.

Indeed, free moral choice, like patriotism, was the kind of
heroic luxury which Lessing felt happy to do without. A few
years after the completion of *Emilia Galotti*, in his commentary on Karl Wilhelm Jerusalem's essay on the freedom of the
will, Lessing wrote:

> was verlieren wir, wenn man uns die Freiheit abspricht? Etwas — wenn
> es Etwas ist — was wir nicht brauchen; was wir weder zu unserer Tätig-
> keit hier, noch zu unserer Glückseligkeit dort brauchen. Etwas, dessen
> Besitz weit unruhiger und besorgter machen müßte, als das Gefühl seines
> Gegenteils nimmermehr machen kann. — Zwang und Notwendigkeit,
> nach welchen die Vorstellung des Besten wirket, wie viel willkommner
> sind sie mir, als kahle Vermögenheit, unter den nämlichen Umständen
> bald so, bald anders handeln zu können! Ich danke dem Schöpfer, daß
> ich *muß*; das *Beste* muß.[13]

The dramatist's highest task is to create an image of the moral
design of the universe. Human beings are not free agents, and
any attempt to execute their own designs, good or ill, will —
as we are reminded at every twist and turn of the plot of
Emilia Galotti — be rewarded with frustration and possibly
with tragedy. Controlling all is a Providence which we must
assume to be working for the best. It does not however intervene arbitrarily in individuals' lives, but works internally,
through their characters. This means that the tragic necessity
which operates in this play is not ultimately moral — in the
sense of a compulsion to moral choice — but psychological,
and that the characters' moral aims and attitudes are to be
seen in the light of their general psychological dispositions
and of their mental and emotional states at given moments.

Nowhere is this more crucial than in the climactic scene in
which father and daughter appear on stage together for the
first and only time. The catastrophe is brought about by the
interaction of their characters, attitudes, and states of mind
in a situation of profound emotional, moral, and psychological

[13] G viii. 448 f. On Jerusalem, cf. below, p. 181, and H. Schneider, *Lessing.
Zwölf biographische Studien* (Munich, 1951), pp. 94–109.

stress. Everything that goes before is designed to lead up to this final confrontation: the first four acts are in effect, as in a tragedy by Racine, nothing but a protracted exposition. Act I introduces us to the Prince and Marinelli and the relations between the Prince and the Galottis, and gives us our first hint of the character of Odoardo: 'Ein alter Degen; stolz und rauh; sonst bieder und gut!' (I, 4). Act II shows us the Galottis and their vulnerability: the corruption of their servants, the confusion into which Emilia has been thrown, the weakness of those whose duty it is to protect her — her mother, her fiancé, even (already at this stage) her father, who comes rushing in full of slightly hysterical, even if in fact all too justified, anxiety, takes a quick look and utters a few stern moral pronouncements, and then rushes off again. In Act III the first of Emilia's protectors is removed, and she is brought face to face with the Prince. After this, other protectors appear, one by one: first Claudia, then Orsina — an unlikely, but through their very rivalry, a potential ally for Emilia against the Prince's designs — and finally Odoardo. Orsina's decisive contribution to the mechanics of the action is, of course, to furnish Odoardo with the fatal dagger. For characteristically — quick to react and to strike a moral posture, but ill-equipped to put any decision into practice — he has come unarmed:

Da steh' ich nun vor der Höhle des Räubers — (*Indem er den Rock von beiden Seiten aus einander schlägt, und sich ohne Gewehr sieht*) Wunder, daß ich aus Eilfertigkeit nicht auch die Hände zurück gelassen! (IV, 7)

And from this point on the motif of Odoardo's hand, the hand which is ultimately to execute the fatal design, recurs with mounting insistence.

Sending the women back to town, Odoardo now assumes total responsibility for Emilia: 'Bleibt der Vater nicht in der Nähe?' (IV, 8). Orsina's intention was presumably that he should use the dagger to kill the Prince; but the next time we meet him, he seems firmly to have rejected any such idea:

Und doch ließ ich mich fortreißen: und von wem? Von einer Eifersüchtigen; von einer für Eifersucht Wahnwitzigen. — Was hat die gekränkte Tugend mit der Rache des Lasters zu schaffen? Jene allein hab' ich zu retten. (V, 2)

But despite a characteristic display of moral indignation, he
has no idea what he is actually going to do; and his repeated
resolve to keep calm and cool is each time rapidly forgotten
(V, 2; V, 4). Seeing his intentions so easily defeated by Marinelli's schemings, he almost yields to the impulse to use the
dagger after all — but once again draws back (V, 5). It now
dawns on him that the only remaining possibility is to kill
Emilia; but *this too he rejects*, abandoning now all hope of
action and leaving Emilia to the mercy of Providence:

— Da denk' ich so was: So was, was sich nur denken läßt. — Gräßlich!
Fort, fort! Ich will sie nicht erwarten. Nein! — (*Gegen den Himmel*)
Wer sie unschuldig in diesen Abgrund gestürzt hat, der ziehe sie wieder
heraus. Was braucht er meine Hand dazu? Fort! (*Er will gehen, und
sieht Emilien kommen*) Zu spät! Ah! er will meine Hand; er will sie!
(V, 6)

It is in truth Odoardo's hand which must perform the fatal
deed. But even now he will only act, like Appiani, when his
blood is 'in Wallung geraten': he strikes the blow only as a
result of repeated and increasingly desperate provocation
from Emilia herself. As Claudia has said, Emilia is 'die Furcht-
samste und Entschlossenste unsers Geschlechts. Ihrer ersten
Eindrücke nie mächtig; aber nach der geringsten Überlegung,
in alles sich findend, auf alles gefaßt' (IV, 8). Odoardo cannot
act calmly and rationally; Emilia has — for the moment — no
difficulty in being calm and rational, but her acceptance of
the necessity of 'ruhig sein' (V, 7) is dependent upon her con-
fidence that her father will now take her away:

Den wenn der Graf tot ist; wenn er darum tot ist — darum! was ver-
weilen wir noch hier? Lassen Sie uns fliehen, mein Vater!   (V, 7)

Her response to the discovery that this cannot be, that she is
to remain in den Händen [des] Räubers', is articulated in a
crescendo of indignation and determination to assert her will:

Ich allein in seinen Händen? — Nimmermehr, mein Vater. — Oder Sie
sind nicht mein Vater. — Ich allein in seinen Händen? — Gut, lassen Sie
mich nur; lassen Sie mich nur. — Ich will doch sehn, wer mich hält, —
wer mich zwingt, — wer der Mensch ist, der einen Menschen zwingen
kann ... was nennen Sie ruhig sein? Die Hände in den Schoß legen? Leiden, was man nicht sollte? Dulden, was man nicht dürfte? ... Reißt mich?

bringt mich? — Will mich reißen; will mich bringen: will, will! Als ob
wir keinen Willen hätten, mein Vater!   (ibid.)

Here we are reminded of Odoardo's outburst in V, 4: 'Wer
will das? Wer darf das? — Der hier alles darf, was er will?'
And similarly, Emilia's indignation is not to be taken as a sign
of moral strength, but rather of weakness — or, at any rate,
of extreme mental and emotional confusion: it reveals her
reaction to the final and crucial blow to fall upon her, the
realization that her father has failed her. 'Ich allein in seinen
Händen? — Nimmermehr, mein Vater. — Oder Sie sind nicht
mein Vater.'[14] Now it is she who determines upon death, and
Odoardo who seeks to prevent her, dissuading her from killing
herself with the hairpin ('Was? Dahin wär' es gekommen?
Nicht doch; nicht doch! Besinne dich') and then snatching
from her the dagger which, as if mesmerized, he has allowed
her to coax from him the moment before ('Sieh, wie rasch! —
Nein, das ist nicht für deine Hand'). Then there comes another
crescendo, this time of despair and disillusion at her abandonment by the man on whom all her hopes were pinned and
from whom all her ideals were drawn:

Es ist wahr, mit einer Haarnadel soll ich — (*Sie fährt mit der Hand nach
dem Haare, eine zu suchen, und bekömmt die Rose zu fassen*) Du noch
hier? — Herunter mit dir! Du gehörest nicht in das Haar einer, — wie
mein Vater will, daß ich werden soll! . . . Ehedem wohl gab es einen
Vater, der seine Tochter von der Schande zu retten, ihr den ersten den
besten Stahl in das Herz senkte — ihr zum zweiten das Leben gab. Aber
alle solche Taten sind von ehedem! Solcher Väter gibt es keinen mehr!
                    (ibid.)

And it is this reproach which at last stings Odoardo into a
typically hasty action — which he immediately regrets:

Doch, meine Tochter, doch! (*indem er sie durchsticht*) Gott, was hab'
ich getan!   (ibid.)

Emilia's reply, 'Eine Rose gebrochen, ehe der Sturm sie entblättert', seems an expression of gratitude and joy: if the play
were to end here, we might well admire her as a martyr.[15]

---

[14] Cf. my essay, 'Eine bürgerliche Virginia', *GLL* NS xvii (1964), 304–12.
[15] In Crisp's play Virginius speaks similar words over his daughter's body:
'Sweet hapless flow'r!/Untimely cropt by the fell planter's hand!'

But in their final exchanges father and daughter seem rather
to be anxious each to relieve the other of responsibility for a
crime:

> DER PRINZ. Grausamer Vater, was haben Sie getan?
> ODOARDO. Eine Rose gebrochen, ehe der Sturm sie entblättert. — War
> es nicht so, meine Tochter?
> EMILIA. Nicht Sie, mein Vater — Ich selbst — ich selbst —
> ODOARDO. Nicht du, meine Tochter; — nicht du! — Gehe mit keiner
> Unwahrheit aus der Welt. Nicht du, meine Tochter! Dein Vater, dein
> unglücklicher Vater!   (V, 8)

And it is indeed as a crime that Odoardo in his final speech
describes what he has done, and as a criminal that he demands
to be judged — not as a 'tragic hero' in the traditional mould,
or even in the mould of a Mellefont:

> Aber Sie erwarten, wo das alles hinaus soll? Sie erwarten vielleicht, daß
> ich den Stahl wider mich selbst kehren werde, um meine Tat wie eine
> schale Tragödie zu beschließen. — Sie irren sich. Hier! (*indem er ihm
> den Dolch vor die Füße wirft*) Hier liegt er, der blutige Zeuge meines
> Verbrechens! Ich gehe und liefere mich selbst in das Gefängnis. Ich gehe,
> und erwarte Sie, als Richter. — Und dann dort — erwarte ich Sie vor
> dem Richter unser aller!   (ibid.)

It does however look as though Odoardo expects to be judged
with mercy, if not in this world then at all events in the next.
And indeed the 'Richter unser aller' must surely judge
Odoardo technically guilty but not morally responsible — and
the same verdict must be passed on Emilia too. This is the
very opposite of Schiller's Maria Stuart, with her 'Gott wür-
digt mich, durch diesen unverdienten Tod/Die frühe, schwere
Blutschuld abzubüßen'[16] — technically innocent, but a free
and therefore responsible (responsible, and therefore free)
moral agent. But Lessing has here moved beyond the position
of making and inviting moral judgements on his characters and
their actions, as he did in *Miß Sara Sampson* and apparently,
though with fatally damaging ambiguity, in *Philotas*. Different
though his tragic vision is from Schiller's, it is in its paradoxicality a truly tragic vision none the less.

The language of the play, as our examples will have shown,

---

[16] Schiller, *Maria Stuart*, 1. 3735 f.

is a simple, natural but not over-colloquial prose, closely akin to that of the Banks translation in the *Dramaturgie*. Karl commented on this when he read the manuscript, writing to his brother on 3 February 1772, 'In Deiner Emilia Galotti herrscht ein Ton, den ich in keiner Tragödie, so viel ich deren gelesen, gefunden habe: ein Ton, der nicht das Trauerspiel erniedrigt, sondern nur so herunterstimmt, daß es ganz natürlich wird, und desto leichter Eingang in unsere Empfindungen erhält.'

The play begins with broken, elliptical utterances — as had *Miß Sara Sampson*; but whereas the earlier work had very soon abandoned simplicity and psychological realism for elaborate rhetoric, Lessing sustains throughout *Emilia Galotti* a language appropriate to his individual characters and their states of mind. The variations of the Prince's speech in particular would repay close study: obviously a man capable of formal and polished utterance, he is more often shown to us as distracted, following associative rather than logical trains of thought, as in the opening monologue; as absent-minded, not listening to Conti (I, 4) or fully taking in what Rota is saying (I, 8); or as helplessly confused, as in his conversations with Marinelli or in his embarrassed and maladroit speech of 'welcome' to Emilia in III, 5 (this, incidentally, is the longest speech in the whole play). Careful, polished prose is more typically reserved for other characters, and with them too it is significantly varied: cool, rational, and detached in Marinelli, more intense and emotional in Emilia and Appiani. The latter is sometimes sententious and, we may feel, excessively analytical in a way which recalls the characters of *Miß Sara Sampson*; but here this kind of language is used not indiscriminately, for general, undifferentiated, and hence unconvincing emotional intensification, but as a precise instrument of psychological delineation:

Ach meine Mutter, und Sie können das von Ihrem Sohne argwohnen? — Aber, es ist wahr; ich bin heut' ungewöhnlich trübe und finster. — Nur sehen Sie, gnädige Frau; — noch Einen Schritt vom Ziele, oder noch gar nicht ausgelaufen sein, ist im Grunde eines. — Alles was ich sehe, alles was ich höre, alles was ich träume, prediget mir seit gestern und ehegestern diese Wahrheit. Dieser Eine Gedanke kettet sich an jeden andern, den ich haben muß und haben will. — Was ist das? Ich versteh' es nicht.

(II, 8)

Odoardo speaks a more heated version of Appiani's language, Orsina a more heated version of Marinelli's. In all these figures, language is an essential part of character. Indeed, many of these people strike us as *talkers*, in a significant sense (not undifferentiatedly, as in *Miß Sara Sampson*): notably Odoardo, Appiani, and Orsina (evidently Lessing found a 'Philosophin' (IV, 3) acceptable in a relatively minor role!),[17] together with Conti, who is ready to give a lecture on Art at the drop of a hat. But the enormous speeches of *Miß Sara Sampson* are gone, though there are a number of monologues, skilfully used for reflection and self-revelation: more than twice as many as in the earlier play, in fact, though nowhere approaching them in length. Rhetorical ornament is used sparingly: Emilia's dream of pearls (II, 7) is presented with much greater psychological plausibility than is Sara's more elaborately prophetic dream (*Miß Sara Sampson*, I, 7), and her final 'Eine Rose gebrochen, ehe der Sturm sie entblättert', obvious and familiar symbol though it is, is rendered convincing by its integration with a piece of realistic stage-business (the rose in her hair).[18] Similarly, the pathetic, rhetorical outburst with which the Prince concludes the play is entirely in character: a typical piece of self-deception. There are only a few instances in the play of purely decorative rhetoric, such as Claudia's 'Was kümmert es die Löwin, der man die Jungen geraubet, in wessen Walde sie brüllet?' in III, 8; or of the slightly awkward use of 'witty' language in a context of tragic emotion, such as Odoardo's 'Ha, Frau, das ist wider die Abrede. Sie wollten mich um den Verstand bringen: und Sie brechen mir das Herz', to Orsina in IV, 7.[19]

Curiously, the language of the servants is rather less realistically differentiated than that of their masters; it tends to be stylized like that of the servants in comedy. This is particularly noticeable in the scene between Pirro and Angelo (II, 3): it begins with a typical comic servant's complaint — the very faintest echo of the porter in *Macbeth* complaining of the

[17] Cf. Staiger, op. cit., p. 44.
[18] On the increased importance of stage action in *Emilia Galotti*, cf. O. Mann, *Lessing: Sein und Leistung* (Hamburg, 1948), p. 258 f. (revised edn., Hamburg 1961, pp. 252 ff.).
[19] On this scene, cf. Schröder, *Lessing: Sprache und Drama*, pp. 191 ff.; also Staiger, op. cit., pp. 38–60.

knocking at Hell-gate — after which a good deal of expository information is got through, with great economy but with rather less concern for linguistic or psychological plausibility. But though the servants in *Emilia Galotti* are plainly descended from the servants of traditional comedy, they are not used for comic effect. Thus Pirro is in origin a stock comic character — the amiable rogue of a servant — but is here metamorphosed into a wholly serious realistic equivalent, the old crook trying to go straight but finding his past catching up on him with disastrous consequences. Nor is it any part of Lessing's intention to make socio-linguistic distinctions between masters and servants: the servants are functional to the plot and so too is the stylized economy of their dialogue. Neither with the principals nor with the servants does Lessing make any attempt to imitiate linguistic idiosyncrasy for its own sake, such as we find in the drama of the 'Sturm und Drang': the archaisms and vulgarisms of *Götz von Berlichingen*, the Jewish dialect of Lenz's *Die Soldaten* and 'Maler' Müller's *Faust*, the malapropisms of Frau Miller and the 'Was?' of the foppish Hofmarschall in *Kabale und Liebe*. These belong to the kind of superficial, over-particular realism he rejected. The language of the play is an integral part of its total design, almost always precisely and functionally related to action and to characterization.

(ii)

All this is very finely calculated. But calculated, in a negative rather than a positive sense, has seemed to many critics of the play an all too appropriate word. 'Und was ist denn nun diese bewunderte und gewiß bewundrungswürdige "Emilia Galotti"?' wrote Friedrich Schlegel in his essay on Lessing in 1797; 'Unstreitig ein großes Exempel der dramatischen Algebra.'[20] Goethe had already expressed a similar view in a letter to Herder as early as July 1772:

Emilia Galotti ist auch nur gedacht, und nicht einmal Zufall oder Caprice spinnen irgend drein. Mit halbweg Menschenverstand kann man das

---

[20] B 25. This and other early critical comments on the play are also quoted in G ii. 709 ff.

Warum von jeder Szene, von jedem Wort, möcht ich sagen, auffinden.
Drum bin ich dem Stück nicht gut, so ein Meisterstück es sonst ist.

Everything, Goethe and Schlegel are saying, is worked out
with admirable skill to achieve the desired effect; every scene,
every word, fits together in a flawless design; yet the play
lacks the immediacy of life and therewith of true poetic inspiration. Some have however criticized the play from a different point of view: the motivation, on which Lessing has
clearly, in accordance with his theories, lavished immense
care, and which Goethe and Schlegel, even if reluctantly,
concede to be flawless, these others have found implausible
and even incomprehensible, and they have found it impossible
to agree on what to Goethe and Schlegel seemed all too obvious, namely, Lessing's true dramatic intention. Many have
taken exception to the sensual weakness Lessing imputes to
his heroine: this criticism too dates back to the year of the
play's appearance, to Matthias Claudius, who wrote in his
well-known Hamburg weekly, the *Wandsbecker Bote*, on 15
April 1772:

Eines kann ich mir in diesem Augenblick nicht recht auflösen, wie nämlich die Emilia sozusagen bei der Leiche ihres Appiani an die Verführung
eines andern und dabei an ihr warmes Blut denken konnte. Mich dünkt,
ich hätte in ihrer Stelle halb nacket durch ein Heer der wollüstigsten
Teufel gehen wollen, und keiner hätte es wagen sollen, mich anzurühren.

Others down to our own day have shared these essentially
moralistic reservations, even to the extent of arguing that
Emilia's words in V, 7 are a deliberate lie, uttered solely in
order to provoke her father into action.[21] Many critics have
failed to recognize the background of philosophical determinism against which Lessing has created his characters: seeing
them accordingly as free agents, they have sought to judge
their actions right or wrong, to apportion praise or blame,
and many have identified some kind of satiric element in the
play, some kind of invitation to *criticize* the beliefs and attitudes which make the characters act as they do.[22] There is, in

[21] Cf. H. Steinhauer, 'The Guilt of Emilia Galotti ', *JEGP* xlviii (1949)
173-85, esp. p. 182.
[22] J. Desch's article, 'Emilia Galotti − a victim of misconceived morality',
Trivium, ix (1974), 88-99, exemplifies a common modern view.

short, no end of critical speculation on the question 'Warum stirbt Emilia Galotti?'[23] And despite Lessing's original avowal to Nicolai that he had 'die Geschichte der römischen Virginia von allem dem abgesondert, was sie für den ganzen Staat interessant machte', despite the similar assertion to his brother in February 1772 that the finished play was 'von allem Staatsinteresse befreit', many have felt that he must have intended some kind of social comment or indeed accusation: for is not *Emilia Galotti*, with its devastating exposure of the workings of a typical eighteenth-century petty principality — despite the Italian veneer, it could well be a German principality, even Brunswick-Wolfenbüttel itself — what the unfinished *Spartacus* was avowedly intended to be, an 'antityrannische Tragödie'?

These criticisms, doubts, and uncertainties, though they come from many different and often seemingly irreconcilable standpoints, are all related. For they reveal that there is in *Emilia Galotti*, if not to the extent that there is in *Philotas*, a discrepancy between Lessing's intention and his achievement. The play is a disturbing one. Lessing's characterization, his dramatic structure, and above all his creation of atmosphere are such that a good performance, which does not try too hard to interpret but lets the play speak for itself, will be assured of a considerable measure of success: the spectator will identify with the characters, fear for them, and be moved by their fate. Yet in all probability he will feel at the end that something has gone wrong: that the play *ought* not to have ended thus, that Emilia's death is not tragically inevitable, and that something calls for explanation. If he is then offered a sophisticated interpretation of Lessing's intended meaning, he will very probably say, 'Yes, that's all very well; but the *real* reason Emilia Galotti dies is because that's how the Virginia story has to end.' And indeed this simple, common-sense reaction is essentially correct. Emilia provokes her father into emulation of the Roman Virginius, and thereby, just like Marwood threatening to emulate Medea, explicitly and deliberately identifies herself and her father as *actors in a*

---

[23] H. Weigand, 'Warum stirbt Emilia Galotti?', in *Fährten und Funde* (Bern and Munich, 1967), pp. 39–50; A Wierlacher, 'Das Haus der Freude oder Warum stirbt Emilia Galotti?', *LYB* v (1973), 147–62.

tragedy.[24] But, as Odoardo's subsequent refusal to kill himself as in 'eine schale Tragödie' rather awkwardly reminds us, Lessing's characters, if they are convincing, are not that: they are complex, modern human beings inhabiting a complex, modern world, and tragedy is essentially simple and archaic. Lessing has in fact written a complex and essentially modern play, and imposed upon it a conventional tragic ending for theoretical reasons: because it was a tragedy that he had set out to write, and because he was convinced of the ideal superiority of the tragic genre. Or rather, since such an account inverts Lessing's actual procedure, he has taken the Virginia story, rejected, for reasons which I have indicated, the original — utterly simple and totally comprehensible — motivation, and devised a completely new psychological motivation of his own, highly complex, sophisticated, and problematic — too much so, in fact, for the still essentially simple tragic ending of the original story.[25]

The result is a blurring of focus, essentially similar, though neither as radical nor therefore as damaging, to that involved in the modernization of the Medea legend in *Miß Sara Sampson*. It is surely profoundly significant that the two full-length tragic works which Lessing, amidst so many plans and fragments, managed to complete are both modern-dress versions of ancient tragic themes. It indicates the problematic nature of the attempt to write tragedy in the eighteenth century: a fusion — or an uneasy compromise? — between ancient and modern worlds.

Emilia Galotti is of course superior in every respect — in characterization, in setting, in dialogue — to his earlier tragedies. It is a less perfect work than *Minna von Barnhelm*, in which intention and achievement more fully coincide. But it is, I believe, a greater one. Lessing has set himself a more difficult task, and has all but succeeded. And in the depth of its portrayal of character and background it raises grave and profound questions — including some of those which, as I

---

[24] Cf. Schröder, *Lessing: Sprache und Drama*, p. 206; Neumann, op. cit., p. 41.

[25] To this extent one must agree with F. O. Nolte, 'Lessing's *Emilia Galotti* in the Light of his *Hamburgische Dramaturgie*', *Harvard Studies and Notes in Philology and Literature*, xix (1938), 175–95 (German version in B), though the particulars of Nolte's argument seem to me quite wrong.

suggested, *Minna von Barnhelm* answered a little too blandly.

Let us first consider the question of Emilia's sensuality, which so shocked Claudius. Now there can be little doubt that Lessing *means* Emilia's words — 'Ich habe Blut, mein Vater; so jugendliches, so warmes Blut, als eine. Auch meine Sinne, sind Sinne. *Ich stehe für nichts. Ich bin für nichts gut'* — to be shocking. But they are not intended simply to be shocking to the audience, and not at all so in the sense of causing moral revulsion and thereby weakening the audience's sympathy for Emilia. Far more importantly, they are the revelation of something profoundly shocking *to Emilia herself*, and therefore an essential part of Lessing's network of psychological motivation: an essential contributory factor to the mixture of shame, anger, and despair which motivate her desire for death. Her virtue, to which she attaches such importance, is threatened not only from without but from within, by the sensual, irrational side of her own nature. The 'es' that speaks to her in church (II, 6) is indeed her own Freudian id,[26] something which she seeks to repress. But critics who have perceived this often seem to suggest that her virtue is a mere chimera like Philotas's patriotic heroism, and that she is foolish to prefer death to dishonour, just as Antiphila is foolish to prefer her husband's tomb to the living world outside. Now this surely cannot be the case. Even if, as I have argued, the moral impulses which drive Emilia to her death are to be seen as essentially psychological in their functioning, this does not mean that they have no objective moral substance, that 'Tugend' is, as Mellefont had tried to persuade Sara (I, 7) nothing but a 'Gespenst'.[27] If Emilia is not meant to be seen as a martyr, nor is she the victim of a delusion. Her virtue is for her creator as for herself a symbol of her worth and integrity as a rational human being: as the Prince's mistress she would lose that integrity — she would become a mere material possession, like her picture (I, 5).[28]

Nor is it necessary to suppose, with Goethe and others, that

[26] Neumann, op. cit., p. 46.

[27] Ibid., pp. 50 ff.

[28] Cf. Seeba, op. cit., p. 80; M. Durzak, 'Das Gesellschaftsbild in Lessings "Emilia Galotti"', in *Poesie und Ratio: Vier Lessing-Studien* (Bad Homburg, 1970; originally in *LYB* ii), p. 79.

Emilia is really in love with the Prince, or that she does not really love Appiani.[29] What has happened is that the encounters with the Prince, at the Grimaldis' *vegghia* and then in church, have made her aware for the first time of an element in her own nature which she fears she cannot control, which her upbringing has perhaps not equipped her to deal with, and which her marriage to Appiani would keep within the bounds of reason and morality — if indeed it ever allowed her to become aware of it. Of course Emilia loves Appiani, dutifully, genuinely, innocently; and Appiani is worthy of the love of such a girl, brave, noble, upright as he is. To us today he may well appear something of a bore and a prig; but we should reflect that the only character in the play who takes a negative view of Appiani is the play's most negative character, Marinelli. Thus Appiani's resolve 'in seinen väterlichen Tälern sich selbst zu leben', which Odoardo so enthusiastically commends (II, 4), is more cynically viewed by Marinelli:

Er will mit seiner Gebieterin nach seinen Tälern von Piemont: — Gemsen zu jagen, auf den Alpen; und Murmeltiere abzurichten. — Was kann er Beßres tun? Hier ist es durch das Mißbündnis, welches er trifft, mit ihm doch aus.

— a view which the Prince does not share (I, 6). Marinelli would no doubt agree with Oscar Wilde's Lord Henry Wotton that 'anybody can be good in the country.'[30] But we have no right to assume that Emilia's marriage to Appiani, if it were allowed to happen, would not be happy. We may well infer that it would not be passionate, but that is not the same at all.

Lessing himself undoubtedly took a very negative view of erotic passion. The love of which he approves, the love which animates the happy couples in *Der Misogyn, Der Freigeist,* and *Minna von Barnhelm,* is not this, but a rational affection based upon the recognition of moral worth — as was indeed the love of Lessing and Eva König. Sara Sampson, the victim of passion, asks that her daughter be brought up 'gegen alle Liebe auf ihrer Hut zu sein'; and in *Nathan der Weise* erotic attraction yields to fraternal affection. Wholly characteristic

[29] Goethe to Riemer, March 1812 (quoted in G ii. 714); Brüggemann, op. cit.; J. Poynter, 'The Pearls of Emilia Galotti', *LYB* ix (1977), 81-95.
[30] Oscar Wilde, *The Picture of Dorian Gray,* ch. 19.

is Lessing's reaction to Goethe's *Werther*, the novel based partly on the suicide of Karl Wilhelm Jerusalem (the young man whom both Lessing and Goethe had known). The depression which led to Jerusalem's suicide had been occasioned chiefly, or so Lessing believed, by philosophical and religious doubts; and he found it impossible to approve of a hero who had killed himself for such an unworthy reason as unrequited sexual passion, as Goethe's novel seemed to suggest. As Lessing wrote to Eschenburg on 26 October 1774,

ja, wenn unsers Jerusalems Geist völlig in dieser Lage gewesen wäre, so müßte ich ihn fast — verachten. Glauben Sie wohl, daß je ein römischer oder griechischer Jüngling sich *so* und *darum* das Leben genommen? Gewiß nicht. Die wußten sich vor der Schwärmerei der Liebe ganz anders zu schützen . . .

But Jerusalem had shot himself with a copy of *Emilia Galotti* open before him; and Goethe retains this detail, unexplained, in *Werther*. Perhaps we are to understand that Werther sees in the relationship between Emilia, Appiani, and the Prince a reflection of his own situation: Lotte is innocently and happily engaged to the worthy but prosaic Albert, but her meeting with the sensitive Werther has introduced her (or so, at least, Werther would like to believe) to emotions of an intensity and a profundity of which she had never dreamed.[31]

The relationship is paralleled again in that of Anna, Ottavio, and Giovanni in Mozart's opera *Don Giovanni* of 1787, which for good measure adds in Donna Elvira a figure closely corresponding to Orsina as well. Here the parallels are presumably totally fortuitous, but this suggests all the more that the characters, their relationships, and — most important — their sensibilities are characteristic of the period. What in fact was happening was a profound revaluation of erotic passion: one of the most important elements in the revolution of sensibility which we call the Romantic movement — as the everyday meaning of the adjective suggests. Lessing's attitudes are those of the older generation. But as the great realist he was, he clearly saw and faithfully portrayed many of the phenomena of change, even where he disapproved of them or did not

[31] Cf. L. W. Forster, 'Werther's Reading of *Emilia Galotti*', *PEGS* xxvii (1958), 33–45.

perhaps fully comprehend them. Emilia's latent 'romantic' passion is one such phenomenon. Like her creator she mistrusts and condemns it, but recognizes it as inescapably part of her nature. Lessing's psychological insight was too modern for the old-fashioned Claudius: it was an insight into the future.

The same is perhaps even more significantly true of Lessing's insight into the social relations of his characters and the social world which they inhabit. Here again, as with *Minna von Barnhelm* and *Philotas*, critics draw different conclusions from their observations, often telling us more about themselves than about the play: generally speaking, those of a liberal or progressive persuasion assume that Lessing must have intended some kind of social or even political criticism, those of a conservative disposition that he did not. The view of the play as a deliberate attack on princely absolutism is most vigorously propounded by Marxist critics, following upon Marx's own eulogy of Lessing as the 'anti-establishment' writer *par excellence.*[32] Lessing's declarations that the play was 'von allem Staatsinteresse befreit' are ignored, interpreted as ironies, or ingeniously got round. Thus we are told that the subjects from Roman history which attracted Lessing at various times from 1750 to 1770 — Brutus, Lucretia, Virginia, Spartacus — are all highly charged with libertarian and indeed republican ideological associations (which is true), that Lessing's turning to such subject-matter represents an attempt to overcome the limitations of the purely private 'bürgerliches Trauerspiel' (which is plausible — but this does not necessarily imply an interest in the political material for its own sake), and that Lessing's omission in *Emilia Galotti* of the political sequel to Virginia's death — the overthrow of the tyrants — only makes stronger the *implicit* political charge of the 'purely human' tragedy (which is distinctly tendentious — at any rate as a statement of Lessing's *intentions*).[33] Critics who take this line tend to see the bourgeois characters of the play as idealized or exemplary; but others have pointed out that they

[32] Cf. S. S. Prawer, *Karl Marx and World Literature* (Oxford, 1976), p. 49 f.

[33] Riedel, op. cit., pp. 107 ff. (though Riedel himself criticizes the views of other Marxist critics). Cf. also P. M. Lützeler, 'Die marxistische Lessing-Rezeption (ii): Darstellung und Kritik am Beispiel der *Emilia Galotti*-Interpretation in der DDR', *LYB* viii (1976), 42-60.

make themselves, by their attitudes and their unwillingness or inability to act, too easy prey for their aristocratic predators, and the play has even been called 'an indictment of bourgeois passivity'.[34] But it has also been held that Lessing was simply concerned to write a tragedy, and that the social or even political thematic material is — as I argued above in respect of the moral-religious thematic material of *Miß Sara Sampson* — in itself indifferent, being merely made use of for that further, purely aesthetic purpose.[35]

Lessing's intention and the meaning of the finished play may however not be the same thing. He may not have intended to write a work of social criticism; indeed, writing when he did, he hardly could have intended to write such a work as we might understand it; and yet, whatever he intended, he has in fact written a play in which the system of princely absolutism, the situation of the middle classes under that system, and their reactions to its workings are subjected to a profound critical analysis.[36]

In his general attitudes Lessing was indifferent, perhaps even hostile, to the doings of the great: his brother Karl in his biographical sketch describes him as 'ein Plebejaner'.[37] We have observed his reactions to the Seven Years' War and the Prussia of Frederick the Great in connection with *Philotas* and *Minna von Barnhelm*. His views were, broadly speaking, liberal and humanitarian, but there is little evidence in his voluminous writings of any systematic thought on social or political matters. Fritz Jacobi wrote that Lessing 'in Staatsverfassungen kein Arg hatte', and if, as Jacobi goes on to tell us, he once went so far as to declare that 'die bürgerliche Gesellschaft müsse noch ganz aufgehoben werden',[38] this may well indicate not revolutionary radicalism or even anarchism so much as a sceptical, resigned — or perhaps despairing — turning away from political concerns, like Aridäus's 'Glaubt ihr Menschen, daß man es nicht satt wird?' It may be that in

---

[34] R. R. Heitner, '*Emilia Galotti*: an Indictment of Bourgeois Passivity', *JEGP* lii (1953), 480-90. Cf. also Brüggemann, op. cit., esp. B, p. 122: 'die Bankerotterklärung der bürgerlichen Welt des Vorsubjektivismus'.

[35] Cf. my 'Lessing and the "Bürgerliches Trauerspiel"'.

[36] Cf. J. Schulte-Sasse, *Literarische Struktur und historisch–sozialer Kontext. Zum Beispiel Lessings "Emilia Galotti"* (Paderborn, 1975), esp. p. 54.

[37] D 592.   [38] Ibid., p. 519 f.

Wolfenbüttel, as the servant of a ruling prince, Lessing began to appreciate social and political questions as he had not done before; certainly the one work in which he addresses himself directly to such questions, the series of Masonic dialogues *Ernst und Falk*, dates from this period of his life. But *Ernst und Falk*, unlike his writings on aesthetics or theology — subjects which deeply engaged him — is abstract and elusive, and it certainly does not advocate revolution. Moreover, Lessing seems to have been surprisingly undisturbed by one of the major political scandals of the Duchy of Brunswick, the sale of mercenaries to fight in America,[39] whereas Schiller's indignation at similar goings-on in Württemberg is plainly, even stridently, recorded in *Kabale und Liebe*. In *Emilia Galotti* Lessing set out to produce as good a tragedy as possible, in accordance with the theories he had developed in Hamburg. He will therefore have been concerned above all with the motivation of his action and the plausibility of his characters. But what has happened is that in pursuit of this end he has given his characters, both in their individual personalities and in their mutual relationships, a social concreteness much greater than anything we find in his earlier work, and this has in effect restored or even reinforced the political meaning of the original story which he set out to remove. It is not by any means clear that he realized this.

In the closing numbers of the *Hamburgische Dramaturgie* Lessing had appeared to greet with a certain scepticism Diderot's suggestion that the theatre should portray *conditions* rather than characters. But in *Emilia Galotti* (applying, we note, a theory developed in respect of comic characters to the creation of tragic ones!) Lessing has created personages whose individual characters — their attitudes and modes of behaviour — are profoundly representative of, indeed to a large extent determined by, their social position. Herder pointed out in an essay of 1794 how Lessing 'zeigt den Charakter des Prinzen in seinem Stande, den Stand in seinem Charakter', seizing the opportunity offered by every dramatic

---

[39] Cf. H. Schneider, op. cit., p. 205–10; M. Durzak, 'Gesellschaftsreflexion und Gesellschaftsdarstellung bei Lessing', *ZfdPh* xciii (1974), 546–60; and K. Eibl, 'Identitätskrise und Diskurs. Zur theoretischen Kontinuität von Lessings Dramatik', *JDSG* xxi (1977), 138–91, esp. p. 159 f.

situation 'das Prinzliche dabei zu charakterisieren'.[40] But the same is true of all the characters, in whom individuality is indissolubly fused with social rank and identity. Moreover, Lessing has taken the trouble to bring before us a complete panorama of his little society, from the Prince, his current favourite, and his about-to-be-discarded mistress, through Appiani and the Galottis, down to the common people and the criminal lower fringes of society. Even such minor, almost episodic, figures as Conti and Rota have their precise places in the social picture and serve to make it more complete.[41] It is a picture such as Lessing might have observed with his own eyes in Wolfenbüttel. Indeed, when the play was performed in Brunswick the Prince was taken to be modelled on the Erbprinz, the Duke's heir, and Orsina (whose role, according to Nicolai, was absent, or at any rate less highly developed, in the earlier version of the play)[42] on the Erbprinz's mistress, the Marchioness Branconi, whose 'großen, hervorragenden, stieren, starren Medusenaugen' as the Prince unflatteringly describes them (I, 4), still gaze out there from her portrait in the ducal picture gallery.[43]

The personages of *Emilia Galotti* occupy a moral as well as a social hierarchy; and the two broadly coincide. The characters are of course, as we have noted, no longer painted in simple black and white like those of *Miß Sara Sampson*. Nevertheless, it is broadly true in *Emilia Galotti* that virtuous attitudes are shown to be characteristic of the middle-class characters, notably Odoardo and Emilia. Claudia is of course attracted to the court and its values, while conversely Appiani has thrown in his lot with the middle classes, making, as Marinelli observes, a *mésalliance* which will close society's doors to him. The Prince himself, as his response to Marinelli's remarks indicates (I, 6), is attracted to the values which the middle class embodies, though in the event, of course, he

[40] Herder, *Briefe zu Beförderung der Humanität*, ed. Kruse (Weimar, 1971), i. 190 (37. Brief).
[41] Cf. Durzak, 'Das Gesellschaftsbild in Lessings "Emilia Galotti".
[42] D 193 f. and 353 f.
[43] Cf. E. L. Stahl (ed.), *Lessing. Emilia Galotti* (Oxford, 1946) (Blackwell's German Texts), p. 71. Lessing had met both Branconi and her portraitist, Anna de Gasc, whose husband was a colleague of Ebert and Eschenburg at the Collegium Carolinum in Brunswick.

succumbs to the habits of his own class — the aristocratic morality (or lack of it) more typically represented by Marinelli and Orsina. At the other end of the social scale we find a similar moral shading-off from the Galottis through Pirro to Angelo: though the attachment of Pirro to the Galotti household may be held to betoken aspirations to a virtuous way of life, the rest of the 'Pöbel' characteristically show as little inhibition in the pursuit of their selfish and nefarious ends as do the 'Leute von Stande'. Social and moral hierarchies thus quite closely correspond. A modern critic may see this as the masking of what is really a social conflict by its projection in moral terms,[44] but as with the conflict of Emilia's virtue and her sensuality, Lessing himself undoubtedly shares, in essentials, his middle-class characters' moral attitudes. He does however show them as problematic: that is, he shows us that Odoardo — and Appiani — find it difficult, even impossible, to translate their moral principles into resolute moral action. And this, as we have observed before, is characteristic of the middle-class morality of Lessing's generation, even finding its reflection in his theories of the moral efficacy of tragedy.

Indeed, the state of affairs which Lessing brings before us in *Emilia Galotti* is not only socially but historically very precisely determined. The setting is sometimes described as 'Renaissance',[45] but whatever the dates and circumstances of the historically attested Gonzagas of Guastalla, Lessing — exploiting to the full the dramatist's right to use historical names and facts for his own ends — is surely here showing us the Germany of his own day, in which the values, but not yet the political power, of princely absolutism were being challenged by middle-class 'Empfindsamkeit'. Marinelli indeed describes Appiani as an 'Empfindsamer' (I, 6), using the word which Lessing had coined himself;[46] and as we have seen, the Prince himself is not immune to the new outlook — which is unwelcome to Marinelli, for it embodies a potential threat to the absolutist system to which he owes his position and livelihood.

---

[44] Cf. Seeba, op. cit., p. 95.

[45] e.g. Durzak, *Poesie und Ratio*, p. 75.

[46] Lessing suggested 'empfindsam' to Bode as a rendering of 'sentimental' in Sterne's *A Sentimental Journey* (cf. LM xvii. 256). In fact the word was widely used: cf. Sauder, op. cit., pp. 4 ff.

He must however serve his master's desires; no doubt he thinks that the Prince will tire of Emilia, as Marwood thinks Mellefont will tire of his 'Landmädchen', and he can in the meantime use the opportunity to pay off an old score with Appiani, whom as an aristocrat hostile to the system and the traditional habits of his class he particularly detests. Odoardo's and Appiani's turning away from the corrupt urban society of Guastalla to return to their country estates smacks strongly of Rousseau. And the historical context is underlined by another, seemingly gratuitous little touch: by the 'Romantic' view of art propounded by the painter Conti, in which (how unlike Lessing's own views!) inspiration is all, execution ultimately of no account: 'Oder meinen Sie, Prinz, daß Raphael nicht das größte malerische Genie gewesen wäre, wenn er unglücklicher Weise ohne Hände wäre geboren worden?' (I, 4) — another detail echoed in *Werther*.[47]

Lessing thus shows us that his characters' attitudes and behaviour reflect their social and historical identity. But he also shows us that their attitudes and relationships to each other, and the courses of action which are open to them, are conditioned by their respective positions in an all-embracing social system. This realization was completely absent in the early comedies and in *Miß Sara Sampson*, which take place in a social vacuum: the characters are presented purely as 'Menschen', and specifically social (e.g. master-servant) relationships are taken for granted, or at any rate not seriously examined for their own sake. And even in *Minna von Barnhelm*, despite its much more concrete historical and social setting, there is very little concern with the social structure of the characters' relationships: in the traditional comic parallel of 'high' and 'low' characters, even if (or even because) the

---

[47] Cf. Ilse Appelbaum-Graham, 'Minds without Medium. Reflections on *Emilia Galotti* and *Werthers Leiden*', *Euph.* lvi (1962), 3–24 (German version in B, 362–75). Conti's image of the 'handless' Raphael does of course adumbrate that of the 'handless' Odoardo Galotti in IV, 7. Lessing surely does not 'endorse Conti's view', as R. Wellek claims (*A History of Modern Criticism*, i. 163): his own aesthetic theory, with its stress on 'Absicht' and audience reaction, is emphatically a communicative one, not an inspirational one such as Conti proclaims and as the 'Stürmer und Dränger' were to espouse. It is nevertheless true of his own works, of none more so than *Emilia Galotti*, that, as Mendelssohn wrote to him in November 1757, 'Ihre Gedanken finden den Weg nach der Hand ziemlich spät'!

two levels are brought closer together than was previously usual, there is an unproblematic acceptance of the existing relations between the classes, and all the characters ultimately live their lives as individuals, free of any serious hierarchical restrictions. In *Emilia Galotti*, however, the characters no longer enjoy the luxury, so dear to Lessing and his contemporaries, of being simply 'Menschen': they are part of a system of hierarchical dependences (the relations between the classes under princely absolutism) and their lives are subject to the working of its mechanisms. Which is to say that whatever Lessing may have intended, the essential meaning of the Virginia story is and remains inescapably political: it is a story of the abuse of power, and amongst the reasons why Odoardo and his daughter fall victim to the machinations of their adversary, numerous and complex though those reasons may be, not the least is the simple fact that their adversary is in a position of power over them. More clearly than in *Miß Sara Sampson*, the original meaning of the story emerges despite Lessing's attempted reinterpretation. It may be 'tragisch genug, und fähig genug . . . die ganze Seele zu erschüttern' without our reflecting on any remedies for the evils it portrays. It may well be that Lessing believed that he had devised a 'Reihe von Ursachen und Wirkungen', largely or even entirely psychological in its functioning, 'nach welcher jene unwahrscheinliche Verbrechen nicht wohl anders, als geschehen müssen'. But by his rooting of character, attitude, and behaviour in a precisely observed society he has made the systematic working of that society not less but more important as a cause of the tragedy. Again, the evils which result from the characteristic functioning of princely absolutism Lessing may well have regarded as belonging to what in *Ernst und Falk* he calls the 'unvermeidlichen Übeln, welche, eine gewisse Staatsverfassung angenommen, aus dieser angenommenen Staatsverfassung nun notwendig folgen';[48] and while commending to the public-spirited citizen the mitigation of such evils, Lessing does not advocate or even appear to contemplate any action against the system itself. Nor should it be forgotten that the play was approved by the Duke and performed on a court

---

[48] G viii. 467 (*Ernst und Falk*, Drittes Gespräch).

occasion, though Lessing himself, in a letter to the Duke at the beginning of March 1772, offered to stop the performance if the work should be thought unsuitable. To some, of course, this may merely seem to illustrate Swift's dictum that 'Satyr is a sort of Glass, wherein Beholders do generally discover every body's Face but their Own';[49] and from the portrait of absolutism which Lessing had drawn, others could readily draw radical or even revolutionary conclusions.

The play is very much a play of and for its time. It achieved Lessing's aim of a serious drama with specifically contemporary appeal, and pointed forward to future developments, to the introduction of still more realistic and critical depiction of contemporary social issues into the drama and to the writing of plays in which such depiction, rather than the satisfaction of traditional dramatic canons of 'tragedy' or 'comedy', however reinterpreted, was to become the writer's principal intention. In this Lessing has taken tragedy, at any rate tragedy as conceived by the Enlightenment,[50] to its limit — and indeed perhaps already overstepped it, weakening his own play as a tragedy in so doing. For if Emilia's choice between death and dishonour is the product of the particular society in which she lives, is it really illustrative of the whole human condition? Is the case depicted not too particular and insufficiently general? And if Emilia's death is the result of human institutions, are not those institutions susceptible of change? Does not the spectator come away feeling not emotional satisfaction ('catharsis'?) occasioned by the recognition of inevitability, but intellectual — that is, critical — dissatisfaction occasioned by the recognition that these things need not and ought not to have happened, as in Brecht's 'epic theatre'?[51]

As I have suggested in connection with *Minna von Barnhelm*, the development of realistic drama since Lessing's day, a development to which his own work made such a vital initial contribution, makes it inevitable that we should ask such questions. To Lessing the answer to them lay in a theodicy, in a demonstration of the workings of Providence, and it was

---

[49] Preface to *The Battle of the Books*: Swift, *A Tale of a Tub*, etc., ed. Davis (Oxford, 1939), p. 140.
[50] Cf. Steinmetz, 'Aufklärung und Tragödie'.
[51] Cf. Brecht, 'Vergnügungstheater oder Lehrtheater?', Werkausgabe xv. 265.

in his view the task of the tragic dramatist to provide such a
demonstration: to create, in the words of the *Hamburgische
Dramaturgie*, a 'Schattenriß von dem Ganzen des ewigen
Schöpfers', a symbolic representation of the 'ewiger unend-
licher Zusammenhang aller Dinge' (No. 79). The dramatist
creates a closed, coherent system in which everything — the
characters, their interdependence, even place and time — is
significant: 'Nichts unter der Sonne ist Zufall' (IV, 3). Within
this system, this 'possible world' in the Leibnizian sense, he
shows events to be inevitable. The characters get into a situation from which only a miracle could save them, and indeed
Odoardo prays for one (V, 6); but for Lessing the workings of
a benevolent Providence do not extend to arbitrary intervention in human affairs[52] — and so catastrophe ensues. The best
that can be hoped for, in this image of the 'best of all possible'
worlds, is the preservation of Emilia's honour. Through
Odoardo's hand, this is ensured; father and daughter are reconciled in the moment of her death; Odoardo faces the
'Richter unser aller' repentant, but confident of mercy.

Yet this does not completely satisfy us, even if we share
(or are willing imaginatively to share) Lessing's belief in Providence. We feel rather that here as elsewhere — in *Philotas* and
in *Minna von Barnhelm*, and as we shall see in *Nathan der
Weise* — Lessing shows us Providence not simply directing
human beings who respond only passively, but requiring their
active co-operation: the human beings whom Lessing portrays
are, we feel, to some extent free agents with genuine choices
to make, and if (but only if) they retain their faith in 'Tugend
und Vorsicht', they will make the right ones, act correctly,
and be rewarded. Providence is seen as *testing* human beings:
Minna and ultimately Tellheim, Nathan and ultimately the
Templar pass the test, but Emilia and Odoardo fail, as Philotas
failed. Their morality does not stand the test of action. Providence does indeed need Odoardo's hand for the execution of
its design; but it needs his will too, and this he has abdicated.
In spite of his bluster, he has let Marinelli run rings round
him when he ought simply to have insisted on his right to
take his daughter home. We must indeed abide by the decisions

[52]   Cf. below, p. 214.

of Providence and remain 'ruhig', but this does not mean helpless passivity: Emilia is all too right to ask her father 'Was nennen Sie ruhig sein?' But if Odoardo cannot regain a proper faith in 'Tugend und Vorsicht', then Emilia, totally dependent upon him as she is at this moment, must lose hers too. Seen in this light their action is, like Philotas's, one of 'wütende Schwermut'. It is not deliberately self-induced in quite the same way and so not in the same degree censurable, but our pity is still clouded with a certain disapproval, a certain intellectual dissatisfaction. The pure emotional effect, the 'Mitleid' which Lessing held to be the sole and self-sufficient aim of tragedy, is compromised. Ultimately, Lessing's attempt to combine tragedy and theodicy has not succeeded.

Goethe was less than fair in describing *Emilia Galotti* as 'nur gedacht': its presence on Werther-Jerusalem's desk is evidence of its power to move and to disturb, and it can still hold the stage today. But there is no doubt that it is an intellectual play, and this, as Goethe and Schlegel recognized, is the source of its strength and its weakness. Its strength lies in features which can be intellectually appreciated: its rigorous construction, its realistic depiction of character and of social milieu, its raising, intentional or otherwise, of awkward questions about the world we live in — its social and political structures, even its ultimate governance and design. Its weakness — though also from a historical and biographical point of view a considerable part of its interest — lies in its attempt to combine, for theoretical reasons, things which are ultimately incompatible. The adaptation of the ancient art-form of tragedy to the presentation of the lives and circumstances of specifically modern characters is in fact for Lessing an intellectual exercise, and this is made evident when he finds it necessary to remind us, through the mouth of his heroine, that what we have been watching is essentially intended as 'weiter nichts als die alte römische Geschichte der Virginia in einer modernen Einkleidung'.[53] Lessing has had recourse to the tragic form once again not to express a tragic view of life, but because of a traditional, uncritically accepted, abstract belief in the superiority and timeless validity of the tragic

[53] Lessing, letter to the Duke of Brunswick, March 1772 (G ii. 707).

genre, and in the consequent necessity of writing a successful tragedy to demonstrate the coming of age of German literature. But if, as I believe, *Emilia Galotti* is a greater play than *Minna von Barnhelm* it is because its insistent and disturbing modern content has overflowed the archaic vessel it was designed to fill.

VII

'Lessings Lessing': *Nathan der Weise*

(i)

Emilia Galotti marks the climax, and the end, of Lessing's programme for the renaissance of the German theatre. It was greeted with enthusiasm by his friends — Ebert hailed the first performance in Brunswick with the words 'O Shakespear-Lessing!'[1] — and soon performed elsewhere, in Berlin and even in Vienna. The Vienna performance was not good, to judge by the description in Eva König's letter to Lessing of 15 July 1772, but when Lessing himself visited Vienna three years later, he was rapturously received, and granted an audience by Maria Theresia.[2] However, very soon after the completion of *Emilia* we begin to find in his letters the familiar expressions of distaste and disillusion with the theatre. As early as 22 April 1772 he complains to Nicolai that he wants to get on with other work, but that he cannot do so until he has rid his mind of dramatic affairs. The conditions under which he had to work in Wolfenbüttel were far from ideal; very soon dissatisfaction with his job set in, combined with friction with his courtly employers, and persisted to the point of his seriously contemplating resignation. But he did not wish to return to the theatre: again he wrote to Karl on 2 February 1774 of his 'Ekel gegen alles, was Theater ist und heißt', and to Bode on 9 March 1775 that he was 'fest entschlossen, auf keine Weise etwas weiter für das Theater zu arbeiten'.

One reason for this is that he was less than satisfied with the results of his emancipation of the German drama from the shackles of Gottschedian neo-classicism. He had proclaimed the freedom of the 'genius' from mechanical rules, but, as he

---

[1] Ebert to Lessing, 15 March 1772.   [2] D 358 ff.

wrote to Wieland on 8 February 1775, in answer to Wieland's
request for a contribution to his periodical the *Teutscher
Merkur*, 'Was für Beiträge erwarten Sie von mir? Arbeiten des
Genies? Alles Genie haben itzt gewisse Leute in Beschlag genommen, mit welchen ich mich nicht gern auf einem Wege
möchte finden lassen.' He had encouraged the Germans to
read and study Shakespeare, but the fruits of the veritable
Shakespeare mania which swept Germany in the seventies
could not be to his taste: historical costume-dramas, much
like the old 'Haupt- und Staatsaktionen' of the days before
Gottsched, with a lot of unnecessary scene-changes and gratuitous improprieties — the reference is obviously to Goethe's
Götz von Berlichingen.[3] He was also predictably displeased
with Lenz's *Anmerkungen über das Theater*, in which the
relevance of Aristotelian authority to modern drama is
roundly denied.[4] He did however have some praise for Lenz's
dramatic work — even if the occasion is mistaken: for the
play in question is H. L. Wagner's *Die Kindermörderin*, an
essay in a similar, if greatly inferior, style of social realism to
Lenz's, which Lessing wrongly attributed to the latter. Karl
Lessing had made an adaptation of *Die Kindermörderin* for
performance in Berlin, and commenting upon this, in a letter
of 8 January 1777, his brother observes, 'Lenz ist immer noch
ein ganz anderer Kopf als Klinger, dessen letztes Stück [pre-
sumably *Sturm und Drang* itself] ich unmöglich habe auslesen
können.' Unlikely as it seems after this, Lessing did nevertheless, according to one account, recognize the talent of Klinger,[5]
as well as that of Leisewitz and 'Maler' Müller (with both of
whom he enjoyed friendly personal relations) and, despite his
aberrations, of Goethe. One wonders, though, what he would
have thought of Schiller's *Räuber*, which appeared in the year
of his death.

In 1776 the theatre beckoned more temptingly. In the
summer of that year, after his return from Italy, when his
relations with the ruling house of Brunswick were at their
worst, he was approached by the Palatine court in Mannheim,
and although nominally the offer made to him was merely of
membership of the Palatine Academy of Arts and Sciences, it

[3]   Ibid., 377 f.; cf. Lessing's letter to his brother Karl, 30 April 1774.
[4]   D 357.   [5]   Ibid., p. 435.

was clear that what was in the minds of the Elector and his minister, Baron Hompesch, was that Lessing should assume the direction of the Mannheim court theatre, which was now to bear the proud if ill-omened title 'Deutsches Nationaltheater'. Lessing was at pains to assure his fiancée Eva König that he did not intend to accept: Eva was not favourably disposed to his giving up the modicum of stability and economic security which was his in Wolfenbüttel and which afforded their only real hope of being able to marry. But in September Lessing was already actively engaged in looking for actors for Mannheim; negotiations with Hompesch continued throughout the autumn and winter, and it seems to have been widely known that Lessing was at least contemplating taking up the directorship, for in his correspondence we find a letter dated 27 December 1776 from one Johann Hornung, *'Decorateur* und Theatrall Maschinist auf dem K. Königl. Hof Theater zu Inßprug in Thiroll', offering his services for the 'Neüe Theatrall Schaupihne' [= -bühne] in Mannheim. Lessing was apprehensive, as he wrote to Karl on 8 January 1777: 'Denn mich schaudert, wenn ich nur daran denke, daß ich mich wieder werde mit dem Theater bemengen müssen.' One of the concerns which most exercised him, after his bitter experience in Hamburg, was that the running of the theatre should be kept out of the hands of impresarios or actor-managers. To this end, he proposed to Hompesch that strict supervision should be exercised by the Court and by the Academy in Mannheim:[6] rather remarkable proposals from a supposedly 'anti-establishment' writer, but he had expressed similar views in a letter to Eva of 15 November 1771 regarding the establishment of a National Theatre in Vienna. However, in March 1777 the negotiations broke down, and Lessing returned to theology, which since his arrival in Wolfenbüttel had more and more come to engage the best of his intellectual energies.

It is a matter of enduring debate what Lessing's religious views actually were. Not only did they change and develop over the years, but they are often expressed obliquely, sometimes disguised for tactical reasons, sometimes overlaid by the surface brilliance of the polemics which, since he took

---

[6] Cf. Karl Lessing, *G. E. Lessing's Leben*, i. 382 ff., quoted in LM xviii. 223 f.

such delight in controversy, develop a life of their own almost independent of their occasion. Lessing is often regarded as one of the foremost representatives of the Enlightenment, and therefore as essentially sceptical if not actually hostile towards religion; but he has also been seen as the founder of 'existential' Protestantism, as fundamentally an orthodox Lutheran, even as a crypto-Catholic.[7] Recent studies of his theological and philosophical writings have stressed their transitional nature: as in his dramatic theory and practice, so here too Lessing stands on a historical watershed, 'inchoately breaking through the a-historical and static conceptualism of the Aufklärung and laying the foundations for an evolutionary interpretation of man based upon a historically constructed anthropology'.[8] But from his earliest essays to *Die Erziehung des Menschengeschlechts*, despite the differences in approach, in emphasis, even in apparent conclusion, certain themes remain constant. First among these is the omnipotence and ultimate benevolence of God or, to use the less personal term so often favoured by eighteenth-century writers, of divine Providence. This dogma or axiom, as we may well describe it, corner-stone of Christianity and of rational deism alike, is an assumption which Lessing never questions, even at moments of deepest personal tragedy. Then come two problems which are the subject of unceasing enquiry: the meaning of truth, and the relation between cognition of the truth and right conduct — in Kantian terminology, between theoretical and practical reason. Finally, another axiom which Lessing unwaveringly maintains: the right and duty of every man to exercise his reason (both theoretical and practical) in his own way, free of restriction or intervention by religious or, by implication, secular authority. The necessary corollary of this is that intellectual and religious tolerance of which Lessing is rightly regarded as the champion.[9] But characteristically, tolerance, the public aspect of the question, is really only its passive, negative side: the positive, active emphasis is on the intellectual

[7]   The fullest treatment of the subject is G. Pons, *G. E. Lessing et le christianisme* (Paris, 1964). For a somewhat hostile view, cf. H. Chadwick (ed. and trans.), *Lessing's Theological Writings*, (London, 1956).

[8]   L. P. Wessell, *Lessing's Theology: a Reinterpretation* (The Hague, 1977), p. 139.

[9]   Cf. H. Schultze, *Lessings Toleranzbegriff* (Göttingen, 1969).

and moral initiative of the individual. However, the virtues which Lessing commends are unquestionably 'gesellschaftliche Tugenden', virtues to be exercised by man not in isolation but in the society of his fellows.

These preoccupations are apparent from Lessing's earliest religious writings onward. The unpublished *Gedanken über die Herrnhuter*, written probably in 1750, is already concerned with the evident disharmony between theoretical and practical reason: 'Der Mensch ward zum Tun und nicht zum Vernünfteln erschaffen . . . Der Erkenntnis nach sind wir ['enlightened' moderns] Engel, und dem Leben nach Teufel.'[10] The *Rettung des Hieronymus Cardanus*, his first major published essay on a religious subject, compares Christianity, Judaism, and Mohammedanism on intellectual, moral, and what one might call existential grounds, and the comparison is not to Christianity's advantage. These early works no doubt reflect the emancipation of the young Lessing from the strict, indeed narrow-minded Lutheranism of his family and background. But after about 1760 he began to take a more positive and sympathetic interest in Christianity. In Breslau he made extensive studies in the origins and early history of the Christian Church, and by January 1771 he could write to Moses Mendelssohn of his present concern for 'Wahrheiten, die ich längst für keine Wahrheiten mehr gehalten'.[11] And in the Wolfenbüttel years he published a series of works dealing with the meaning of religious truth, beginning in the autumn of 1770 with *Berengarius Turonensis*, an essay (somewhat in the manner of the earlier *Rettungen*) on an important eleventh-century heretic, and culminating in his intellectual testament, the *Erziehung des Menschengeschlechts*, in 1780.

The most momentous undertaking of the Wolfenbüttel years was the publication of the so-called Reimarus fragments. The *Fragmente eines Ungenannten* (Lessing never admitted his knowledge of their authorship) were excerpts from an extensive critique of Christianity on rationalistic grounds, entitled *Apologie oder Schutzschrift für die vernünftigen Verehrer Gottes*, by the Hamburg scholar Hermann Samuel

---

[10] G iii. 683 and 688.
[11] Cf. E. S. Flajole, S. J., 'Lessing's Retrieval of Lost Truths', *PMLA* lxxiv (1959), 52–66.

Reimarus (1694–1768). Reimarus did not publish his *Apologie*, and indeed it was not published in its entirety until 1972.[12] Lessing, it seems, never met Reimarus himself, but during his stay in Hamburg became well acquainted with his daughter Elise and her brother; it may be that Elise herself gave him a copy of her father's manuscript for the express purpose of publication, or there may, as Lessing claimed, have been a copy in the library at Wolfenbüttel already, since versions of it had been privately circulated. Lessing's first excerpt, *Von Duldung der Deisten*, appeared in 1774, but seems to have aroused relatively little comment: the furore began with the five fragments published in 1778. These were accompanied by 'counter-propositions' (*Gegensätze*) of Lessing's own, in which he defends — or appears to defend — Christianity against Reimarus's arguments; but the orthodox did not welcome Lessing as an ally. The ensuing controversies reached their climax in a ferocious battle between Lessing and the Hamburg pastor Johann Melchior Goeze, whom we have already encountered as an enemy of the theatre. A stream of polemical essays and pamphlets flowed from Lessing's pen; as the dispute grew fiercer, his brother and his Berlin friends warmed to his writings on a subject they had previously thought unworthy of his attentions. 'Nun verzeihe ich Dir gern', wrote Karl to him on 7 February 1778, 'in diesem Jahr kein Schauspiel geliefert zu haben. Du hast eine theologische Kömodie gegeben'; to which he replied on 25 February, 'Besonders freue ich mich, daß Du das haut-comique der Polemik zu goutieren anfängst, welches mir alle anderen theatralischen Werke so schal und wäßrig macht.' Goeze for his part objected to Lessing's 'Theaterlogik', a charge to which Lessing replied in the second of his *Anti-Goeze*. But in the summer of 1778 the controversy was abruptly ended. The ecclesiastical authorities persuaded the Duke of Brunswick to withdraw the freedom from censorship which Lessing as ducal librarian had hitherto enjoyed, and he was forbidden to engage in further theological debate.

Thus silenced, he at last returned to the drama. 'Ich habe in vergangener Nacht', he wrote to Karl on 11 August, 'einen

[12] H. S. Reimarus, *Apologie oder Schutzschrift für die vernünftigen Verehrer Gottes*, ed. G. Alexander (Frankfurt, 1972).

närrischen Einfall gehabt. Ich habe vor vielen Jahren ein
Schauspiel entworfen, dessen Inhalt eine Art von Analogie
mit meinen gegenwärtigen Streitigkeiten hat, die ich mir
damals wohl nicht träumen ließ.' And to Elise Reimarus he
wrote on 6 September, 'Ich muß versuchen, ob man mich auf
meiner alten Kanzel, auf dem Theater wenigstens, noch un-
gestört will predigen lassen.' A subscription was raised to
finance publication. Exactly when the earlier sketch to which
Lessing refers was made, we do not know: possibly, as he
later told Karl, on his return from Italy, that is, at the time of
the approach from Mannheim. But, as always with Lessing,
though an idea might lie dormant for years, once the vital
spark was fired completion did not take long. *Nathan der
Weise* was published by Voss in the spring of 1779.

(ii)

In his letters to his brother and to Elise Reimarus, Lessing
cites as his major source and the 'key' to his play Boccaccio's
tale (*Decameron* i. 3) of Sultan Saladin and the Jew Melchise-
dech. In answer to Saladin's question about the truth of
Christianity, Judaism, and Islam, the Jew tells him the parable
of the three indistinguishable rings given by a father to his
three equally beloved sons, and thereby wins the friendship
of the Sultan, who in the first place had only wanted to trap
the Jew into lending him money. Lessing had similarly been
pressed by Goeze (though Goeze was in deadly earnest) to
declare himself unequivocally on the truth of Christianity,
and he writes his play as Nathan-Melchisedech tells his parable:
to get himself out of a tight corner, and to give to a pressing
question what may seem to be an evasion rather than an
answer, but in fact demonstrates that the question cannot be
answered in the terms in which it is posed. The historical
truth of a particular religion cannot be established: it is right
conduct that matters. But the parable is only part of the play,
and the relativity of religious truth is only part of the play's
message. Moreover, though the telling of the parable occupies
a central position in the play — and indeed a position of great
dramatic importance — it is not in itself dramatic. To turn
this into a play, Lessing had to devise a complete dramatic

action in which to embed it. And it is this dramatic action
which not only exemplifies the ethical message of the ring
parable in practical application, but also links it with the
wider theme, common to both Lessing's theological essays
and, as we have seen, to his earlier plays, of the workings of
divine Providence and of man's relation to it.

The framework is provided by an elaborate mistaken-iden-
tity plot, in which a Christian knight and the foster-daughter
of a Jew discover that they are in fact brother and sister and
the children of a Moslem prince. It may owe something to
Voltaire's *Les Guèbres, ou la tolérance* (1769), in which we
likewise find a benign, tolerant ruler, a wise stepfather, a fanatical, bloodthirsty high priest, and a young couple ignorant
of their true identity; and the combination of the brother-sister
motif, the Near-Eastern setting, and the theme of religious
conflict and fanaticism had been used by Voltaire in two
earlier tragedies, *Zaïre* and *Mahomet*.[13] But the detailed
working-out is very much Lessing's own, the violence and
melodrama of Voltaire's tragedy are completely absent, and
the whole work, even the villainous figure of the Patriarch,
transposed into a lighter, brighter key, much as Lessing had
transposed the earnest sentimentality of *Le Fils naturel* in
Minna von Barnhelm.[14] The design is an intricate one, in
which every character, every encounter, every concealment
or partial revelation of the truth has its precise dramatic consequence: the final dramatic climax is, of course, the final unravelling of the mystery, and a large part of the audience's
pleasure derives, as in any detective story, from this unravelling
and from the consequent realization of the way in which all
the pieces of the design fit together. The plot is essentially of
the kind we associate with romantic comedy, lacking only in
the betrothal with which we normally expect such a play to
end: this Lessing quite deliberately avoids, though he originally intended, it seems, to end the play with Recha, or Rahel
as she is called in the earlier draft,[15] betrothed to Saladin and

---

[13] Cf. F. O. Nolte, 'Voltaire's *Mahomet* as a source of Lessing's *Nathan der
Weise* and *Emilia Galotti*'.
[14] The brother–sister motif occurs in *Le Fils naturel* too: it is a favourite of
the period.
[15] G ii. 724-47.

the Templar to Sittah — a double betrothal like that which ends *Der Freigeist*. In the final version, in keeping with the generally negative view which Lessing took, as we have seen, of erotic love, such love functions only as a *retarding* element in the plot. It threatens the Templar's friendship with Nathan almost as soon as it is formed; while still under its influence, the Templar ruefully observes 'Daß/ Ein einz'ger Funken dieser Leidenschaft/ Doch unsers Hirns so viel verbrennen kann!' (V, 3); and when at last cured of it, he can say to Nathan, 'Ihr gebt/ Mir mehr, als Ihr mir nehmt! unendlich mehr!' (V, 8). This is a new and very characteristic variation on the familiar comic motif (*Der Misogyn* furnishes a perfect example) of young lovers circumventing the opposition of a parent or guardian; and it is by no means clear that we should agree with those who have criticized Lessing for failing to be conventional.[16]

Nor, on the other hand, should we pay much attention to the criticism, though it is one very often repeated, that the plot is improbable or artificial. Plots of this kind *are* improbable and artificial: they are full of, indeed they *consist* of, coincidences and symmetries far exceeding those of ordinary life. In tragedies, such as Voltaire's, or dramas pretending to a realistic depiction of ordinary life, such as Diderot's, such devices may legitimately be criticized as tending to weaken the credibility upon which the dramatist's intended effect depends. But in *Nathan der Weise* Lessing is aiming neither at tragedy nor at mimetic realism. Though so much of his earlier dramatic work, both in theory and in practice, had been directed to those ends, in *Nathan* he has left them behind and created a work whose essential configuration is quite plainly symbolic. It is indeed a 'Schattenriß von dem Ganzen des ewigen Schöpfers', and whereas in *Minna von Barnhelm* or *Emilia Galotti* we may feel a certain tension between the self-containedness of an artistic design ('comedy' or 'tragedy') and the evident attempt at a realistic portrayal of contemporary reality, in *Nathan* we need not hesitate to admire and delight in the artifice of Lessing's design for its own sake and for that of the higher truth which it is intended to convey.

[16] Cf. P. Demetz, 'Vom Mythos der Komödie', in *Lessing: Nathan der Weise* (Dichtung und Wirklichkeit, xxv; Frankfurt and Berlin, 1966), pp. 154 ff.

This does not mean that Lessing has abandoned reality completely, or that the characters who enact this elegantly artificial design are mere lay figures. Lessing still plainly holds with Diderot that the dramatist should seek to 'rendre les hommes tels qu'ils sont',[17] even if on this occasion he allows them to inhabit a world more self-evidently controlled by a benevolent Providence than the world with which we are familiar.[18] In particular the play's two most important characters, the Templar and Nathan, are full of a reality as deeply felt as it is keenly observed. Indeed, both of them contain elements of their creator's own character and experience.

The Templar is a character of a kind we have met before in Lessing: the resemblance to Tellheim is particularly strong. Unhesitatingly selfless, brave, and generous, he has, like Tellheim, earned the gratitude and hence the love of one to whom the conventional loyalties of his calling should have made him an enemy. Like Tellheim's, his generosity is of a kind which finds it hard to accept thanks, and his pride and self-reliance make it difficult for him to recognize the mutuality upon which human relationships must be founded. Like Tellheim, he comes to doubt the loyalties of his calling and undergoes a crisis of faith in humanity and Providence, coming to the brink of total misanthropy and pessimism; though whereas Tellheim regains his faith not only in 'Tugend und Vorsicht' but also in the King of Prussia, the Templar seems at the end to have left Christianity — and certainly the extreme fanaticism which, we are told (II, 1), distinguishes his Order in particular — behind him. Like Tellheim, he is hot-tempered and impatient, quick to jump to conclusions. Mendelssohn, noting the affinity between such characters and Lessing himself, also described them as younger versions of Odoardo Galotti.[19] Nathan's reaction to the Templar — 'Fast macht/ Mich seine rauhe Tugend stutzen' (II, 5) — indeed recalls Claudia Galotti's comments on her husband (II, 5). The Templar's encounters with his fellow human beings are similarly marked by a brusqueness amounting to brutality:

[17] Diderot, Œuvres ésthetiques, p. 160.

[18] Cf. D. von König, Natürlichkeit und Wirklichkeit. Studien zu Lessings "Nathan der Weise" (Bonn, 1976).

[19] D 578. On Lessing's own 'Irascibilität' see the sketch Unterbrechung im theologischen Kampf, G viii. 349 f.

> Von heut' an tut
> Mir den Gefallen wenigstens, und kennt
> Mich weiter nicht. Ich bitt' Euch drum. Auch laßt
> Den Vater mir vom Halse. Jud' ist Jude.
> Ich bin ein plumper Schwab. (I, 6)

His self-doubt is turned against his fellow men, taking the form of suspicious misanthropy:

> DAJA. Die Menschen sind nicht immer, wie sie scheinen.
> TEMPELHERR. Doch selten etwas Bessers. (ibid.)

We are reminded of Odoardo Galotti's finding 'alles . . . verdächtig, alles strafbar' (II, 5), and likewise of Tellheim's contemptuous retort to Werner:

> WERNER. Herr Major! (*ärgerlich*) ich bin ein Mensch —
> TELLHEIM. Da bist du was Rechts! (V, 11)

But whereas Odoardo Galotti persists in the proud isolation from the world which makes him at the crucial moment unable to cope with its dangers, the Templar learns, like Tellheim, to emerge from his misanthropic self-absorption and to cultivate the 'gesellschaftliche Tugenden' of friendship and of willingness to receive as well as to give.

The process begins in the very first scene between him and Nathan, in which he confesses that what he is undergoing is in fact a religious crisis: 'Ihr stutzt,/ Daß ich, ein Christ, ein Tempelherr, so rede?' (II, 5). Spared from death by the caprice of a Mohammedan sultan to save in his turn the life of a Jewish girl, the Christian Crusader has lost his *raison d'être*, and is in consequence plunged into melancholic introspection. And melancholy is self-indulgent: warned by the Lay Brother that eating too many dates 'macht melancholisches Geblüt', the Templar replies that perhaps he *wants* to be melancholy (I, 5). However, if he can see no sense in the bizarre pattern of events which have befallen him, he can see enough to reject the Patriarch's perverted view that God has destined him 'zu großen, großen Dingen' — namely, espionage and murder. Nathan's message of the religion of humanity, 'Sind Christ und Jude eher Christ und Jude,/ Als Mensch?', falls upon receptive ears (II, 5). But welcome though the message may be, it is as yet only an abstraction: it has to be tested in practice. And of course the Templar all but fails the test. Led astray,

as we have noted, by his impulsive love for Recha, he miscon-
strues the temperance of Nathan's friendship (III, 9), seizes
upon the revelations of Daja — who of course knows only
part of the truth — and allows himself to be driven into the
arms of the Patriarch after all, extricating himself only when
it is almost too late (IV, 2). His relapse takes him to the point
at which Saladin can rebuke him with the angry words, 'Sei
ruhig, Christ!' (IV, 4); and the epithet recurs yet more vehe-
mently when a partial recovery has led to another, even more
perilous relapse:

> TEMPELHERR (*aus seiner wilden, stummen Zerstreuung*
> *auffahrend*).   Wo? wo ist
>   Er, dieser Bruder? Noch nicht hier? Ich sollt'
>   Ihn hier ja treffen.
> NATHAN.   Nur Geduld!
> TEMPELHERR (*äußerst bitter*).   Er hat
>   Ihr einen Vater aufgebunden: — wird
>   Er keinen Bruder für sie finden?
> SALADIN.   Das
>   Hat noch gefehlt! Christ! ein so niedriger
>   Verdacht wär über Assads Lippen nicht
>   Gekommen.   (V, 8)

The stage directions remind us of Tellheim at the end of the
penultimate scene of *Minna von Barnhelm*, when he '*vor Wut*
an den Fingern naget, das Gesicht wegwendet, und nichts
höret'. But as with Tellheim, when the Templar is in possession of the full truth there can be no further relapse. When
the design of Providence is revealed, there can be no further
reason for a man to mistrust his fellows or to misinterpret
their actions.

Presiding over the whole play and guiding all the other
characters towards the truth, which of course not even he is
fully aware of at the beginning, is Nathan, the wise Jew. He
is, as Al-Hafi tells Saladin and Sittah,

> Ein Jude freilich übrigens, wie's nicht
> Viel Juden gibt. Er hat Verstand; er weiß
> Zu leben; spielt gut Schach . . .   (II, 2)

He has emancipated himself from the limitations of his ances-
tral faith, and has brought up Recha to revere God, but without

the forms of any conventional religion. Yet, as he muses in his monologue before the encounter with Saladin, if he does not wish to appear a 'Stockjude', nor would he seem to be 'ganz und gar nicht Jude' (III, 6). Indeed, the Templar comments with admiration upon the fact that he 'so ganz nur Jude scheinen will' (III, 9), and in delineating him Lessing has boldly made use of a number of traditional, even stereotyped features of the Jew as perceived by his Gentile European neighbours. First among these is, of course, his association with money, for, as the as yet unenlightened Templar observes to Daja, 'Seinem Volk ist reich und weise / Vielleicht das Nämliche' (I, 6). Nathan is a rich capitalist, like Shylock (who of course also loses his daughter to a Christian). Nathan even alludes wryly to the stereotype himself, as he reflects upon Saladin's question:

> Wie Geld in Sack, so striche man in Kopf
> Auch Wahrheit ein? Wer ist denn hier der Jude?
> Ich oder er?   (III, 6)

Here Lessing, as he had done in *Die Juden* so many years before, boldly confronts the stereotypes of anti-Semitism. Like the traveller in the earlier play, Nathan is a wealthy man and has no reason to be ashamed of his wealth, for he makes wise and generous use of it.[20] Some of the aspects of his wisdom too seem particularly, or at any rate characteristically, Jewish. The ironical quibbling, the pouncing on words, the quizzical dissection and definition which permeate the play from its very first lines —

> DAJA. Er ist es! Nathan! — Gott sei ewig Dank,
>   Daß Ihr doch endlich einmal wiederkommt.
> NATHAN. Ja, Daja; Gott sei Dank! Doch warum *endlich*?
>   Hab' ich denn eher wiederkommen wollen?
>   Und wiederkommen können?

— have a distinctly rabbinical (if also very Lessingian) flavour. They give rise to some of the play's most characteristic wit:

---

[20] Cf. P. Hernadi, 'Nathan der Bürger: Lessings Mythos vom aufgeklärten Kaufmann', *LYB* iii (1971), 151-9.

DAJA.   Er läßt sich wieder sehn! Er läßt
    Sich wieder sehn!
NATHAN.   Wer, Daja? wer?
DAJA.   Er! er!
NATHAN. Er? Er? — Wann läßt sich *der* nicht sehn! — Ja so,
    Nur euer Er heißt er.   (I, 4)

Or:

NATHAN.   — Doch wie? Sollt' er auch wohl
    Die Wahrheit nicht in Wahrheit fodern? — Zwar,
    Zwar der Verdacht, daß er die Wahrheit nur
    Als Falle brauche, wär' auch gar zu klein! —
    Zu klein? — Was ist für einen Großen denn
    Zu klein?   (III, 6)

Or:

TEMPELHERR.   Und so fiel mir ein,
    Euch kurz und gut das Messer an die Kehle
    Zu setzen.
NATHAN.   Kurz und gut? und gut? — Wo steckt
    Das Gute?   (V, 5)

But most important of all, Lessing shows us Nathan as a wise
man whose wisdom has not been easily won, but gained
through the profoundest suffering — like that of Job, cited in
the *Rettung des Cardanus* as the archetype of the Jewish experience.[21] Like the Templar, Nathan has found himself at a
loss to understand the workings of Providence — and where
the Templar is confused by the apparent meaninglessness of *for-
tunate* events, Nathan has been confronted with what can
only seem senseless suffering and disaster, the slaughter of his
wife and seven sons by the Christians. But, as he relates to
Brother Bonafides, this was for him a practical test of an abstract and theoretical wisdom. After coming to the verge of
despair in God and humanity, he yields to the 'gentle voice' of
reason:

            — Ich stand! und rief zu Gott: ich will!
            Willst du nur, daß ich will!   (IV, 7)

---

[21] G vii. 23.

Nathan has triumphantly passed the severest possible test of his faith in 'Tugend und Vorsicht' and solved the problem which Odoardo Galotti could not solve, that of reconciling his own will with the designs of Providence. By this he qualifies to act as the principal agent of Providence, within the play, in guiding and enlightening the others. And it may be that, as Judaism is historically prior to Christianity and Islam, Nathan's role of educator, leading Christian (Recha and the Templar) and Mohammedan (Saladin) to enlightenment, is to be seen as also essentially connected with his Jewishness.[22]

There is much in the figure of Nathan to suggest a portrait of Lessing's wise, chess-playing Jewish friend, the 'merchant-philosopher' Moses Mendelssohn.[23] Mendelssohn, though he became one of the leading figures of the German Enlightenment never renounced his Jewish identity — indeed, he kept up far more of the formal observances of Judaism than Nathan seems to do. In 1769 he declined a challenge from the egregious Lavater either to refute the claims of Christianity to exclusive truth, or to permit himself to be baptized:[24] another real-life parallel to Saladin's challenging of Nathan. And Lessing has given Nathan's daughter, in the final version of his play, the name of Mendelssohn's daughter. But Nathan's tragedy is a reflection rather of that bitterest moment in Lessing's own life, the loss of his wife and son. Lessing and Eva König, engaged for five years, were finally married on 8 October 1776, and enjoyed a year of rich happiness and companionship. A son was born to them on Christmas Day 1777, but he lived only for a few hours; Eva lay unconscious, rallied in the New Year, but relapsed and died on 10 January 1778, and was buried two days later. 'Meine Frau ist tot', wrote Lessing to his friend Eschenburg, 'und diese Erfahrung habe ich nun auch gemacht. Ich freue mich, daß mir viel dergleichen Erfahrungen nicht mehr sein können zu machen.' It is one of a number of similar letters expressing with laconic bitterness what must have been the hardest test of his own

---

[22] Cf. G. Rohrmoser, 'Lessing: *Nathan der Weise*', in B. von Weise (ed.), *Das deutsche Drama* (Düsseldorf, 1964), i. 118.

[23] Cf. A. Altmann, *Moses Mendelssohn: A Biographical Study* (London and Alabama, 1973), p. 569.

[24] Ibid., pp. 201–21.

faith in the benevolent design of the universe. But he regained the courage to live and fight on, to reaffirm in his last works his faith and trust in Providence, and to love and care for his stepdaughter Malchen König — like the exemplary foster-father who crowns the series of otherwise tragically frustrated father-figures running through the plays.[25]

Most of the other characters of *Nathan der Weise* are more conventional, less three-dimensional, but they are all neverthe-less vividly brought to life, and all have their parts to play in the setting-forth of Lessing's argument. Recha in particular, like a good many romantic heroines, is defined largely in terms of others' (including the audience's) expectations of such a figure: young, innocent, (presumably) beautiful, emo-tionally vulnerable, but possessed in full measure of the 'Frömmigkeit und Gehorsam' which Lessing had come to regard as the highest virtues in a young girl.[26] Her most indi-vidual characteristic is one not often found in such heroines, and indeed one which fits the role slightly awkwardly: her in-tense intellectual seriousness. Though brought up, as she tells Sittah, without the dubious benefits of 'tote Buchgelehrsam-keit' (V, 6), she has certainly acquired her foster-father's habit of intellectual dissection, so that she can, for example, pounce upon Daja's phrase 'sein Gott' and deliver her a lecture on the inappropriateness of such phrases (III, 1). She is a very Les-singian heroine, but a serious and rather subdued one: Lessing's idea of the character appropriate to such a figure seems to have changed, perhaps darkened, since the creation of the lively Hilaria of *Der Misogyn* or of Minna von Barnhelm. One cannot quite imagine Recha saying 'Kann man denn nicht la-chend sehr ernsthaft sein?' (*Minna* IV, 6), though it would not serve ill as a motto for *Nathan* as a whole.

The play's most purely comic characters are Daja and the Lay Brother Bonafides: both simple, even naïve figures at whose innocence a good deal of unmalicious fun is poked. Both are easily recognizable comic types: the garrulous old maid, and the dim servant-messenger who cheerfully reveals the secret he is meant to keep. Both are, of course, also Chris-tians, and Lessing uses them to comment on a certain kind of

---

[25] Cf. Neumann, op. cit.
[26] Cf. letter to Karl Lessing, 10 February 1772.

naïve Christianity. In the *Gegensätze* to the Reimarus fragments, Lessing had defended this kind of simple faith against
the destructive arguments of the sceptic: 'Aber was gehen
dem Christen dieses Mannes Hypothesen, und Erklärungen
und Beweise an? Ihm ist es doch einmal da, das Christentum,
welches er so wahr, in welchem er sich so selig *fühlet*.'[27] In
Nathan der Weise he takes a slightly more critical view. The
simple Christian piety of Daja and the Lay Brother may give
them a subjective spiritual satisfaction, but it equips them ill
for dealing with the world. Daja's inability to keep secret any
longer the — for her vital, but for Lessing trivial — fact that
Recha is the baptized child of Christian parents could have
had disastrous consequences. And Brother Bonafides' desire
to escape the wicked world leads him into the service of the
wicked Patriarch, whom he must obey, even when his natural
human instincts tell him it is wrong to do so, for 'Wär's sonst
gehorchen, lieber Herr?' (I, 5). But of course the possible evil
consequences of their actions are not allowed to happen, and
we are left with a predominantly favourable impression of
these characters and of their good intentions. There is satire
here, but of a very tolerant kind. Bonafides in particular
emerges in a very positive light: it was, after all, he who entrusted Recha to Nathan in the first place, and it is to him,
precisely because of his 'fromme Einfalt', that Nathan tells
the story of his bereavement and of the effort of will it cost
him to accept his place in the providential scheme of things
(IV, 7). To some extent, then, Lessing is still willing, as he
was in the *Gegensätze* (and, many years before, in the *Gedanken über die Herrnhuter*), to allow the simple Christians their
simple faith.

With the Patriarch it is a different matter, for here we have
to deal not with simple faith, but with bigotry and fanaticism
hand in glove with power politics. The Patriarch is a perverter
of the designs of Providence, an enemy of reason — 'die stolze
menschliche Vernunft' is the principal target of the 'sermon'
he preaches the Templar (IV, 2) — and a stickler for the letter
of the law at its most inhuman, insisting that 'der Jude wird
verbrannt' and refusing to admit of any mitigating circum-

[27] G vii. 458.

stances — until, that is, he remembers (having been previously carried away by his own eloquence) that the Templar enjoys Saladin's favour, and that it is therefore impolitic to hector him in this fashion. There is certainly a more biting satire here. It is however noteworthy that Lessing has chosen to make his Patriarch not so much a genuinely threatening and evil figure — like his historical prototype, the appalling Patriarch Heraclius — as a figure of satirical fun.[28] The Patriarch recalls not so much Heraclius as Lessing's adversary Pastor Goeze, from his physical presence — 'ein dicker, roter, freundlicher Prälat' — down to his contemptuous references to the theatre. His 'sermon' is a parody of Goeze's style as surely as anything in the *Axiomata* or the *Anti-Goeze* — where there is indeed, despite the seriousness of Lessing's purpose, a good deal of sheer theatricality; Goeze was right about this. But histrionics are no stranger to the pulpit, as Lessing's parody reminds us (IV, 2). It is also noteworthy that Lessing saves the Patriarch up for one scene, which is the major comic set-piece of the play, just like the Riccaut scene which occupies the exactly corresponding position in *Minna von Barnhelm*. The Patriarch even has his catch-phrase, his thrice-repeated 'Tut nichts, der Jude wird verbrannt'; Lessing can hardly have imagined that in the twentieth century these words would regain a genuinely sinister, even terrifying undertone.

Through the medium of satire Lessing gives his Christian public a good deal of food for thought about the Christian faith and, above all, its ethical implications. He also uses his Mohammedan characters, Sultan Saladin and his sister Sittah, to voice direct criticism of Christian claims to the exclusive possession of the truth. Lessing thought of the religion of Mohammed as a simple faith with few if any superstitious accretions, as close as any actual religion might be to the ideal 'natural religion' of the eighteenth-century Deists: a view shared by many of his contemporaries, though others saw the Prophet as an impostor.[29] In the *Rettung des Cardanus* the Mohammedan claims that his own faith contains nothing 'das nicht mit der allerstrengsten Vernunft übereinkomme', and

---

[28] Cf. Demetz, *Nathan der Weise*, ed. cit., pp. 137 ff.

[29] Cf. H. B. Nisbet, '*De Tribus Impostoribus*: On the Genesis of Lessing's *Nathan der Weise*', *Euph.* lxxiii (1979), 365–87.

challenges the Christian, 'Du mußt beweisen, daß der Mensch zu mehr verbunden ist, als Gott zu kennen, und tugendhaft zu sein.'[30] Saladin's challenge to Nathan similarly has every appearance of strict rationality — 'Von diesen drei/ Religionen kann doch eine nur/ Die wahre sein' — though Nathan's answer takes us beyond simple rationalism. Saladin is also shown, in accordance with the reputation history has generally given him, as a benevolent ruler, brave, generous to a fault (another Tellheim!), tolerant — 'Ich habe nie verlangt,/ Daß allen Bäumen Eine Rinde wachse' (IV, 4) — fanatical only in his enmity to fanaticism. Yet there is in Saladin a certain irresponsibility too, as Al-Hafi observes (I, 3); and the sparing of one Templar's life is just as much the action of an arbitrary despot as the execution of the other nineteen (I, 5) — even if it proves to be part of a providential design. This is also true of Sittah's scheme to play a trick on Nathan in order to force him into advancing Saladin money (II, 3): in Sittah we catch a glimpse of the capriciousness of a Minna von Barnhelm. Saladin and his sister are both fundamentally well-intentioned and sympathetic characters, imperfect but capable of enlightenment; and through the action of the play and with the guidance of Nathan, they are indeed raised at the end of the play to a higher level of awareness — leaving the unreformed Christians behind.

Left behind too is the last character we must mention, the Dervish Al-Hafi. He is yet another of those Lessingian characters in whom moral idealism leads to the rejection of a world which cannot measure up to their impossibly high standards. Unlike the other figures in *Nathan* whom we have considered, he is not to be thought of as representing any particular religion: though he is called a Dervish, that is, a kind of Mohammedan monk or friar, there are contrary suggestions that he is in fact a Parsee or Guebre, an adherent of the pre-Islamic religion of Persia and the Near East (like the protagonists of Voltaire's *Guèbres*). Al-Hafi surprises his old friend Nathan by accepting the office of treasurer to Saladin; and sure enough, his compromise with the world does not last long. He has taken on the job because 'Warum man ihn recht bittet,/

---

[30] G vii. 24 f.

Und er für gut erkennt: das muß ein Derwisch' (I, 3). He has
rightly taken the opportunity to be of service to his fellow
men. But Nathan's gentle mockery of the 'Kerl im Staat' is
enough to provoke a violent disillusionment and even self-
denunciation:

> Laßt *meiner* Geckerei
> Mich doch nur auch erwähnen! — Was? es wäre
> Nicht Geckerei, an solchen Geckereien
> Die gute Seite dennoch auszuspüren,
> Um Anteil, dieser guten Seite wegen,
> An dieser Geckerei zu nehmen? Heh?
> Das nicht?   (ibid.)

Al-Hafi is too intolerant of the world's imperfections; as in
Minna von Barnhelm, we are not invited to approve such cen-
soriousness. As Nathan, now only half jokingly, says, Al-Hafi's
virtue is of a kind which can only exist in isolation: 'Ich
fürchte,/ Grad' unter Menschen möchtest du ein Mensch/ Zu
sein verlernen' (ibid.). Al-Hafi has no sense of proportion.
What finally damns Saladin in his eyes is — his refusal to take
a game of chess seriously; and Al-Hafi returns to the desert,
where Nathan, for all his affection, even admiration for him
('Der wahre Bettler ist/ Doch einzig und allein der wahre
König!') cannot follow (II, 9). Al-Hafi resolves, like Appiani,
'ihm selbst zu leben' (II, 9), but this withdrawal from society
is not Lessing's ideal.[31] Yet in such a character there is more
than a touch of Lessing himself, of the Lessing who told Fritz
Jacobi that 'die bürgerliche Gesellschaft müsse ganz aufgehoben werden.' Perhaps Nathan, and in him Lessing, continued
to hope that Al-Hafi might be brought back into human
society (as Philinte hopes to bring back Alceste at the end of
Molière's *Misanthrope*), for Lessing talked of adding a 'Nachspiel' to *Nathan*, to be entitled *Der Derwisch*; but this was
never written.[32]

The play thus presents us with an array of characters, of
different historic religions or of none, of different shades of
naïvety or sophistication, acting from a variety of motives
(though only one is positively ill-intentioned) and with varying

[31] Cf. Hernadi, 'Nathan der Bürger', and von König, op. cit., esp. pp. 58 ff.
[32] Cf. G ii. 722 f. For a real-life model for Al-Hafi, cf. D 195 f., and Altmann,
op. cit., p. 569.

degrees of insight into the providential plan of which they are
nevertheless all agents. It shows us that, as the ring parable
teaches, right conduct is independent of any particular religious faith or any particular conception of the 'truth'. The
three sons in the parable are wrong to argue about the authenticity of their rings, for the three rings are 'gleich wahr und
gleich falsch', as Lessing writes of historic religions in *Über
die Entstehung der geoffenbarten Religion*;[33] or indeed, in
the words of the Latin motto of the *Erziehung des Menschengeschlechts*, 'All these things are in certain respects true for
the same reason that they are in certain respects false.'[34] And
just as Lessing follows up his essay *Über den Beweis des
Geistes und der Kraft*, in which the historical evidence for the
truth of Christianity is probed with philosophical rigour, with
the dialogue *Das Testament Johannis*, in which all such argu-
mentation is brushed aside in favour of the simple ethical
message 'Kinderchen, liebt euch!',[35] so Nathan follows up
the first, traditional part of the parable, which demonstrates
the undemonstrability of religious truth, with the sequel, not
in Boccaccio's version of the tale, in which the judge advises
the three brothers to strive to make themselves 'vor Gott und
Menschen angenehm' by their own efforts. But though Lessing is plainly convinced (in contradiction to the orthodox
Lutheran view) of the inefficacy of faith without good works,
he undoubtedly regards the performance of good works as
dependent upon some kind of faith: the power of the original
ring is, it seems, effective only for the wearer who 'in dieser
Zuversicht ihn trug', and the last, but by no means the least,
of the qualities which the judge tells the brothers they will
need in order to show forth the power of their rings is 'in-
nigst[e] Ergebenheit in Gott' (III, 7). 'Submission to the will
of God' is of course, as Lessing noted,[36] the literal meaning
of the word 'Islam'; and Nathan characterizes his own actions,
in his narration to Brother Bonafides, as those of 'der gottergebne Mensch' (IV, 7) — whereas, as Nathan tells Daja, the
Christian's '"Sich Gott um so viel näher fühlen",/ Ist Unsinn
oder Gotteslästerung' (I, 2). Lessing's message therefore is

[33] G vii. 283.   [34] G viii. 489.
[35] G viii. 17.   [36] G ii. 744.

not a purely secularized gospel of social ethics;[37] its sheet-anchor is a faith in the ultimate wisdom and benevolence of God. 'Tugend und Vorsicht' are, as ever, intimately connected.

But as the action of the play makes clear, divine Providence moves in a mysterious way. It does not work by means of miraculous, supernatural intervention: for if such intervention were necessary, it would cast doubt upon the wisdom and benevolence of God's original creation.[38]

> Der Wunder höchstes ist,
> Daß uns die wahren, echten Wunder so
> Alltäglich werden können, werden sollen.   (I, 2)

The human agencies through which it operates are, as Nathan insists to Daja and Recha, 'miraculous' enough:

> Sieh! eine Stirn, so oder so gewölbt;
> Der Rücken einer Nase, so vielmehr
> Als so geführet; Augenbrauen, die
> Auf einem scharfen oder stumpfen Knochen
> So oder so sich schlängeln; eine Linie,
> Ein Bug, ein Winkel, eine Falt', ein Mal,
> Ein Nichts, auf eines wilden Europäers
> Gesicht: — und du entkömmst dem Feur, in Asien!
> Das wär' kein Wunder, wundersücht' ges Volk?
> Warum bemüht ihr denn noch einen Engel?   (ibid.)

It seems to attach not very much significance to the moral intention behind an action. Lessing's great contemporary Kant was to distinguish rigorously in his moral philosophy between 'Handlungen aus Pflicht', actions undertaken for the sake of duty, and 'pflichtgemäße Handlungen', actions which merely happen to conform to it, and to reserve moral approbation in the strict sense for the former.[39] But Kant believed in man's absolute moral freedom, and Lessing did not. It does not seem to matter very much whether an action is, like Nathan's fostering of Recha, an example of 'was sich der gottergebne Mensch/Für Taten abgewinnen kann' (IV, 7) (which sounds

---

[37] As argued, for example, by H. Politzer, 'Lessing's Parable of the Three Rings', *GQ* xxxi (1958), 161-77 (German version in B, 343-61). Nor is the 'Zuversicht' merely a psychological factor, as suggested by Nisbet, op. cit., p. 383.

[38] This point is expounded in the third of the *Gegensätze*, G vii. 468-72.

[39] Kant, *Grundlegung zur Metaphysik der Sitten*, i: *Werke*, ed. W. Weischedel, iv (Wiesbaden, 1956), p. 22 f.

almost Kantian); or, like the Templar's rescue of Recha from
the fire, a semi-instinctive act of selfless courage; or, like
Saladin's sparing of the Templar's life, the indulgence of an
impulse. A good deed is a good deed; and as Saladin himself
observes — the lines are an expression of wonder, not of com-
placency —

> Wie aus Einer guten Tat,
> Gebar sie auch schon bloße Leidenschaft,
> Doch so viel andre gute Taten fließen!   (III, 7)

Moreover, the designs of Providence can be furthered by
actions which are morally neutral or even dubious — the
thoughtless revelations of Daja and the Templar, the selfish,
if not actually malicious, scheming of Sittah, even the positively evil intentions of the Patriarch: as Nathan tells the
Templar (V, 5) it is thanks to the Patriarch that the full truth
is finally revealed. Perhaps this means that men are after all
to be judged by their faith and their intentions rather than by
their actions, for it is not for their actions that they are
responsible:

> Gott! wie leicht
> Mir wird, daß ich nun weiter auf der Welt
> Nichts zu verbergen habe! daß ich vor
> Den Menschen nun so frei kann wandeln, als
> Vor dir, der du allein den Menschen nicht
> Nach seinen Taten brauchst zu richten, die
> So selten seine Taten sind, o Gott!   (V, 4)

But Nathan says 'selten', not 'niemals'. Providence may indeed employ some surprising agents for the execution of its
designs, but it is not true that, as the Patriarch claims, God
does not need man's help at all:

> Zu dem, was hat
> Der Jude Gott denn vorzugreifen? Gott
> Kann, wen er retten will, schon ohn' ihn retten.   (IV, 2)

God will have man's hand, as Odoardo Galotti had realized;
he wills, as Nathan puts it, that man shall will — shall understand to the full the role which has been allotted to him in
the scheme of things and shall actively strive to perform it.
Unaided by man, Providence would no doubt accomplish its

design, but it would take an infinity to do so; with man's active co-operation, infinity is brought a little closer.[40] As Lessing put it in the 'Ankündigung' with which he invited subscriptions for the play, 'die Welt, wie ich mir sie denke, ist eine eben so natürliche Welt, und es mag an der Vorsehung wohl nicht allein liegen, daß sie nicht eben so wirklich ist.'[41]

Mendelssohn was right to describe *Nathan der Weise* as a 'Lobgedicht auf die Vorsehung':[42] faith in Providence is the ground of Lessing's ethical message and of his demonstration of the equal positive (as well as negative) potential of all religions. It was therefore absolutely necessary, quite apart from the lack of actual *dramatic* substance in Boccaccio's anecdote, for him to devise a plot which, with its complex interrelations all leading inevitably to the final happy ending, presents us with a model of the workings of divine Providence: a theodicy, a 'Schattenriß von dem Ganzen des ewigen Schöpfers'.

The plot is designed with an economy perhaps even greater than that of *Emilia Galotti*. As we have seen, all the characters play their part in the working-out of the action, and every scene contributes both to the exposition and eventual completion of the dramatic pattern, and to the discussion of Lessing's themes in a more immediate and obvious sense.[43] Sometimes this discussion may to modern tastes drag a little: for example in Nathan's lesson to Recha and Daja on the subject of miracles (I, 2). It might seem that Lessing, having already discussed this topic in the *Gegensätze*, is being rather self-indulgent in giving space to it in his play. But quite apart from the fact that it occupies an essential place in his conception of the working of Providence, reference to this and other topics familiar from Lessing's theological investigations of the mid–70s would no doubt be appreciated by his intended audience as 'pungent allusions to current affairs'[44] such as

---

[40] The interaction, at the level of moral action, between human effort and providential guidance is closely paralleled at the level of congition by the interaction of human reason and divine revelation which is the subject of *Die Erziehung des Menschengeschlechts*.

[41] G ii. 749. Cf. von König, op. cit.   [42] D 581.

[43] Cf. K. Heydemann, 'Gesinnung und Tat. Zu Lessings *Nathan der Weise*', *LYB* vii (1975), 69–104.

[44] Altmann, op. cit., p. 573; cf. Nisbet, op. cit., p. 380.

are a regular staple of comedy, though the affairs there alluded to are usually of a more mundane sort. Even in *Der junge Gelehrte*, we recall, Lessing had used the Berlin Academy's philosophical essay competition to add topical spice to his portrayal of a recurrent comic type. The discursive and allusive material in *Nathan* is skilfully woven in with material of a more purely dramatically functional kind, and Lessing is careful to vary the register of his dialogue, intellectual seriousness being constantly blended with wit, humour, and the occasional touch of pathos. Even the discussion of miracles does not come across as cold, for it has a powerful emotional effect on Recha.

The blending of effects is most strongly evident in the ring parable scene which occupies the centre of Act III. Embodying as it does so much of the play's ethical message, the parable is conceived as a great set-piece, almost an aria, in which Nathan appears as the spokesman of Lessing's ideals. But this does not mean that Lessing is holding up the dramatic action to indulge in gratuitous preaching through the mouth of a favourite character (though when it is as brilliantly done as this, we may well feel in any case disposed to pardon the dramatist his self-indulgence). On the contrary, the parable scene fulfils a vital dramatic function. By his parable, Nathan changes Saladin: from a purely passive tolerance ('Ich habe nie verlangt,/ Daß allen Bäumen Eine Rinde wachse') and an arbitrary, capricious benevolence, he is won over to a more active realization of his part in the providential scheme of things (his 'Ich Staub! Ich Nichts!' marks the moment of this realization, analogous to Nathan's 'Ich stand und rief zu Gott . . .')[45] and Nathan has gained a powerful ally whose support is essential to the resolution of the dramatic action. Saladin's 'Nathan, lieber Nathan! . . . Geh! — Aber sei mein Freund' is one of the high points of the action, and a powerful assurance of the inevitability of a happy ending despite the complications which, of course, begin to develop very soon afterwards. Lessing had to devise a dramatic action to show off his parable, as the ring shows off the opal; but he has rightly made his parable the centre of his play.[46]

[45] Heydemann, op. cit., p. 100.
[46] Cf. F. M. Fowler, 'Why Lessing's Nathan had to be *der Weise*: on the Inte-

Even the opening scenes of Act V are not without relevance, although they seem to make little contribution to the action, introduce extra characters who are not directly involved in it, and are often omitted in performance. Lessing evidently felt it necessary, as with Tellheim, to show us the restoration of Saladin's wealth: a 'Bettler' can be a king only to himself, but a rich man is in a position to act socially, by sharing his wealth with others. The scene also, incidentally, illustrates the hastiness of Al-Hafi's judgement on Saladin's 'Geckerei', just as the outcome of the parable scene proves Al-Hafi wrong in telling Nathan that Saladin never listens to advice. And Lessing is also concerned to show us that the achieved harmony of his ending is not to be thought of as a Utopian state of perfection, but part of a continuing history which will bring new challenges to be faced.[47] He makes Saladin refer to his impending 'Abtritt' (V, 1), and we learn that 'Die Tempelherrn sind wieder rege' (V, 2). In historical fact the truce between Saladin and the Crusaders under Richard Lionheart, during which the action of the play takes place, ended in 1192, and Saladin died in the following year.

Lessing has, of course, not striven for historical accuracy, but as he himself noted '[sich] über alle Chronologie hinweg gesetzt.'[48] We should expect nothing else from the man who had written that the dramatist 'braucht eine Geschichte nicht darum, weil sie geschehen ist, sondern darum, weil sie so geschehen ist, daß er sie schwerlich zu seinem gegenwärtigen Zwecke besser erdichten könnte' (*Dramaturgie*, No. 19). Boccaccio's story had introduced the historical figure of Saladin, and Lessing was thereby presented with a historical and geographical setting which could not have been better suited to his theme and to his symbolic purpose. The Holy Land at the time of the Crusades provides the only possible setting to bring together the representatives of the three great religions:

> DAJA.   O! das ist das Land
> Der Wunder!

---

gration of Play and Parable', *NGS* vii (1979), 17–22.
    [47] Cf. R. K. Angress, '"Dreams that were more than dreams" in Lessing's *Nathan*', *LYB* iii (1971), 108–27.
    [48] G ii. 744.

TEMPELHERR. (Nun! — des Wunderbaren. Kann
  Es auch wohl anders sein? Die ganze Welt
  Drängt sich ja hier zusammen.)   (III, 10)

But as the lines remind us, Lessing's theme is universal. He is not at all interested in the history for its own sake, though he studied historical source-material, such as Marin's *Histoire de Saladin* (1758); he uses the truce between Saladin and the Crusaders to provide a plausible occasion for the action, and he includes a few little historical touches that had taken his fancy, such as Marin's information[49] that a Templar might not offer for his ransom 'mehr als den ledern Gurt . . . und höchstens seinen Dolch' (I, 2), or colourful, unfamiliar words like 'Defterdar', 'Ginnistan', or 'Jamerlonk'. But the effect of things like this is not one of genuine historical authenticity. It is rather that of a kind of exoticism found in several other eighteenth-century works, from Montesquieu to Mozart, in which an Oriental frame is used to adorn a mirror held up to European issues, implying that they are of more than merely European significance. (The idea of a universal humanity is of course very largely a creation of eighteenth-century Europeans.) The purpose of the Oriental colouring is not to give an authentic portrait of the Eastern world, but on the contrary to intimate that the work is to be read symbolically rather than literally. In style and atmosphere it is completely different from Lessing's three earlier full-length plays, all of which aim in different ways and with differing degrees of success at the representation of characters and settings drawn from contemporary real life.

Lessing had of course made a number of attempts at such a style and such an atmosphere before *Nathan. Kleonnis* and *Philotas* had employed another and traditionally more familiar form of *éloignement*, the setting of classical antiquity, to underline the intended universality of their thematic content. More exotic settings had been assayed in *Fatime* and *Der Horoscop*, both of which also employ blank verse. In *Alcibiades* the worlds of ancient Greece and Persia were to meet, and here the motif of religious conflict would have played a part. All these experiments formed a part of Lessing's search

[49] Ibid.

for a new kind of serious drama, and *Nathan* may justly be
regarded as their final fruition. But they were of course all
experiments in *tragedy*, and Lessing was only able to bring
them to fruition when, thanks to the compelling force of his
theme and subject-matter, he was able to put the formal
requirements of tragedy behind him.

Nathan der Weise is described as 'ein dramatisches Gedicht'.
Obviously it is not a tragedy; nor is it a comedy of a satirical
kind — as Lessing wrote to Karl on 20 October 1778, 'Es
wird nichts weniger, als ein satirisches Stück, um den Kampf-
platz mit Hohngelächter zu verlassen. Es wird ein so rührendes
Stück, als ich nur gemacht habe.' But with its blend of
humour, wit, intellectual seriousness, and sentiment it surely
comes very close to what Lessing had proclaimed in the
Theatralische Bibliothek as the ideal of 'wahre Komödie'.[50]
Hugo von Hofmannsthal wrote in 1929 that it should be performed 'ganz als das geistreichste Lustspiel, das wir besitzen',[51] and a number of memorable productions in recent
years have confirmed that this is indeed the way in which it
most surely makes its effect.

One wonders, then, why Lessing did not designate it a
comedy. Perhaps he had come to the conclusion that Diderot
was right after all: that the requirements of the modern theatre
and the modern public were to be met, not by the continuation or revival of the traditional dramatic genres, but by the
creation of new, intermediary ones. But the exoticism of
Nathan takes it, as we have seen, away from the kind of drama
that Diderot stood for. It is more likely that Lessing was no
longer interested in questions of genre or even of theatrical
effect for their own sake: the play was written because he had
something that demanded to be said, the form is created by and
for the content, and the resultant work demands to be taken
on its own terms, without reference to any pre-established
generic norms.[52] Nor, however, is it to be understood as a
deliberate rebellion against such norms, as the term 'Schau-

[50] Cf. above, p. 26.

[51] Hofmannsthal, 'Gotthold Ephraim Lessing. Zum 22 Januar 1929', in *Aus-
gewählte Werke* (Frankfurt, 1957), ii. 773.

[52] For a view of *Nathan* as a 'polemical reversal' of a kind of play of which
Lessing disapproved, and hence grounded in dramatic theory, see R. K. Angress,
'Lessing's Criticism of Cronegk: *Nathan in Ovo?*', *LYB* iv (1972), 27–36.

spiel', much favoured by the 'Stürmer und Dränger', might have implied. But the idol of the younger dramatists has surely cast a little of his shadow here too. If one looks for parallels and precedents for the form of *Nathan der Weise*, one can only say that it is more like Shakespearian romance — *The Winter's Tale* or *The Tempest* — than any other work of the classical German dramatic repertory.

Lessing's handling of form in *Nathan* is by no means careless or ineffectual. It is certainly care*free*, but with this relaxation goes an instinctive sense of pace and contrast: in register and effect, in the use of different characters and groupings, and of course of different settings. For *Emilia Galotti* Lessing had self-consciously proclaimed his intention to make use of 'alle Freiheiten der englischen Bühne', but had finally produced a work essentially classical in its scale and concentration. The twelve scene-changes of *Nathan* create quite a different atmosphere. Lessing moves freely back and forth between four principal settings: Nathan's house, Saladin's palace, the Patriarch's monastery (the setting, like the character, appears only once) and the grove of palm-trees where the Templar wanders, plucking dates. Many hours must have been spent by readers searching the text of *Nathan* in vain for the familiar quotation 'Es wandelt niemand ungestraft unter Palmen', which actually comes from Goethe's *Wahlverwandtschaften*:[53] unlike the landscape of Goethe's novel, the palm-trees of *Nathan* are not an ominous or sinister setting, but (despite the Lay Brother's warning of the ill-effects of eating too many dates) essentially a bright, serene, and cheerful one. Indeed, one imagines the whole action taking place under a bright sun and cloudless Mediterranean blue skies (perhaps, after all, a product of that Italian journey on which Lessing seemed to have *seen* so little); and this atmosphere is surely one of the features which justify the epithet 'poetic'.

Another such feature is of course the fact that it is written in verse. Lessing anticipated that this would surprise his friends, and attempted to offer some explanation. To Ramler, with whom he had in earlier days discussed the question of verse drama and the appropriate choice of metre, he wrote on

---

[53] *Wahlverwandtschaften*, Part ii, chapter 7: Goethe, ed. cit., vi. 416.

18 December 1778, 'Ich habe wirklich die Verse nicht des Wohlklanges wegen gewählt: sondern weil ich glaubte, daß der orientalische Ton, den ich doch hier und da angeben müsse, in der Prose zu sehr auffallen dürfte.' This looks a curiously 'unpoetic' argument, but in fact it emphasizes the move away from realism: the adoption of the exotic tone leads to the abandonment of the medium whose virtues, as expounded by Lessing in theory and as exemplified in the best of his dramatic practice hitherto, are essentially realist virtues. And to his brother Karl he had written on 7 December that the choice of verse would further rather than impede the work's speedy completion: 'Meine Prose hat mir von jeher mehr Zeit gekostet, als Verse. Ja, wirst Du sagen, als solche Verse! — Mit Erlaubnis; ich dächte, sie wären viel schlechter, wenn sie viel besser wären.' Again an 'unpoetic' argument, but again it signals the essentially poetic purpose, the abandonment of deliberate realism. The prose of *Emilia Galotti* had been a finely-tuned instrument for recording reality, and for achieving that 'Herunterstimmung' of conventional tragic rhetoric upon which Karl had so approvingly commented. Even the 'indeklamable Stellen' in *Miß Sara Sampson*, as Lessing had written to Moses Mendelssohn on 14 September 1757, represented an attempt to help the actors and actresses feel their way into their parts, and so to reproduce the characters and their feelings more convincingly: 'ihre Einbildungskraft durch mehr sinnliche Bilder zu erhitzen, als freilich zu dem bloßen Ausdrucke meiner Gedanken nicht nötig wären.' That is, even the rhetoric of *Miß Sara Sampson* is, paradoxically, governed by notions of mimetic realism. In *Nathan der Weise* Lessing is no longer bothered by such considerations: concerned only with 'dem bloßen Ausdrucke meiner Gedanken', he has left behind him both 'tragedy' and mimetic realism, and created a work whose style and language are utterly and uniquely its own.

Since the most important of all the ideas seeking expression in *Nathan der Weise* is that of a symbolic theodicy, it is appropriate that the play is cast in a medium which immediately announces that it is to be read symbolically rather than literally: hence, verse rather than prose. But the humanitarianism of Lessing's message forbids anything grandiloquent or rhetorical, anything in the least smacking of the heroic.

> Der große Mann braucht überall viel Boden;
> Und mehrere, zu nah gepflanzt, zerschlagen
> Sich nur die Äste. Mittelgut, wie wir,
> Findt sich hingegen überall in Menge.
> Nur muß der eine nicht den andern mäkeln.
> Nur muß der Knorr den Knuppen hübsch vertragen.
> Nur muß ein Gipfelchen sich nicht vermessen,
> Daß es allein der Erde nicht entschossen.   (II, 5)

Hence the deliberate unpretentiousness of this verse, its familiarity, its colloquialisms, its rough-and-ready rhythms (often rendered almost unrecognizable by frequent enjambment and change of speaker in mid-line). In this sense it is indeed 'unpoetic'. But that Lessing was not unconcerned with its acoustical properties is shown by his attention to punctuation. He claimed to have devised a new scheme designed to aid the actors' delivery. Sending an instalment of the manuscript to Karl for printing on 15 January 1779, he requests that the printer shall pay particular attention to the distinction between dashes (—) and points (...), which evidently indicate different kinds of pause. He intended to explain his new punctuation in a preface, but the play turned out so long that there was not room for it; it was therefore deferred, to appear separately together with the 'Nachspiel' *Der Derwisch*, but after the publication of *Nathan* itself we hear no more of this. Actor, producer, and reader are thus left to themselves to ponder on the subtleties of Lessing's punctuation, just as they are with Arno Holz or Samuel Beckett.

The verse of *Nathan der Weise*, then, is once again more carefree than the prose of Lessing's other plays — though it has strong affinities with the often more characteristically Lessingian prose of his critical and polemical writings: lively, informal, ironical, spiced with homely and proverbial expressions. Friedrich Schlegel was observing this affinity when he wrote that the verse of *Nathan* was 'mit die beste Prosa, welche Lessing geschrieben hat', but failing to perceive Lessing's intention when he complained of the dramatic inappropriateness of a princess (Sittah in II, 2) using an expression like 'Noch bin ich auf/Dem Trocknen völlig nicht'.[54] Peter Demetz,

---

[54] B 31.

on the other hand, seeing the style of *Nathan* in terms of a proto-Brechtian 'Verfremdung' rather than of traditional poetic *éloignement*, has described it as a deliberate 'Anti-Vers'.[55] It is certainly very different from the polish and smooth flow of Goethe's *Iphigenie auf Tauris*, or the pathos and grandeur of Schiller's *Don Carlos*, which a few years later sealed the naturalization of the Shakespearian metre as the standard medium for the German classical drama. It is perhaps best described as a medium which distances without heightening, which enhances the exotic flavour while yet preserving familiarity. It is in a sense the reverse of a 'verfremdende Darstellung', which is, in Brecht's own definition, 'eine solche, die den Gegenstand zwar erkennen, ihn aber doch zugleich fremd erscheinen läßt'.[56]

Nathan der Weise is Lessing's most spontaneous and original dramatic creation. Nothing about it is contrived: content, form, and language are in perfect harmony, and there is none of that sense of strain and artificiality which mars *Miß Sara Sampson*, none of that tension between the questions raised by a probing contemporary realism and the too-ready answers provided by the traditional dramatic genres which mars *Emilia Galotti* and, to a lesser extent, *Minna von Barnhelm*. Lessing has also overcome the tension between theory and practice which can be felt in his earlier work; or rather, he has freed himself of this tension simply by abandoning most of the conflicting requirements of his theory. There is namely a major conflict within the theory itself, between, on the one hand, attachment to the traditional forms and insistence upon strict genre-definition, backed by appeals to Aristotelian authority, and, on the other, recognition and acceptance of the new style of contemporary realism represented by Diderot; but in *Nathan* both traditional genre and contemporary realism are forgotten. There is also a tension within the theory between an insistence on purely theatrical *effect*, closely associated with genre-specification ('die Tragödie ist ein Gedicht, welches Mitleid erreget'), and a strong, at times almost Gottschedian insistence on the moral, even didactic purpose of the true artist, the 'Absicht' which distinguishes the real genius

[55] *Nathan der Weise*, ed. cit., p. 131.
[56] Brecht, *Kleines Organon für das Theater*, §42 (Werkausgabe, xvi. 680).

from the 'kleinen Geistern, die nur dichten, um zu dichten' —
which reasserts the primacy of *content*. Lessing's theory of
catharsis is an attempt to resolve that tension, but I have already suggested that it is an over-elaborate and not very convincing one; and it is perhaps significant that it is after that
most searching exploration of the *effect* of drama that Lessing
returns to the view that the highest purpose of artistic creation
is to convey a 'Schattenriß von dem Ganzen des ewigen
Schöpfers'. The same tension is evident in the plays. They are
plainly designed to be models of their respective genres, and
thus to contribute to the renaissance of the German theatre,
to further a cultural and social programme which must be
achieved 'wenn auch wir einst zu den gesitteten Völkern gehören wollen, deren jedes *seine* Bühne hatte'.[57] And yet there
remains in the case of each of them a nagging conviction that
Lessing must have intended some specific message or moral —
combined, as we have seen, with uncertainty or even total
disagreement as to what the message is. But when he wrote
Nathan der Weise, Lessing had abandoned his hopes for a
German literary renaissance, or seen them overtaken by the
forms which that renaissance was in the 1770s actually taking.
And he was no longer concerned with 'culture' in the narrower sense, but with more important issues — with truth,
with the rights of man (if not in any directly political application), and with his duty to his fellows. Accordingly in *Nathan*
he lets the message speak out loud and clear, and creates a
uniquely appropriate form for it to do so. Again, though
Lessing was nothing if not an intellectual, his theories tend to
dwell on the emotional appeal of serious drama;[58] but *Nathan*
is a frankly intellectual play — which does not make it cold
or solemn or over-serious, nor even rule out the element of
'Rührung' itself. For Lessing, the use of the intellect is itself
one of the richest sources of pleasure and delight.

It is surprising that Schlegel did not see this. Carried away
by his Romantic love of paradox to invert the accepted valu-
ation of Lessing's 'poetic' and 'non-poetic' works, and by his

---

[57] Cf. above, p. 48.
[58] Cf. H. Steinmetz, 'Emotionalität versus Rationalität: Gegensätze von Theorie
und Praxis des Dramas bei Lessing', in E. P. Harris and R. E. Schade (eds.), *Lessing
in heutiger Sicht* (Bremen and Wolfenbüttel, 1977), pp. 165-8.

Romantic (Contiesque!) conception of the creative personality to assert that Lessing the man 'war mehr wert, als alle seine Talente',[59] he failed to see that the work he himself dubbed 'Lessings Lessing'[60] crowns his career not least by its harmonious unification of the diverse and many talents of its creator.

(iii)

Nathan der Weise was published in April 1779. Apart from the *Erziehung des Menschengeschlechts* it was Lessing's last important published work. After it appeared he returned to his theological studies, and planned a defence of his publication of the Reimarus fragments, for which he was now threatened with actual prosecution by the ecclesiastical authorities. But his work on *Nathan* seems to have rekindled an interest in those theatrical matters which he had declared after writing *Emilia Galotti* that he found so irksome; or perhaps it was only for financial reasons that in the summer of 1780 he signed a contract to write two plays a year for the Hamburg theatre. He proposed to begin by making an adaptation of the Jacobean play *The London Prodigal*, a work originally (though plainly wrongly) attributed to Shakespeare. On 9 November 1780 he wrote to Eschenburg requesting, among other works, a copy of this play: 'Ich soll und soll für das Hamburger Theater etwas machen, und da denke ich, daß ich mit meiner alten Absicht auf dieses Stück am ersten fertig werden will.' What the 'alte Absicht' was we do not know; but it is interesting to see his thoughts turning once more to the English drama. It is also noteworthy, however, that when he returns from writing a play designed to express his own vision to writing one designed to meet the requirements of the theatre, we find him thinking again in terms of the traditional dramatic genres. On 15 November he wrote to Elise Reimarus that he was uncertain whether to make the play a tragedy or a comedy. Elise recommended a happy ending (which, incidentally, is what the original has), and in December Lessing wrote to her that he had indeed so decided, but that the work would have to be put aside because of the latest, more

---

[59] B 20. [60] Ibid., p. 28.

threatening developments on the theological front. It is not clear that Lessing in fact did any serious work on this project; if so, nothing of it survives. Nor do we hear any more of *Der Derwisch*, the proposed 'Nachspiel' to *Nathan der Weise*; nor, unsurprisingly, of the tragedy which, Lessing had grimly suggested in a letter to Elise of 14 May 1779, could be written on the subject of the Good Samaritan, 'nach der Erfindung des Herrn Jesu Christi'. It would indeed have been a bitter irony if under the blows he had suffered in those last years he had gone so far as to revoke, as it were, the optimistic vision of *Die Juden*. But in the winter of 1780 the final deterioration in his health set in. He died on 15 February 1781, three weeks after his fifty-second birthday.

VIII

Conclusion

Lessing emancipated the German drama from neo-classicism and created model plays, not only in the traditional genres of tragedy and comedy but in a new form of his own. His example, if it was followed at all, was soon abandoned. Within a few years of his death Goethe and Schiller were moving towards a classicism of their own, and writing dramatic works in which the spirit of seventeenth-century France is once more influential. *Minna von Barnhelm* created no traditon of German comedy; and when Goethe in *Iphigenie auf Tauris* and *Torquato Tasso*, and later Schiller in *Wilhelm Tell*, turned to writing serious non-tragic drama as a vehicle for the exploration of moral and intellectual problems and the expression of ideas, the result was in style and in emotional effect far closer to classical tragedy than to Lessing's model in *Nathan der Weise*. His most influential work was undoubtedly *Emilia Galotti*, which, whatever their conscious critical reaction, exerted a powerful effect on the 'Stürmer und Dränger'. The mode of contemporary realism, allied to a now more deliberate social criticism, is continued by Lenz and Wagner, and by Goethe in *Clavigo* and (with interesting variation) in *Stella*; Schiller essayed the 'bürgerliches Trauerspiel' only once, in *Kabale und Liebe*, but motifs recalling *Emilia Galotti* are found in all his three early prose tragedies, notably *Fiesco*; and Lessing's choice of Italy as the setting for his play may well have influenced the similar choices of Leisewitz and Klinger in such plays as *Julius von Tarent, Die Zwillinge*, and *Simsone Grisaldo*. But the younger generation soon abandoned Lessing's sober realism, finding that their newly reawakened sense of the tragic contradictions of life and the tragic movement of history called for larger-than-life modes of expression — the melodrama of the 'Sturm und Drang', the return to elevated classicism in the mature Schiller, the transcendence of all bounds of space, time, and earthly reality in Goethe's *Faust*. Domestic realism survived for the time only in the hands of lesser dramatists like Iffland, who enjoyed a considerable degree of popular success while the literary theatre withdrew to a cultural isolation of a kind from which Lessing had hoped to rescue it. But the German classical drama, great though its achievement was, was in many ways an anachronism. It was the last great literary flowering of the European Renaissance; but it came at a time when men's eyes were already being opened to prosaic contemporary realities in a way which undermined the assumptions underlying the Renaissance grand style. 'Es ist verflucht', wrote Goethe as he worked on *Iphigenie auf Tauris*, 'der König von Taurien soll reden, als ob kein Strumpfwirker in Apolda hungerte.'[1] Later Hebbel (in *Maria Magdalene*) and the more radical Büchner were to return to the realistic manner, and Ibsen, Strindberg, and the Naturalists were to follow them. Goethe and Schiller had turned the German drama on to a very different course from that set by Lessing; but it was Lessing who had set the course for the future.[2]

Seen from the point of view of his own age and his immediate successors, Lessing's achievement in the drama was that of a liberator. He did indeed succeed in what he set out to do, to free the German drama from the dead hand of a misunderstood and mechanically imitated tradition. If his successors then found their own way back to a version of that tradition, unencumbered by such externals as the pedantry of the Unities or the clatter of the alexandrine, Lessing, with his profound reverence for true tradition as he conceived it, would not necessarily have been displeased. He would probably have been more shocked by the pathological and nihilistic elements in Büchner's realism (and shared Goethe's reaction to the similar streak in Kleist), and agreed with his great admirer Franz Mehring on the tendency of the Naturalists to become 'Dekadenzjünger, Fäulnispiraten und Verfallsschnüffler'.[3] Little

---

[1]   To Charlotte von Stein, 6 March 1779. Cf. Goethe, ed. cit., v. 403.

[2]   Cf. Peter Demetz, 'Die Folgenlosigkeit Lessings', *Merkur*, xxv (1971), pp. 727-41.

[3]   Mehring, *Ästhetische Streifzüge* (1892), quoted in R. Hamann and J. Hermand, *Naturalismus (Epochen der deutschen Kultur von 1870 bis zur Gegenwart*, vol. ii) (Munich, 1972), p. 27.

though he respected false 'Delicatesse',[4] we know that he did not hold it to be the artist's business to reproduce nature warts and all, simply because nature looked like that: he believed that the artist should show us, in Schiller's terminology, not 'die wirkliche' but 'die wahre Natur'.[5]

But Lessing's plays are still performed today, more so than those of his classical successors: indeed, *Minna von Barnhelm* has been in the course of the last quarter-century the most frequently performed of all German plays. *Emilia Galotti* and even *Miß Sara Sampson* are still revived; the modern audience is more concerned with stocking-weavers than with Kings of Tauris, agrees with Lessing that 'Das Unglück derjenigen, deren Umstände den unsrigen am nächsten kommen, muß natürlicher Weise am tiefsten in unsere Seele dringen', and recognizes and admires his attempts at realism even where, as in *Sara*, they soon founder or even sink beneath a weight of rhetoric too great for mere 'Menschen' to bear. In all the plays we sense an emergent modernity, sense Lessing's own awareness, if sometimes only partial or reluctant, of a new world of greater complexity, and a new humanity with greater aspirations, than can be accommodated within traditional forms, whether of literary and dramatic expression or, by implication, of social and political organization. The prose plays are in particular very much documents of their time, but for that very reason can speak strongly to ours. *Emilia Galotti* is the classic drama of an age of transition — an age moving beyond 'tragedy' and the view of the world that that implies; and *Emilia Galotti* can still move us because we have not yet successfully completed that transition. I have suggested that *Minna von Barnhelm* disappoints by failing to pursue to the bitter end some of the awkward issues it appears to raise, leaving Frederick the Great secure on his throne after a modest rocking, and thereby perhaps implying that the Prussia of 1763 is, after all, as near to an ideal state as we are likely to get or have any right to demand. But it is also a powerful source of the play's appeal that it provides its happy ending not for paragons of virtue in a never-never land of perfect

---

[4] Cf. above, p. 51.
[5] Schiller, *Über naive und sentimentalische Dichtung*, in *Sämtliche Werke*, ed. Göpfert etc. (4th edn., Munich (Hanser), 1967), v. 755.

harmony, but for imperfect human beings in an imperfect (though maybe, as Leibniz had taught, the best *possible*) world. *Nathan der Weise* has enjoyed a predictable spate of revivals in post-Nazi Germany, often for the wrong reasons, which have encouraged over-solemn productions. But properly understood, it conveys the same essentially anti-Utopian message: men (and women) of good will can make of the world as it is a more than tolerable place to live in. The sober optimism, the realistic humanitarianism of Lessing's plays is one of the pillars of his greatness. (It remains to be seen whether any director will attempt to present *Philotas* as a parable for our age of terrorist hi-jackings, as Dieter Hildebrandt suggests.)[6]

The plays are also, of course, highly accomplished pieces of dramatic craftsmanship. With their modest-sized casts and their unfussy observance of a limited spatial and temporal scale, they occupy a happy mean between the excessive concentration, to modern tastes, of French classicism and the kind of extravagance which Shakespeare could apparently afford, but which nowadays seems best left to the cinema. They are well proportioned and well paced. And last but by no means least, they are the work of a master of dramatic language. Lessing was never more truly himself than when he was arguing; and in his plays never more himself than in scenes of argument. These may be actual quarrels (Sara and Marwood, Appiani and Marinelli) or scenes of discussion and persuasion (Minna and Tellheim, Nathan and Saladin). They can even be soliloquies, in which characters argue with themselves: Mellefont's 'Was für ein Rätsel bin ich mir selbst' (IV, 2), Odoardo Galotti's 'Wie? — Nimmermehr!' (V, 4), Nathan's 'Hm! hm! wunderlich! — Wie ist/ Mir denn? (III, 6), or the Templar's 'Ins Haus nun will ich einmal nicht' (V, 3). But typically, speeches in which, rather than exploring, analysing, or criticizing, characters seek to talk themselves into predetermined attitudes, such as Sara's 'Wenn man mir es vor Jahr und Tag gesagt hätte' (III, 4), or Philotas's 'Götter! Näher konnte der Blitz, ohne mich ganz zu zerschmettern', the longest soliloquy in all Lessing's dramatic output (sc. 4), are less persuasive,

---

[6]   Cf. Hildebrandt, *Lessing*, p. 227.

although not without the authentic Lessingian flavour. His language is characteristically intellectual rather than emotional: we know that he disapproved of passionate emotion and of the egocentricity which it implies. There are indeed a number of convincingly portrayed egocentrics in the plays; but they are either wholly or predominantly negative characters, whose egoism has tragic consquences (Marwood, the Prince) or they are characters in crisis, whose self-preoccupation is cured before such consequences can occur (notably, Tellheim). And there is a passionate rationality, a passionate common sense even, in characters like Minna and Nathan, and a genuine moral passion (again, notably, allied to doubt and questioning rather than the striking of attitudes) in Emilia's 'Aber was nennen Sie ruhig sein? Die Hände in den Schoß legen? Leiden, was man nicht sollte? Dulden, was man nicht dürfte?' (V, 7). And if Lessing cannot give us, or does not choose to give us, a sympathetic portrait of powerful emotion, this is not to say that he cannot portray affection: the warmth of feeling between Minna and Tellheim, the shy, innocent, even awkward love of Emilia and Appiani, are conveyed with a tact and reticence wholly appropriate to such feelings and to Lessing's approval of them.

What of the significance of the drama in Lessing's work as a whole? Quantitatively it occupies a sizeable, but not the largest place: one and a half of the eight volumes of the latest reasonably complete edition, with a further volume devoted to dramatic theory and criticism. The remainder (apart from half a volume of verse) is taken up by critical prose writings on other subjects: language, literature, the art of classical antiquity, theology, the philosophy of history, and some more unlikely topics. His prose is masterly, and everywhere we turn we can recognize his mind at work: Gleim wrote that Lessing would be Lessing even if he were to write about venereal disease – which indeed he once actually planned to do.[7] Though he disclaimed the title of a scholar,[8] there can be no doubt that Lessing loved books, loved scholarship, and loved intellectual controversy for its own sake, sometimes, it

---

[7]   Cf. Gleim to Lessing, 10 November 1770; D 337; LM xv. 390.
[8]   G v. 788. Cf. P. Raabe, 'Lessing und die Gelehrsamkeit', in *Lessing in heutiger Sicht*, pp. 65–88.

seems, irrespective of the occasion which gave rise to it. He attacked various opponents — Gottsched in the *Literaturbriefe* and elsewhere, Lange in the *Vade mecum*, Klotz in the *Briefe, antiquarischen Inhalts*, and finally Pastor Goeze, with a polemical ferocity verging on scurrility, which can make the unbiased observer doubt rather than assent to the justice of Lessing's cause. He fought uncompromisingly for tolerance; but he could be the reverse of tolerant himself. He fought for freedom of speech; but though he commended to Nicolai the courage with which others had spoken out 'für die Rechte der Untertanen, . . . gegen Aussaugung und Despotismus',[9] he made little use of his formidable rhetorical talents in such causes as these. He attacks pomposity and pretension; but he often attacks the person rather than the issue, leaving his own views on the latter tantalizingly — or suspiciously — unclear. In *Laokoon*, for example, he grossly misrepresents the arguments of Joseph Spence for his own purpose, without its being at all plain what that purpose actually is;[10] and at least one usually sympathetic critic has found that in the confrontation between Lessing and Goeze it is not Lessing who cuts the more admirable figure.[11] Many readers seem to have accepted Schlegel's rating of the polemical prose works higher than the 'poetic' works in genuine linguistic power; they are certainly virtuoso performances by a master of every trick of the rhetorician's trade; but one is perhaps entitled to enquire a little more closely into the substance of the matter under discussion, the purpose to which the tricks are ostensibly being put.

Where we have less cause to doubt the seriousness of Lessing's concern with the matter for its own sake, we often find that it is a matter of specialized, antiquarian, or even, as it now seems, outmoded interest. It is noteworthy that the two literary genres on which Lessing produced reasonably completed treatises are two which the current of literary history has left behind — the fable and the epigram;[12] the same might

---

[9] Letter to Nicolai, 25 August 1769.

[10] Cf. Donald T. Siebert, Jr., '*Laokoon* and *Polymetis*: Lessing's Treatment of Joseph Spence', *LYB* iii (1970), 71–83.

[11] O. Seidlin, review of *Lessing contra Goeze*, ibid. 228.

[12] *Abhandlungen über die Fabel*, G v. 355–419; *Zerstreute Anmerkungen über das Epigramm*, ibid. 420–529.

well be said of the epic, which furnishes the principal literary subject-matter of the *Laokoon*, and even of tragedy, the major concern of Lessing the dramatic theorist. There can be little doubt that the real interest of Lessing's theory of the drama is to be found in its complex and sometimes contradictory relation to his own dramatic practice. The *Laokoon* is a document of immense significance in the history of the 'tyranny of Greece over Germany';[13] but the intrinsic interest of its basic argument is only theoretical, and one has the impression that a distinction which works well enough at a common-sense level and within common-sense limitations is being stretched by Lessing, with immense forensic ingenuity, to a point of supposed logical precision and absoluteness which it will not actually bear. The theological writings are also of considerable importance to an understanding of the plays, and their intrinsic interest too is great — to the theologian: for despite another of Lessing's characteristic disclaimers, 'Ich bin Liebhaber der Theologie, und nicht Theolog',[14] they are in fact highly technical. The simple believer, or even the simple hungerer after truth and righteousness, may well find himself turning back on Lessing his own comment on Reimarus, 'Was gehen dem Christen dieses Mannes Hypothesen, und Erklärungen und Beweise an?'[15]

The theological and philosophical writings are also of immense interest and importance to the historian of ideas, as marking a stage in the development from a Christian eschatology to a secularized philosophy of history. But even from this point of view they may be found wanting, lacking as they do the kind of substance which a genuine interest in history for its own sake — in the material conditions of human life and in the specificity of different social and cultural manifestations, such as we find already so highly developed in Herder — can provide. The author of one of the most stimulating recent studies of Lessing's historical thought has criticized him, and his successors in the German tradition of the philosophy of history, for just this excessive abstraction and lack of concrete historical substance, for a Utopian faith in progress, for a lack of true psychological and sociological

[13] Cf. E. M. Butler, *The Tyranny of Greece over Germany* (Cambridge, 1935).
[14] *Axiomata*, G viii. 130.   [15] *Gegensätze*, G vii. 458.

insight.[16] But we have seen that in his mature prose plays Lessing is concerned to establish a concrete sense of everyday reality, and that in the motivation of his characters and in their relation to the world they inhabit he reveals often profound psychological and sociological insights, even though he may have lacked a theory and a terminology to express them abstractly. And we have seen that *Nathan*, though it may be said to embody a vision of progressive human enlightenment, and although it is removed from our own prosaic surroundings, nevertheless conveys a sober, realistic ethical optimism based upon a recognition and tolerance of the imperfections of the real, historical world.

Scholars will continue to find in Lessing's critical prose writings abundant fuel with which to stoke the fires of intellectual controversy. But the best of Lessing, his humanity, his sympathy and concern for the lives and fortunes of ordinary men and women, and his vision of what those lives might be, is to be found in the plays.[17] They are his enduring monument, and it is through them that he speaks to humanity at large.

---

[16] Wilm Pelters, *Lessings Standort. Sinndeutung der Geschichte als Kern seines Denkens* (Heidelberg, 1972), p. 105.

[17] Pelters himself comes to a similar conclusion (ibid., p. 109). I am sorry to see, however, that he takes a negative view of *Nathan*: cf. his paper, 'Anti–Candide oder die Apotheose der Vorsehung', in *Lessing in heutiger Sicht*, pp. 251-8.

Bibliography

(i) Collected Editions of Lessing's Works

The principal scholarly editions, to which reference is made in this book, are:

Lessings sämtliche Schriften, ed. Karl Lachmann, 3rd. edn. revised by Franz Muncker, 22 vols. (Stuttgart, 1886–1924) (LM).

Lessings Werke, ed. Julius Petersen and Waldemar von Olshausen (etc.), 25 vols. (Berlin, n.d.) (plus 5 vols. of notes and indices) (PO).

Lessings Werke, ed. H. G. Göpfert (etc.), 8 vols. (Munich, 1970–9) (G).

(ii) Editions of Individual Plays, etc.

These will be found useful:

Miß Sara Sampson, ed. K. Eibl. (Frankfurt, 1971) (Commentatio, ii).

Philotas, ed. W. Grosse (Stuttgart, 1979) (Reclams Universalbibliothek, 5755).

Minna von Barnhelm, ed. D. Hildebrandt (Frankfurt and Berlin, 1969) (Dichtung und Wirklichkeit, xxx).

Emilia Galotti, ed. E. L. Stahl (Oxford, 1946) (Blackwell's German Texts).

Nathan der Weise, ed. P. Demetz (Frankfurt and Berlin, 1966) (Dichtung und Wirklichkeit, xxv).

Briefwechsel über das Trauerspiel (Lessing, Mendelssohn, Nicolai), ed. J. Schulte-Sasse (Munich, 1972).

Hamburgische Dramaturgie, ed. O. Mann (Stuttgart, 1958) (Kröners Taschenausgabe, 267).

(iii) Secondary Literature

The following is a check-list of all the books or articles about Lessing (and the more important of the more general works) referred to in this book, together with a few others of particular value; except that articles in the *Lessing Yearbook* have not been separately listed.

A. Altmann, *Moses Mendelssohn: A Biographical Study* (London and Alabama, 1973).

I. Appelbaum-Graham, 'Minds without Medium. Reflections on *Emilia Galotti* and *Werthers Leiden*', *Euph.* lvi (1962), 3–24 (German version in B).

H. Arntzen, *Die ernste Komödie. Das deutsche Lustspiel von Lessing bis Kleist* (Munich, 1968).

A. Aronson, *Lessing et les classiques français* (Montpelier, 1935).

W. Barner, *Produktive Rezeption: Lessing und die Tragödien Senecas* (Munich, 1973).

E. M. Batley, 'Rational and Irrational Elements in Lessing's Shakespeare Criticism', *GR* xlv (1970), 5-25.

G. and S. Bauer (eds.), *Gotthold Ephraim Lessing* (Darmstadt, 1968) (Wege der Forschung, ccxi) (B).

D. Borchmeyer, 'Corneille, Lessing und das Problem der "Auslegung" der aristotelischen Poetik', *DVJS* li (1977), 208-21.

H. Bornkamm, 'Die innere Handlung in Lessings *Miß Sara Sampson*', *Euph.* li (1957), 385-96.

F. A. Brown, 'The Conversion of Lessing's "Freygeist"', *JEGP* lvi (1957), 186-202.

—— —— *Lessing* (New York, 1971) (Twayne's World Authors Series).

W. H. Bruford, *Theatre, Drama and Audience in Goethe's Germany* (London, 1950).

—— —— *Germany in the Eighteenth Century* (Cambridge, 1952).

F. Brüggemann, 'Lessings Bürgerdramen und der Subjektivismus als Problem', *Jahrbuch des freien deutschen Hochstifts*, 1926 (reprinted in B).

J. Clivio, *Lessing und das Problem der Tragödie* (Zurich, 1928).

C. von Dach, *Racine in der deutschen Literatur des 18. Jahrhunderts* (Bern, 1941).

R. Daunicht, *Die Entstehung des bürgerlichen Trauerspiels in Deutschland* (Berlin, 1963).

—— —— (ed.), *Lessing im Gespräch* (Munich, 1971).

P. Demetz, 'Die Folgenlosigkeit Lessings', *Merkur*, xxv (1971), 727-41.

J. Desch, 'Emilia Galotti – a victim of misconceived morality', *Trivium*, ix (1974), 88-99.

D. Droese, *Lessing und die Sprache* (Zurich, 1968).

M. Durzak, *Poesie und Ratio. Vier Lessing-Studien* (Bad Homburg, 1970).

—— —— 'Gesellschaftsreflexion und Gesellschaftsdarstellung bei Lessing', *ZfdPh* xciii (1974), 546-60.

K. Eibl, 'Identitätskrise und Diskurs. Zur thematischen Kontinuität von Lessings Dramatik', *JDSG* xxi (1977), 138-91.

C. Enders, 'Der geistesgeschichtliche Standort von Lessings *Horoskop*', *Euph.* 1 (1956), 208-16.

E. S. Flajole, S. J., 'Lessing's Retrieval of Lost Truths', *PMLA* lxxiv (1959), 52-66.

L. W. Forster, 'Werther's Reading of *Emilia Galotti*', *PEGS* xxvii (1958), 33-45.

F. M. Fowler, 'Why Lessing's Nathan had to be *der Weise*: on the Integration of Play and Parable', *NGS* vii (1979), 17-22.

G. Fricke, 'Bemerkungen zu Lessings *Freigeist* und *Miß Sara Sampson*', in H. Moser etc. (eds.), *Festschrift Josef Quint* (Bonn, 1964), 83-120.

W.-H. Friedrich, 'Sophokles, Aristoteles und Lessing', *Euph*. lvii (1963), 4-27.

H. B. Garland, *Lessing, the Founder of Modern German Literature* (London, 1937) (2nd edn., 1962).

D. R. George, *Deutsche Tragödientheorien vom Mittelalter bis zu Lessing* (Munich, 1971).

H. Göbel, *Bild und Sprache bei Lessing* (Munich, 1971).

O. G. Graf, 'Lessing and the Art of Acting', *Papers of the Michigan Academy of Science, Arts and Letters*, xl (1955), 293-301.

F. Gundolf, *Shakespeare und der deutsche Geist* (2nd edn., Berlin, 1914).

K. S. Guthke, 'Problem und Problematik von Lessings Faustdichtung', *ZfdPh* lxxix (1960), 141-49.

——— ——— *Das deutsche bürgerliche Trauerspiel* (Stuttgart, 1972) (Sammlung Metzler, cxvi).

——— ——— 'Der Glücksspieler als Autor. Überlegungen zur "Gestalt" Lessings im Sinne der inneren Biographie', *Euph*. lxxi (1977), 353-82.

E. P. Harris and R. E. Schade (eds.), *Lessing in heutiger Sicht. Beiträge zur internationalen Lessing-Konferenz, Cincinnati 1976* (Bremen and Wolfenbüttel, 1977).

R. R. Heitner, '*Emilia Galotti*: an Indictment of Bourgeois Passivity', *JEGP* lii (1953), 480-90.

——— ——— 'Lessing's Manipulation of a Single Comic Theme', *MLQ* xviii (1957), 183-98.

——— ——— 'Concerning Lessing's Debt to Diderot', *MLN* xlv (1960), 82-8.

——— ——— *German Tragedy in the Age of Enlightenment* (Berkeley and Los Angeles, 1963).

A. Henkel, 'Anmerkungen zu Lessings Faust-Fragment', *Euph*. lxiv (1970), 75-84.

P. Hernadi, 'Lessings Misanthropen', *Euph*. lxviii (1974), 113-18.

D. Hildebrandt, *Lessing: Biographie einer Emanzipation* (Munich, 1979).

W. Hinck, *Das deutsche Lustspiel des 17. und 18. Jahrhunderts und die italienische Komödie* (Stuttgart, 1965).

F. van Ingen, 'Tugend bei Lessing: Bemerkungen zu *Miß Sara Sampson*', *ABNG* i (1972), 43-73.

J. Jones, *On Aristotle and Greek Tragedy* (London, 1962).

G. Kettner, *Lessings Dramen im Lichte ihrer und unserer Zeit* (Berlin, 1904).

P. P. Kies, 'The Sources and Basic Model of Lessing's *Miß Sara Sampson*', *Modern Philology*, xxiv (1927), 65-90.

M. Kommerell, *Lessing und Aristoteles* (Frankfurt, 1940 etc.).

D. von König, *Natürlichkeit und Wirklichkeit. Studien zu Lessings "Nathan der Weise"* (Bonn, 1976).

F. Kopitzsch, 'Lessing und Hamburg', *WSA* ii (1975), 47-120, and iii (1976), 273-325.

F. J. Lamport, 'Eine bürgerliche Virginia', *GLL* N.S. xvii (1964), 304-12.

——— ——— 'Lessing and the "Bürgerliches Trauerspiel"', in P. F. Ganz (ed.), *The Discontinuous Tradition. Studies in German Literature in Honour of Ernest Ludwig Stahl* (Oxford, 1970), 14-28.

—— —— 'Patzke's *Virginia*', *NGS* viii (1980), 19-27.

Lessing Yearbook (Munich, 1969–).

K. G. Lessing, *G. E. Lessings Leben. Nebst seinem noch übrigen literarischen Nachlaß* (Berlin, 1793).

O. Mann, *Lessing: Sein und Leistung* (Hamburg, 1948) (revised edn., Hamburg, 1961).

W. Martens, *Die Botschaft der Tugend: Die Aufklärung im Spiegel der deutschen moralischen Wochenschriften* (Stuttgart, 1968).

F. Martini, 'Riccaut, die Sprache und das Spiel in Lessings Lustspiel *Minna von Barnhelm*', in B, 376-426 (originally in *Formenwandel, Festschrift für Paul Böckmann*, Hamburg, 1964).

M. M. Metzger, *Lessing and the Language of Comedy* (The Hague, 1966).

P. Michelsen, 'Die Erregung des Mitleids durch die Tragödie. Zu Lessings Ansichten über das Trauerspiel im Briefwechsel mit Mendelssohn und Nicolai', *DVJS* xl (1966), 548-66.

—— —— 'Die Verbergung der Kunst. Über die Exposition in Lessings *Minna von Barnhelm*', *JDSG* xvii (1973), 192-252.

R. Mortier, *Diderot en Allemagne* (Paris, 1954).

K.-D. Müller, 'Das Erbe der Komödie im bürgerlichen Trauerspiel: Lessings *Emilia Galotti* und die commedia dell'arte', *DVJS* xlvi (1972), 28-60.

P. H. Neumann, *Der Preis der Mündigkeit: Über Lessings Dramen* (Stuttgart, 1977).

H. B. Nisbet, '*De Tribus Impostoribus*: On the Genesis of Lessing's *Nathan der Weise*', *Euph.* lxxiii (1979), 365-87.

V. Nölle, *Subjektivität und Wirklichkeit in Lessings dramatischem und theologischem Werk* (Berlin, 1977).

F. O. Nolte, 'Voltaire's *Mahomet* as a source of Lessing's *Nathan der Weise* and *Emilia Galotti*', *MLN* xlviii (1933), 152-6.

—— —— 'Lessing's *Emilia Galotti* in the Light of his *Hamburgische Dramaturgie*', *Harvard Studies and Notes in Philology and Literature*, xix (1938), 175-95 (German version in B).

W. Oehlke, *Lessing und seine Zeit* (Munich, 1919).

U. Otto, *Lessings Verhältnis zur französischen Darstellungstheorie* (Frankfurt and Bern, 1976) (Europäische Hochschulschriften, i. 154).

W. Pelters, *Lessings Standort. Sinndeutung der Geschichte als Kern seines Denkens* (Heidelberg, 1972).

H. Petriconi, *Die verführte Unschuld* (Hamburg, 1953).

R. Petsch (ed.), *Lessings Briefwechsel mit Mendelssohn und Nicolai über das Trauerspiel* (Leipzig, 1910).

—— —— (ed.), *Lessings Faustdichtung* (Heidelberg, 1911).

L. Pikulik, *"Bürgerliches Trauerspiel" und Empfindsamkeit* (Cologne and Graz, 1966).

H. Politzer, 'Lessing's Parable of the Three Rings', *GQ* xxxi (1958), 161-77 (German version in B).

G. Pons, *G. E. Lessing et le christianisme* (Paris, 1964).

T. J. Reed, 'Critical Consciousness and Creation: the Concept *Kritik* from Lessing to Hegel', *OGS* iii (1968), 87-113.

—— —— 'Theatre, Enlightenment and Nation: A German Problem', *FMLS* xiv (1978), 143-64.

H. Rempel, *Tragödie und Komödie im dramatischen Schaffen Lessings* (Berlin, 1935).

V. Riedel, *Lessing und die römische Literatur* (Weimar, 1976).

J. G. Robertson, *Lessing's Dramatic Theory* (Cambridge, 1939).

V. A. Rudowski, *Lessing's Aesthetica in Nuce: an analysis of the May 26, 1769 Letter to Nicolai* (Chapel Hill, 1971) (University of North Carolina Studies in the Germanic Languages and Literatures, lxix).

W. Sauder, *Empfindsamkeit: I. Voraussetzungen und Elemente* (Stuttgart, 1974).

W. Schadewaldt, 'Furcht und Mitleid? Zu Lessings Deutung des Aristotelischen Tragödiensatzes', *DVJS* xxx (1956), 137-40 (also in B; longer version in Schadewaldt, *Hellas und Hesperien* (2nd edn., Zurich, 1970), i. 194-236).

A. Schilson, *Geschichte im Horizont der Vorsehung: Lessings Beitrag zu einer Theologie der Geschichte* (Mainz, 1974).

E. Schmidt, *Lessing: Geschichte seines Lebens und seiner Schriften* (2nd edn., Berlin, 1899).

J. Schmidt, 'Lessing', in R. von Gottschall (ed.), *Der neue Plutarch*, xi (Leipzig, 1885).

H. Schneider, *Lessing: Zwölf biographische Studien* (Munich, 1951).

J. Schröder, *Gotthold Ephraim Lessing: Sprache und Drama* (Munich, 1972).

—— —— 'Lessing: *Minna von Barnhelm*', in W. Hinck (ed.), *Die deutsche Komödie* (Düsseldorf, 1977).

J. Schulte-Sasse, *Literarische Struktur und historisch-sozialer Kontext. Zum Beispiel Lessings "Emilia Galotti"* (Paderborn, 1975).

H. Schultze, *Lessings Toleranzbegriff. Eine theologische Studie* (Göttingen, 1969).

U. Schulz, *Lessing auf der Bühne. Chronik der Theateraufführungen 1748-1789* (Bremen and Wolfenbüttel, 1977).

H. C. Seeba, *Die Liebe zur Sache. Öffentliches und privates Interesse in Lessings Dramen* (Tübingen, 1973).

E. Staiger, *Stilwandel* (Zurich, 1963).

H. Steinhauer, 'The Guilt of Emilia Galotti', *JEGP* xlviii (1949), 173-85.

H. Steinmetz, *Die Komödie der Aufklärung* (Stuttgart, 1966) (Sammlung Metzler, xlvii).

—— —— (ed.), *Lessing — ein unpoetischer Dichter: Dokumente aus drei Jahrhunderten zur Wirkungsgeschichte Lessings in Deutschland* (Frankfurt, 1969) (Wirkung der Literatur, i).

—— —— 'Aufklärung und Tragödie: Lessings Tragödien vor dem Hintergrund des Trauerspielmodells der Aufklärung', *ABNG* i (1972), 3-41.

—— —— '*Minna von Barnhelm* oder die Schwierigkeit, ein Lustspiel zu verstehen', in A. von Bormann etc. (eds.), *Wissen aus Erfahrungen. Festschrift für Herman Meyer* (Tübingen, 1975), 135–53.

P. Szondi, 'Tableau und coup de théâtre: zur Sozialpsychologie des bürgerlichen Trauerspiels bei Diderot. Mit einem Exkurs über Lessing', in Szondi, *Lektüren und Lektionen* (Frankfurt, 1973).

C. C. D. Vail, *Lessing's Relation to the English Language and Literature* (New York, 1936).

P. Weber, *Das Menschenbild des bürgerlichen Trauerspiels. Entstehung und Funktion von Lessings "Miß Sara Sampson"* (Berlin (DDR), 1970).

H. Weigand, 'Warum stirbt Emilia Galotti?' in Weigand, *Fährten und Funde* (Bern and Munich, 1967) (originally in *JEGP* xxviii (1929)).

L. P. Wessell, *Lessing's Theology: A Reinterpretation* (The Hague, 1977).

B. von Wiese, *Die deutsche Tragödie von Lessing bis Hebbel* (Hamburg, 1948).

—— —— (ed.), *Das deutsche Drama*, i (Düsseldorf, 1964).

K. Wölfel, 'Moralische Anstalt: zur Dramaturgie von Gottsched bis Lessing', in R. Grimm (ed.), *Deutsche Dramentheorien* (Frankfurt, 1971), i. 45–122.

T. Ziolkowski, 'Language and Mimetic Action in Lessing's *Miß Sara Sampson*', *GR* xl (1965), 261–76.

Index

(i) Lessing's Works

(ii) General